THE
FIVE KEYS
TO VALUE
INVESTING

J. Dennis Jean-Jacques

McGraw-Hill

New York   Chicago   San Francisco   Lisbon
London   Madrid   Mexico City   Milan
New Delhi   San Juan   Seoul   Singapore
Sydney   Toronto

Copyright © 2003 by The McGraw-Hill Companies, Inc. All rights reserved.
Printed in the United States of America. Except as permitted under the United
States Copyright Act of 1976, no part of this publication may be reproduced or distributed in any form or by any means, or stored in a data base or retrieval system,
without the prior written permission of the publisher.

1 2 3 4 5 6 7 8 9 0   AGM/AGM   0 9 8 7 6 5 4 3 2

ISBN 0-07-140231-4

This publication is designed to provide accurate and authoritative information in
regard to the subject matter covered. It is sold with the understanding that neither
the author nor the publisher is engaged in rendering legal, accounting, or other professional service. If legal advice or other expert assistance is required, the services
of a competent professional person should be sought.

> —From a Declaration of Principles jointly adopted by a Committee of
> the American Bar Association and a Committee of Publishers.

McGraw-Hill books are available at special quantity discounts to use as premiums
and sales promotions, or for use in corporate training programs. For more information, please write to the Director of Special Sales, McGraw-Hill, Two Penn Plaza,
New York, NY 10121-2298. Or contact your local bookstore.

This book is printed on recycled, acid-free paper containing
a minimum of 50% recycled, de-inked fiber.

Library of Congress Cataloging-in-Publication Data

Jean-Jacques, J. Dennis.
    The five keys to value investing / by
J. Dennis Jean-Jacques.
        p.   cm.
    ISBN 0-07-140231-4 (pbk)
    1. Investment analysis.   3. Securities.   3. Corporations—Valuation.
    4. Investments.   Title.
HG4529.J43   2002
332.6—dc21   2002005972
                                                         CIP

Dedication

To my wife, Bridgette McFadden, and our two girls for their daily encouragement and support. To my parents, Denis and Marie Jean-Jacques, for inspiring their children to pave their own paths.

To the victims and heroes of 9/11.

Contents

Acknowledgments

I AM VERY FORTUNATE to have worked with some of the best and brightest investors, not to mention great individuals at Fidelity Investments and Mutual Series Fund. These individuals, demonstrated—on a daily basis—the level of commitment, focus, and passion that is required to be a successful investor. Thank you to all of my former colleagues and current friends in the investment profession. You know who you are. I would also like to thank my wife, Bridgette, for the tremendous amount of support she has given me throughout this project, and our girls, TAJ and CRJ, for patiently allowing Daddy to write on the weekends. A notable recognition goes to our youngest, (who was five months old when this project began) for sleeping throughout the night (most of the time). Thank you to Stephen Issacs and the staff at McGraw-Hill for making this book a reality. Finally, a special thanks goes to Myra A. Thomas for her assistance with this project.

J. Dennis Jean-Jacques

INTRODUCTION: VALUE MATTERS

I BUY PIECES OF BUSINESSES AND, on behalf of investors, sell them to others at a higher price. I do not "manage" a stock portfolio. I am an investor. I would rather own shares of 8 companies than 80 stocks. While important, beating the S&P 500 Index or the Dow Jones Industrial Average is not the primary objective in this book. The goal is to obtain adequate and consistent performance. Regardless of the performance of the general market, I am looking for a satisfactory return over time, based on the amount of risk taken. The best way to achieve an acceptable level of performance is by purchasing companies one at a time, at a discount to what they are worth. This line of thinking may seem strange to some, but is very common among those in the value investing community.

Value investing is a delicate balance between price and value. You pay a specific price with the expectation of obtaining a certain amount of value. Over the past few years, what was paid for a stock was irrelevant, and the "value" you received in return was overlooked—despite it being measured in unconventional ways, such as on a per "eyeball" basis. As long as share prices continued to rise, nothing else mattered. The world has changed; the great bull run of the 1990s is over. The investment strategy of buy high and sell higher is no longer the norm. Rational behavior has begun to set in. Today, price is important, and now more than ever, value matters.

AN EARLY LESSON

As an analyst at Fidelity Management & Research Company, I remember visiting 30 or so companies in any given year. I met with the chief executives and other members of senior management of every company I visited. Much time was spent questioning these individuals and analyzing the answers. A routine trip to a business would also entail a look at their manufacturing facilities and stores, as well as the survey of their suppliers, key customers, and even their competitors. Some call this type of due diligence "kicking the tires." At Fidelity, we were expected to strip the tire and count the threads.

I understood then, as I do now, that we were not investing in the stock market. Rather, we were investing in what each corporation was truly made up of—ideas, products, and management with a specific set of business goals in mind. Behind every stock symbol or ticker was a CEO about to destroy or create value for his or her shareholders.

THE INDIVIDUAL INVESTOR'S GAINING EDGE

Nothing can replace seeing a company's most valuable assets firsthand and meeting with the decision makers. This is the advantage that professional money managers, like those from such well-funded mutual fund families as Fidelity, Franklin Templeton, and Janus, have over individuals.

While the individual investor does not have the luxury of obtaining access to a corporation's top brass, going on private tours of the company's facilities, or attending Wall Street analyst conferences, there are three factors that are helping individuals compete more effectively for investment opportunities. They include the following.

1.   Technology, media, and the proliferation of the Internet
2.   Regulation Fair Disclosure
3.   The increase in accounting transparency by corporations

Technology in the home has brought management teams closer to investors. Today, individuals can obtain critical U.S. Securities and Exchange Commission documents almost as soon as a company files them. With quarterly emails to shareholders, Web-based telecasts of earnings conference calls with analysts, and the assorted finance Web sites, individuals are able to get much of the same information as professionals. As a result, the competitive nature of the investment business has shifted from those having the best sources of information to those who are best at analyzing the available information.

In addition, the popularity of such programming as CNBC, Bloomberg News Television, and CNNfn has helped individual investors understand management personalities. Television has brought the viewers inside analyst conferences and company shareholder annual meetings. These programs have also helped individual investors understand key business concepts and general stock market terms, as top analysts and money managers come on air to share their thinking with viewers.

Regulation Fair Disclosure (Regulation FD) is an attempt by the Securities and Exchange Commission to rein in the passage of selected information of a company to certain investors. According to the SEC, Regulation FD is "aimed at curbing the selective disclosure of material nonpublic information by issuers to analysts and institutional investors, Regulation FD requires that when an issuer discloses material information, it does so publicly."[1] This may sound obvious, but many believe that such a rule was much needed to help individual investors gain the same quality and flow of information as large, institutional investors.

In combination with the Internet, Regulation Fair Disclosure can have a very profound impact on the information gap between institutions and individuals. Much of the dissemination of information comes by way of SEC filings, Web casts, and press releases.

Senior management is becoming more transparent with their accounting and how they report on the economic health of the companies they run. No more "fuzzy" math. For example, the general investment public was outraged by the collapses of Enron. Its demise has affected the financial system in more ways than one. Perhaps the greatest impact was the fact that the Enron effect helped lawmakers focus on the earnings quality and the questionable use of accounting practices by American corporations. While certain accounting techniques and their applications may be new to the market, self-interest is not. In the history of capitalism, the scenario of personal interest over fiduciary responsibility is certainly not uncommon.

In addition to the use of certain accounting methods, as in the case of Enron and other large corporations, corporate self-interest can and has taken several other forms as well. The long list varies from corporate management teams making decisions that knowingly will have an adverse impact on shareholder value, to corporate boards of directors putting in place structures discouraging unsolicited bids that may enrich shareholders. While the scenario may change, the strong motivating factor of self-interest will probably ensure that some management team down the road will seek some unfair benefit from their shareholder's company.

[1]Unger, L., U.S. Securities and Exchange Commission, "Special Study: Regulation Fair Disclosure Revisited," December 2001, p. 2.

The collapse and eventual bankruptcy of a few visible corporations prompted investors, auditors, and analysts to take a closer look at how companies report their earnings to shareholders. In the process, many are finding out what some investors have known all along—management teams often report company financial data in a manner that is not aligned with the economic realities of their businesses.

As a result of these accounting concerns, investors are reexamining how companies report the numbers in their financial statements. While this skepticism over corporate reporting may prove to be unnecessary for many companies, the Enron effect will have a positive and long-lasting impact on the investment community. Ultimately, companies will be more conscious of how numbers are accounted for. They will also be sensitive to the adequacy, clarity, and amount of information given to shareholders. This increase in clarity will greatly benefit stockholders as they try to evaluate investment prospects. This book will help you make the most use of the increase in better and more transparent financial reporting.

MUTUAL SERIES: THE VALUE THINK TANK

Mutual Series Funds Inc. is a mutual fund company that runs several mutual funds, all based on a value-driven and disciplined approach pioneered by its founder, Max Heine, and popularized by Michael Price. The value approach is essentially like buying a dollar of assets for 60 cents.

The investors at Mutual Series took an analytical approach to every decision that was made. As a group of analysts and portfolio managers, we looked at many different types of opportunities large and small. The most common type of opportunities were:

- Pure value opportunities, such as identifying significantly undervalued companies or well-run cyclical companies at the bottom of their cycles

- Event-driven opportunities, such as corporate restructurings and spin-offs

- Bankruptcies, and mergers and acquisitions

In each area, we worked diligently to uncover the true value of the enterprise and the potential catalyst that would most likely increase shareholder value.

Prior to his semiretirement, Michael Price was essentially the sole portfolio manager of the funds until the decision-making aspects of the firm were reorganized to include a team approach. Under Price, there were seven top lieutenants and nearly a dozen analysts. We all sat in one room about a quarter of the size of a football field. At the center of the room there was a large T-shaped trading desk. Price sat at the head of the T and his traders sat along the sides. All analysts, including myself, sat at individual desks facing Price.

When Price decided only to serve as chairman of the funds and to pare down his day-to-day involvement in managing them, two of his top lieutenants, Peter Langerman and Robert Friedman, assumed his responsibilities. This function was later taken over by David Winters. These three men and the other disciples of Price, including David Marcus, Larry Sondike, Ray Garea, and Jeff Altman, heavily influenced my approach to value investing.

THE ACTIVE, NONPROFESSIONAL INVESTORS

The Five Keys to Value Investing is based on the approaches applied by several value-oriented professional investment managers from various firms. It is written from the perspective of the day-to-day value investor, for the active, nonprofessional investors who invest in the public market for themselves.

How do you know if you are an active, nonprofessional investor? These individuals have the following characteristics: They assess investment opportunities on their own. They are confident and independent, yet humble in how they make investment decisions. They listen to many voices in the marketplace that are giving advice, yet follow no one voice as they continue to rely on their own research to provide the answers. They might be school teachers, doctors, stay-at-home parents, or they might belong to an investment club. Active, nonprofessional investors are ordinary people. If this fits you, read on.

ABOUT THE BOOK

The Five Keys to Value Investing is practical. Therefore, new portfolio theories and broad investment topics are not its focus. Value investors invest in companies one idea at a time—a bottom-up approach. The outcome of such activities is often the accumulation of a limited number of investment holdings that must be monitored over time. The focus of this book is on obtaining and correctly applying a specific set of tools in order to make the best and most rational decisions in investing.

The approach and tools outlined in this book, and used by the value investor, are neither perfect nor new. In fact they are old—very old. Value investors do not try to reinvent the wheel, nor do they try to invent new valuation techniques. Rather, the value investor assembles a bag full of tools and techniques that have stood the test of time. Valuation methods and business analysis procedures that have proven to be robust through various market conditions are specifically discussed here.

As outlined in the book, having the right mental attitude toward investing is one of the most important assets for any individual value investor. The best way to explain value investing is to equate it to the game of golf, in order to drive in a few critical concepts that would otherwise be very difficult to articulate. Some of the similarities between playing golf and investing in the market are obvious, and others are less so.

Perhaps the most critical similarity relates to the mental discipline required for both. You must stay on target in your fundamental approach, even when the world is betting against you. In investing, this requires the acceptance that you may have a few bad quarters or even a bad year, while still not compromising the fundamental tenets of your value investment philosophy. Likewise, good golfers do not abandon their entire approach to the game and fundamentals after a few bad tournaments to merely try a new and untested approach. Nor should you go this route with your investments.

To begin your journey as a value investor, very little is required. Having played a round of golf at some point in your life would be nice, but not necessary. What is required is a sincere drive, hard work, and an eighth-grade math and reading level.

Value investors assess and buy businesses. This requires having a certain set of tools that will prepare one to analyze and dissect the "value" of a business. The best place to start is with the company's SEC filings. There are several excerpts from SEC documents in this book. Reading these filings remains critical to the investment process. While professional investors may spend the bulk of their time visiting companies, individual investors tend to spend most of their time pouring over original sources of information, like the SEC filings. At Mutual Series, reading the various filings was at the center of our due diligence efforts.

WHAT YOU CAN EXPECT

The beginning chapter provides the foundation for the entire book. If this were a book on golf, this is where novice golfers would get the necessary training they need to understand the mental aspects of the game, learn about the different clubs, and their strengths and weaknesses. Similarly, this chapter presents the mental framework of the value investor. It focuses on emotional discipline and introduces you to the Five Keys of Value framework, while also giving you the overall foundation and philosophy of value investing. Discussed in greater detail later, the Five Keys consist of business, value, and price assessments, in addition to catalyst identification and a margin of safety determination.

The book goes on to provide descriptions of the various tools in order to help you understand whether or not a particular investment opportunity is a good company to own. The objective is to build upon your judgment, determining which tools you can use to assess the company.

Once you have determined that the investment opportunity in question is in a good business, *The Five Keys to Value Investing* explores the delicate balance between price and value. The book helps you determine what the current stock price is based on and how much the company is actually worth. Then it bridges the gap between that price and value. Catalysts are also discussed, offering the reader ways to identify and measure the effect of events (or potential events) that will spur stock price appreciation.

The final step in the framework discussed is a description of the proper tools used to determine the individual investor's safety level for the stock. The Five Keys of Value framework supports the notion that once an investor has identified the catalyst needed to get the stock to fair value, a margin of safety analysis (a term popularized by Benjamin Graham) is required in the event that the catalysts identified are delayed or proven ineffective to drive stock price appreciation. This is essentially the investor's downside scenario. The margin of safety analysis is considered by many value investors to be the most important part of the entire investing process.

The Five Keys to Value Investing stresses that once you have the right tools and awareness of the emotional discipline required, no other quality is more important than one's ability to assess properly the specific investment opportunity on the table. This book helps you assess the type of investment that you may face and gives you examples of the tools that other independent value investors have used in such situations.

Like golf, you must first observe others (or "practice") with these tools in similar situations until you have your own "feel" for what is best for you. Two value investors can look at the same company and use different tools when determining its value, yet reach the same conclusion. Likewise, two golfers could be 100 yards from the pin with the same lie, and use different clubs to generate the same outcome. At the end of the day, you have to be comfortable with the tools you know how to use best. This book will provide you with a handful of tools, and it will help you to understand how each is used, but it will be up to you to master them.

After having the proper tools and identifying the situation correctly, it is up to you how you wish to execute. Taking action or "buying right," and your ability and follow-through as an owner of an enterprise once you buy the stock, are essential to your investment success. This is an area that most investment books spend little time on, but as buyers of businesses, this is where a good number of value investors spend most of their time—trying to become better owners of businesses. The value investor knows that the real work begins after you purchase the shares.

The Five Keys to Value Investing concludes by providing a few suggestions on how to generate your own investment ideas, by focusing on specific methods. It provides a discussion about building your own independent portfolio consisting of a few of your best possible ideas. In summary, you will gain the following four skills that will help you prosper as a value investor.

1.   You will have a specific value framework to help you make investment decisions.
2.   You will know how to find the balance between price and value, and how to "buy right."
3.   You will know how to identify events that move stock prices.
4.   You will be able to generate your own value investment targets and build your own portfolio.

With that said, grab your calculator, and let's tee it up!

THE MIND OF THE VALUE INVESTOR

"You've got to look for value. That is all we do."[1]

Michael F. Price

O
N A QUIET DAY IN THE FALL OF **1998,** I was once again under pressure. Gripping his chair with one hand and an annual report in the other, Michael Price, the legendary value investor who *Fortune Magazine* once labeled "the scariest SOB on Wall Street," stood before me. His question to me was direct, as always. "Dennis...is this a good business?" he quickly asked.

"Yes, it is," I responded, after realizing that he was referring to an annual report I placed on his desk earlier that morning.

After a brief pause to gather my thoughts, I continued, "The company has significant market share in the industries in which it competes. While one of the three business segments that the company owns is extremely cyclical, with depressed profit margins, the profitability of the other two has been very strong, and should get stronger. Management is top-notch, and according to my understanding from the most recent proxy statements, their financial incentives are aligned with shareholders."

"What is it worth?" Michael asked.

---

[1] *The Dallas Morning News,* "Michael Price Speaks His Mind," December 15, 1996.

"Shares of the company are selling in the marketplace at private-market valuations, and at a significant discount to take-out valuations. We will probably get an opportunity to pick up shares in the company at around $33, but they are worth at least $50 to $60 apiece based on my sum-of-the-parts and deal valuations. I think we will be able to sell at these price levels in a year or so."

"Go on…"

"Well, the company recently announced that it will be breaking itself into three separate companies. I believe that the breakup will prove to be a potent catalyst to get the stock to its fair value. Also, based on my estimation, we would be getting the company's cyclical business for free at a share price in the low 30s."

"What about the balance sheet?" He demanded.

"Pristine!" I replied. "The company is underleveraged and has plenty of cash on its balance sheet with very little debt. Given the economics of the business, its market share, brand strength, and financial position, I believe that a share price in the low 30s represents ample safety levels."

The interrogation abruptly ended. Michael Price walked away from our discussion. A few weeks later, we purchased as many shares as we could of Varian Associates at our desired price. Our assessment of the businesses and their values paid off. Less than 18 months later, we watched the shares of the individual pieces of the company, after the breakup, trade up first meeting then exceeding their fair values.

Needless to say, the outcome of such conversations varied from one investment to another. The dialogue, however, represents a very typical interaction between the value investors at many investment firms.

THE ESSENCE OF VALUE INVESTING

Value investing is not a technique—it is a philosophy. It is a way of life. In fact, value investors approach what they do inside or outside the world of finance in the same way—taking certain criteria to make a decision, while demonstrating emotional discipline along the way. These patient thinkers tap all available resources to make a judgment call, but follow no one source. They do their own work. Value investors trust their abilities, their instincts, and their philosophy. Their investment style is an extension of their unwavering personalities.

The goal of the value investor is quite simple: to buy solid businesses at exceptional prices in order to achieve adequate after-tax returns over a long period. The mental model is as follows:

Good Business + Excellent Price = Adequate Return over Time

After investors do their homework on a company, an assessment of the firm's value is done, and a reasonable price to pay for the business is determined. The key understanding here is that the most successful investors have a framework and a way of approaching stocks. "It's all simple," says Michael Price. "It's not rocket science. It's Wall Street that makes it complicated. What Max Heine and Warren Buffett did was to boil it all down to buying companies when their value was deeply discounted..."[2] Price explains.

The keys to investing, based on simple rules such as purchasing companies at a discount, are easy to understand. They have worked for a wide range of value investors, such as catalyst-driven investors like Michael Price of Mutual Series and Joel Greenblatt of Gotham Capital, or patient owners such as Warren Buffett of Berkshire Hathaway and John Rogers of Ariel Capital Management. These approaches are well documented, and surprisingly, are not complicated. Implementation, however, is not so simple. The balance between the art of investing, assessing a management team or identifying a good business, and the science of investing, figuring out what price to pay based on what the company is worth, can be difficult for some.

Unfortunately, there seems to be many definitions of what comprises a "good" business; there are also numerous ways that investors can determine if they are getting an excellent price for a company. Even among value investors, you will find differences in opinion on the relationship between business value and price. The objective is to make sure that *your* definition of a "good business" is consistent with *your* definition of an "excellent" price.

The price paid is only meaningful if it is relative to the business' value. Fair value is a destination; price and time help value investors determine if it is worthwhile for them to take that journey. The rewards must justify the risks taken. In a rational market environment, price and value share a delicate balance, as one dictates the degree of the other. They should never be separated.

WE ARE ALL ANALYSTS
At the core, value investors are and will always be investment analysts. Whether they are members of investment clubs, doctors, or professional fund managers by day, they realize that investing requires independent work, analytical thinking, and a relentless work ethic.

[2]*The Dallas Morning News,* "Michael Price Speaks His Mind," December 15, 1996.

While many value investors have a variety of approaches and investment criteria, what binds them together are three basic characteristics: 1) they exude emotional discipline, 2) they possess a robust framework for making investment decisions, and 3) they apply original research and independent thinking.

Value investors also realize that investing is a journey, sometimes over a rather bumpy terrain. But, the decision making must be a patient process, requiring hefty amounts of perseverance and commitment. Most value investors are well equipped to take such a journey. Warren Buffett makes this point in a recent edition of Benjamin Graham's *The Intelligent Investor.* "To invest successfully over a lifetime does not require a stratospheric IQ, unusual business insights, or inside information," Buffett writes. "What's needed is a sound intellectual framework for making decisions and the ability to keep emotions from corroding that framework."[3]

Chapter 1 begins with a discussion on the topic of emotional discipline. The chapter also compares investing to speculating, and lays out the fundamental beliefs of the typical value investor. The chapter then introduces you to the Five Keys—a value investor's framework for making investment decisions. Chapter 1 concludes by revisiting the example of Varian Associates to apply this framework. Throughout this book the analysis draws heavily from original sources of information, specifically from filings to the U.S. Securities and Exchange Commission (SEC). The goal is to show how strongly the link is between SEC filings and independent research.

THE NEED FOR EMOTIONAL DISCIPLINE

Having emotional discipline is a critical asset for any investor, but particularly for those who are value oriented. Even if investors had access to the innermost thoughts of Michael Price or Warren Buffett, they might still fail miserably in the market if their emotions ultimately dictated their actions. Controlling spontaneous reactions and not letting them guide one's decision making is what having emotional discipline is all about.

Emotional discipline is the value investor's greatest strength. It is the foundation upon which all is built. Investors who possess a high degree of emotional discipline have a significant advantage, competing more effectively in the public markets.

Emotions include feelings of fear, anger, greed, et cetera. Discipline is training oneself to act in accordance with a predetermined set of rules.

---

[3]Graham, B. *The Intelligent Investor,* Preface by Warren Buffett (New York: Harper & Row, 1973, p. vii).

Investors are individuals, and therefore, are imperfect. As human beings, we are not machines that analyze data and make buy and sell decisions in a vacuum. People are emotional creatures who are driven by fear, greed, and gambling instincts. There are three basic characteristics of those of us who lack emotional discipline among investors:

1. We often believe what we want to believe, and tend not to take into account what the facts dictate.

2. Short on courage, we at times lack the conviction from our own work.

3. We are often too short-term oriented.

Believing what we want to believe, due to self-denial or overconfidence, is a category into which many investors fall. Overconfidence can be very dangerous for any investor because it often causes rational investors to think irrationally. A less obvious impact is that it can lead investors, often caught up in the moment, to overlook critical facts in their analysis of a situation. Slowly, emotions can take over, as these investors trade in and out of bad investments in a frantic effort to recoup losses, save face, or worse, push their luck during bull markets.

The Internet fuels this danger of overconfidence because of what some call "illusions of knowledge"—the tendency for decision makers to believe that their investment skills increase dramatically simply by getting more information. With so much access to information on a particular company, an overconfident investor can make a case for just about any outcome, no matter how illogical it is—particularly if the information is coming from questionable Web sites. This is a danger for all of us if we lack the training necessary to sift properly through vast amounts of information and interpret them appropriately. As a result, many investors rely heavily on Internet chat rooms, news groups, Web postings, and other research.[4]

We can also be driven by emotions. There are many investors who trade stocks based on what is often coined "market psychology," and their personal mood for the day. If the mood is good, buy; if not, sell. Often, our personal mood and the mood of the market are mixed up. Many investors will trade in and out of stocks frequently, regardless of the economic value of the company shares that they are trading.

There is nothing wrong with professional traders trading stocks—if that is all they do. In fact, there are well-known and well-respected

[4]Nofsinger, J. *The Psychology of Investing* (New Jersey: Prentice Hall, 2002, pp. 14–15).

investors who have benefited tremendously by mastering this highly skilled craft of trading securities. The problem arises when one starts to mix this type of trading—some refer to it as "momentum investing"—with value-based investing, or buying businesses. For the longer-term business buyer, trading is a distraction at best. The small after-tax and transaction gains that result are generally offset by the preoccupation of the investor. Lost in the machinations of day-to-day trading, the investor misses critical signals of asset deterioration of a larger, more meaningful investment. This scenario does not only happen to individual investors; it happens to professional investors as well.

Many of these investors also lack the conviction to support the conclusions from their own work. They tend to be weak on fundamentals and short on courage; they lack confidence in their own research analysis. As a result, they rely on other factors to draw their conclusions. There will always be opposing points of view. That is exactly what happens when one purchases shares of a company—the buyer has a different point of view from the seller. Due to a lack of understanding of the need for fundamental research, or having limited ability to analyze the facts, some investors have no other choice but to invest based on the whims of the market, and this leads to the herding effect.

Investors—even those who are value oriented—often invest in herds. They watch CNBC or hear that Warren Buffett is buying real estate, for example. So, as one would predict, they too must participate because of the fear of being out of step. There is nothing wrong with listening to the herd. However, following the herd can be an emotional decision, and not a judgment based on objective reasoning. Investors get a sense that the herd can't be wrong all of the time.

Focusing on the short term: Investors who lack emotional discipline are often short-term oriented. They want profits, now. They fail to realize that investing is a patient game. Similar to gambling, they trade for short-term profits, an action that fosters strong emotional responses.[5] Short-term investors are not concerned with what a company's management team will do over the next six months or how a company's market position will strengthen over the course of the following year. Rather, these so-called investors are concerned with what the stock will do in the next minute, next hour, or next day. Fundamentals do not drive their decisions. As a result, many short-term investors rely on stock charts to help them make buy and sell decisions, but that too has some skeptics.

[5]Nofsinger, J. *The Psychology of Investing* (New Jersey: Prentice Hall, 2002, p. 72).

There are several reasons why individuals who solely rely on charts to make investment decisions may fall short of achieving adequate investment returns. First, they tend to purchase shares of companies after the shares have risen substantially—succumbing to the buy-high, sell-higher mentality. All else equal, this makes the purchase more risky. Furthermore, the buy and sell "signal" becomes less useful, as more individuals watch for these same market cues. The decision actually creates the opposite effect for the investor, as every *buy* signal actually generates selling. Those who are trying to gauge the technical analyst community understand that when such stock prices are up on technical signals, they are up artificially. Comparatively, fundamental analysis relies on original, proprietary work, and not groupthink.

People are wired to be emotional investors. Peter Lynch, former money manager and Vice Chairman of Fidelity Investments, makes the case that investors continually pass in and out of three emotional states: concern, complacency, and capitulation. He explains that the typical investor becomes concerned after the market has dropped or the economy seems to have faltered, which keeps this particular investor from buying good businesses at excellent prices. Following this logic, after the investor buys at higher prices, he or she gets complacent when the stock continues to rise. This is precisely the time to review the company's fundamentals. However, this type of investor will generally let it ride. Then finally, when the stock falls on hard times, and the price falls below the purchased price, the investor capitulates and sells on a whim.[6]

Even a few so-called long-term investors are only so until the next big drop in stock prices. There is no such thing as long-term investors, if they do not have a tolerance for pain and the ability to ignore the market's panic. True long-term investors are fewer than most believe, as emotional discipline is often in short supply on Wall Street.

OBTAINING EMOTIONAL DISCIPLINE

It is a pretty straightforward process to distinguish someone with a high degree of emotional discipline. Many investors have written about these traits. Peter Lynch indicated that these qualities include patience, self-reliance, common sense, a tolerance for pain, open-mindedness, detachment, persistence, humility, flexibility, a willingness to do independent research, an equal willingness to admit to mistakes, the ability to make decisions without complete or perfect information, and the ability to ignore

[6]Lynch, P. *One Up One Wall Street* (New York: Penguin Books, 1989, p. 70).

panic and euphoria.[7] The investing objective is to ignore the emotions and the whims of the market by controlling the short-term outcomes. "This conflict between desire and willpower occurs because people are influenced by both long-term rational concerns and by more short-term emotional factors."[8]

The vast majority of investors, including value-oriented investors, have some aspect of emotional exuberance at times. Our brains do not function in isolation from our environments and feelings. Rather, the brain may make assumptions often based on emotions in order to come to an analytical conclusion quickly. Knowing about this shortfall helps investors avoid making certain mistakes. There are many ways that we can build upon our emotional discipline in order to invest successfully. Indeed, one does not have to possess all of the best qualities to succeed in this area. The fact that you purchased this book confirms that you already possess the most important quality: the realization that a disciplined framework is critical to any sound investment strategy.

There are several methods that investors use to control their emotions. Legendary investor Benjamin Graham used very rigid control parameters to buy and sell securities. These criteria included buying companies with the current price no greater than 15 times the average earnings of the past 3 years, with current assets at least twice current liabilities, and with an uninterrupted record of payments for at least the past 20 years. His protégé, Warren Buffett, is less stringent. He looks for companies that are relatively simple to understand. These are businesses that are virtually certain to possess enormous competitive strength 10 to 20 years from now, with the intrinsic value of the companies increasing at a satisfactory rate. Michael Price, on the other hand, likes to buy companies with pristine balance sheets and catalysts.

These investment parameters work for them. However, they may not work for you. Investing is an individual sport with individual consequences. It is very similar to golf. You have to approach each investment opportunity or shot in a certain way; you need a set of tools and a defined way of using them with very few compromises. Your approach and the tools you use must all fit together. In order to be successful in both games, you have to master certain fundamentals. It is hard to conceive of an above-average golfer, with a great swing but a poor grip, scoring well consistently. Likewise, a value investor with good business judgment, but poor fundamentals to evaluate opportunities, is very unlikely to outperform on a regular basis. Good

[7]Lynch, P. *One Up One Wall Street* (New York: Penguin Books, 1989, p. 69).
[8]Nofsinger, J. *The Psychology of Investing* (New Jersey: Prentice Hall, 2002, p. 81).

business judgment and good fundamentals fit together. The delicate balance between the rigidity and flexibility of techniques and frameworks is the cornerstone in obtaining emotional discipline.

With an established framework at hand, value investors are more likely to avoid getting caught up with the moods of the market or their own emotional feelings of the day.

THE SEVEN FUNDAMENTAL BELIEFS

Belief #1: The world is not coming to an end, despite how the stock market is reacting.   Investor sentiment has a more pronounced impact on stock prices than fundamentals in the short to intermediate term. In the long term, however, fundamentals always prevail. Throughout the history of American capitalism, the markets have survived and flourished after times of crisis. Since WWII, there have been several recessions and economic setbacks, and the market has recovered from each crisis in a timely manner. History indicates that the vast majority of such declines is normal and will be short term in nature, when the government reacts accordingly.

On October 1, 2001, at the height of investor uncertainty in the marketplace following "September 11," Peter Lynch gives his perspective on the U.S. markets in turmoil: "Although I have been in this field for more than 30 years and have seen many difficult times—the market crash of 1987 (a 23% decline for the Dow in one day) and 5 recessions—I still don't know the answer. I never have. No one can predict with any certainty, which way the next 1000 points will be. Market fluctuations, while no means comfortable, are normal. But it's important for us not to lose focus on why we invest in the stock market. When we invest in the market, we are buying companies." Lynch goes on to say that the events that were hurting the market at the time will have an effect on corporate earnings and the overall economy, "but over the long term, I believe corporate earnings will be higher in 10 years than they are today, and dramatically higher in 20 years. And the markets will follow accordingly."[9]

Based on the data in Exhibit 1.1, in 15 of the 18 economic meltdowns, it has taken only three months for the stock market to return back to positive territory from the event-triggered losses.

---

[9]Lynch, P. *The Wall Street Journal* advertisement, "What's Next? A Perspective from Peter Lynch," October 1, 2001, p. A5.

EXHIBIT 1.1 Dow Jones Industrial Average market crisis.

Crisis Events, DJIA Declines and Subsequent Performance

Event	Reaction Dates	Reaction Date %Gain/Loss	DJIA Percentage Gain Days after Reaction Dates		
			22	63	126
Exchange Closed WWI	07/22/1914–12/24/1914	–10.2	10.0	6.6	21.2
Germany invades France	05/09/1940–06/22/1940	–17.1	–0.5	8.4	7.0
Pearl Harbor	12/06/1941–12/10/1941	–6.5	3.8	–2.9	–9.6
Korean War	06/23/1950–07/13/1950	–12.0	9.1	15.3	19.2
Eisenhower Heart Attack	09/23/1955–09/26/1955	–6.5	0.0	6.6	11.7
Sputnik	10/03/1957–10/22/1957	–9.9	5.5	6.7	7.2
JFK Assassination	11/21/1963–11/22/1963	–2.9	7.2	12.4	15.1
Martin Luther King Assassinated	04/03/1968–04/05/1968	–0.4	5.3	6.4	9.3
U.S. Bombs Cambodia	04/29/1970–05/26/1970	–14.4	9.9	20.3	20.7
Arab Oil Embargo	10/16/1973–12/05/1973	–18.5	9.3	10.2	7.2
Nixon Resigns	08/07/1974–08/29/1974	–17.6	–7.9	–5.7	12.5
Hunt Silver Crash	02/13/1980–03/27/1980	–15.9	6.7	16.2	25.8
U.S. Invades Grenada	10/24/1983–11/07/1983	–2.7	3.9	–2.8	–3.2

10

Event	Reaction Dates				
Financial Panic '87	10/02/1987–10/19/1987	−34.2	11.5	11.4	15.0
Iraq invades Kuwait	08/02/1990–08/23/1990	−13.3	0.1	2.3	16.3
World Trade Center Bombing	02/25/1993–02/27/1993	−0.3	2.4	5.1	8.5
Asian Stock Market Crisis	10/07/1997–10/27/1997	−12.4	8.8	10.5	25.0
WTC and Pentagon Terrorist Attacks	09/10/2001–09/21/2001	−14.3	13.4	21.2	N/A

The 22, 63, and 126 day rate-of-change is calculated from the last day in the reaction dates column.

The first date in the reaction dates column indicates the start of the market reaction or the trading day prior to the event.

1914 data–In 1916 a new list of 20 stocks for the DJIA was adopted and computed back to the reopening of the exchange on 12/12/1914. NDR analysis for this study adjusted the DJIA index level prior to 12/12/1914 to reflect an accurate and " consistent data set." Source: The Dow Jones Averages 1885–1990, Edited by Phyllis S. Pierce.

Days = Market Days

©2001 Ned Davis Research, Inc. All Rights Reserved.

Belief #2: Investors will always be driven by fear and greed, and the over-all market and stocks will react accordingly. This volatility is simply the cost of doing business.   As mentioned earlier in this chapter, the two most common emotional reactions to the stock market are fear and greed. Fear forces stocks below intrinsic value, and greed forces stocks exceed-ingly above intrinsic value. This fear investors have that they will lose all of their money, and stocks will go to zero, causes many in the marketplace to sell at a frantic pace, liquidating their investments in stock holdings and mutual funds. Redemptions from these funds run high, and professional money managers, particularly value money managers—against their own choosing—have to sell shares of companies well below their true worth, pushing stocks down even further. It can ultimately become a vicious cycle. Normal economic cycles or a sudden drop in the stock markets typ-ically gets this cycle going.

Greed has the opposite effect. Investors bid up prices for stocks or refuse to sell overpriced securities in the hopes of squeezing every bit of potential profit possible. Excessive optimism and fear are the enemies of the rational buyer. Therefore, the value investor is often fearful when the market is greedy, and greedy when the market is fearful. The value investor's frame-work controls one's tendency to become too fearful or too greedy.

Belief #3: Inflation is the only true enemy. Trying to predict economic variables and the direction of the market or the economy is a waste of time—focus on businesses and their values, and remember Belief #1. *Inflation* is the overall increase in the price of consumer goods and ser-vices. The federal government measures inflation by comparing a basket of consumer prices today to prices in an historical period to assess the changes. If the current prices increased, investors in companies would demand greater returns on their investment to offset the decline in the investment's purchasing power. The Federal Reserve Board typically steps in. At times of inflation, the Fed will raise the discount rate, causing inter-est rates to increase. With the increase in rates, money becomes expensive, and the demand for it declines. With a decrease in money to purchase goods and services, the demand for goods and services declines as well, which ultimately drives down the price for products. For companies, inflation indicates higher costs to borrow money. Interest rates, unemployment lev-els, etc., react based on what the expectations are for inflation.

Inflation has a devastating impact for investors, and there is little that one can do about it. Buffett says, "The arithmetic makes it plain that infla-tion is a far more devastating tax than anything that has been enacted by our legislature. The inflation tax has a fantastic ability to simply consume capital." Buffett warns, "If you feel you can dance in and out of securities in a way that defeats the inflation tax, I would like to be your broker—but not your partner."[10]

Don't waste time. Accurately predicting economic variables, such as the interest rate or the direction of the stock market, would be very profitable for an investor. But it is not possible, and it will never be possible. Therefore, value investors do not concern themselves with chasing shadows—they focus on what is more substantive.

Belief #4: Good ideas are hard to find, but there are always good ideas out there, even in bear markets. The "stock market" is really a misnomer. Rather, there is a market of stocks. Any individual investor can do well regardless of the overall market. The most disciplined value investor identifies and purchases shares of the best businesses possible at excellent prices. In fact, many value investors believe that the best ideas are found during bear markets, when great companies are attractively priced. This is due to the fact that the market is forward-looking and often discounts the current economic environment. Prudent investors know that bear markets are a natural part of an economic and market cycle, and the fact that every bear market has come to an end after a reasonable length of time provides evidence of this belief.

Therefore, given the notion that bear markets are temporary in nature, and that companies during bear markets are more attractively priced, one can only come to the conclusion that there are good investment opportunities to be had, if not some of the best opportunities, during bear markets. Indeed, the best time to have purchased some of the most valued companies for the long term was in bear-market periods.

Belief #5: The primary purpose of a publicly traded company is to convert all of the company's available resources into shareholder value. As share-owners, your job is to make sure that this happens. Companies are not only "going concerns," they are also resource conversion organizations— converting all of the company's available resources into shareholder value. If this conversion does not take place, then the company is better off shutting its doors or going private. Often, an event—or an ongoing sequence of events— needs to take place to make this transition from resource conversion to wealth

---

[10]Lowe, J. *Warren Buffett Speaks* (New York: John Wiley & Sons, 1997, p. 87).

creation a reality. These events are called *catalysts*. These catalysts can range from the launch of a new product to the break-up of the company.

The best businesses are those with management teams who are most efficient in converting the company's resources into shareholder wealth. The company's resources include its people, capital, brand, property, plant, and equipment, etc. Shareholder wealth develops by converting these resources into shareholder value. An increase in real earnings can be added to share-owners' equity. Free cash flow can be properly reinvested, or dividends can be provided to shareholders, if management cannot properly convert its cash streams to wealth creation for shareowners. Management is the key.

Belief #6: Ninety percent of successful investing is buying right. Selling at the optimal price is the hard part. As a result, value investors tend to buy early and sell early. The market is very consistent, giving value investors the opportunity to buy right by paying a price far less; this is relative to the value they expect to receive without taking on undue risk. In order to buy right, one has to have a framework in place to know exactly when to buy and when to sell. As some have observed, "there is a sucker born every minute—and he exists to buy your investments at a higher price than you paid for them. Any price will do as long as others may be willing to pay more. There is no reason, only mass psychology. All the smart investor has to do is beat the gun—get in at the very beginning."[11]

If you are going to buy, it is best to buy early rather than late. Buying early allows the investor to use dollar cost averaging. *Dollar cost averaging* is buying more shares of a particular company as the share price trades lower in the market place. Assuming that the fundamentals and the reasons for purchasing the company in the first place have not changed, dollar cost averaging can be a very powerful tool. For well-informed value investors, it boosts returns by lowering their average costs per share. It allows the investor to buy right by purchasing shares at more attractive prices.

Belief #7: Volatility is not risk; it is opportunity. Real risk is an adverse and permanent change in the intrinsic value of the company. There is no relation between stock volatility and risk. The value investor disregards the day-to-day movement of the general market. The fair and intrinsic value of a business does not fluctuate as often as its stock price. Benjamin Graham is noted as saying that the market is there to serve you, not to guide

[11]Malkiel, B. *A Random Walk Down Wall Street* (New York: W.W. Norton & Co., 1990, p. 31).

EXHIBIT 1.2   Intrinsic value and stock price.

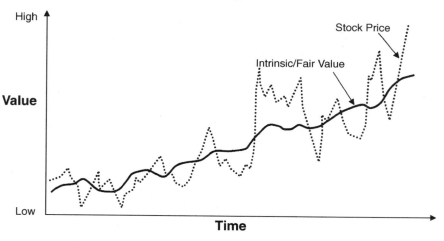

you in making your decisions. Therefore, the market's fluctuations only give the value investor the opportunity to buy and sell at certain prices. Stock prices fluctuate around value. The focus of the value investor should always be on the direction of the intrinsic value of the company. Real risks are the risks to cash flows and the underlying economics of the business. Actual risk also depends on the price paid for the business—determined by the difference between the price paid and the intrinsic value.

The exhibit above illustrates the stock-price-to-intrinsic-value relationship of a typical well-managed, high-quality company. The lines of the graph depict the intrinsic value of the company and its stock price. There are three key understandings from this illustration. The first is that the stock price oscillates around the intrinsic value of the company. Market participants, in attempts to predict the future, react to different variables. These variables include financial news, industry data, general market conditions, portfolio decisions by mutual funds managers, and the actions of large shareholders of the company under consideration. Reacting to these variables creates volatility in the stock price, but the intrinsic value of the company is not as volatile.

The second understanding is that of focus. Informed investors expect this kind of volatile stock behavior to occur with all equity securities. What the value investor looks for and focuses on is the intrinsic worth of the company, by addressing the question, "Has the company's fundamentals changed?" By honing in on the solid line, the investor can take advantage of the situation when the stock price indicates that the market may be overly opportunistic or pessimistic about the company.

Finally, the chart points to the issue of time. Every company and industry is different when it comes to levels of volatility. Technology companies, for example, have stock prices that are more volatile than most industrial manufacturing companies. As a result, investors who purchase a technology-related company below its intrinsic value can expect to exit their investment earlier, given the high volatility in technology shares. The key is to buy below the intrinsic worth of the company—which is often very difficult to determine for technology companies, for reasons we discuss later in this book. In general, value investors are split on the issue of owning technology companies. Warren Buffett stays away. Michael Price is more opportunistic and admits that he is "not a tech investor until they stumble…paying less than net cash per share."[12] This also underscores the need to buy right. The point here is that the market often dictates not only when an investor buys, but also when an individual should sell.

THE FIVE KEYS OF VALUE FRAMEWORK

When it comes to investing, Warren Buffett clearly outlines his investment criteria in a 1998 issue of *Outstanding Investor's Digest*. Buffett says, "Our criteria for selecting a stock are also our criteria for selecting a business. First, we're looking for a business we can understand—where we think we understand its product, the nature of its competition, and what can go wrong over time. Then, when we find that business, we try to figure out whether its economics—meaning its earnings power over the next five or ten or 15 years—are likely to be good and getting better or poor and getting worse. And we try to evaluate its future income stream. Then we try to decide whether we're getting in with people who we feel comfortable being in business with. And finally, we try to decide on what we think represents an appropriate price for what we've seen up to that point."[13]

Comparatively, a reporter once asked Michael Price what an investor should look for when considering what companies to buy. Price responded, "First, a company selling at a discount from asset value. Second, a manage-

[12]*Outstanding Investor's Digest*, "Mutual Series Funds' Michael Price," December 31, 1996.

[13]*Outstanding Investor's Digest*, "Berkshire Hathaway's Warren Buffett and Charlie Munger," September 24, 1998.

ment that owns shares. The more the better. Third, a clean balance sheet—little debt—so there is less financial risk. It doesn't work to buy things that are highly leveraged. If you do these three things, you'll do fine."[14] The reporter interrogated Price a bit further by asking him if his approach was the same as Warren Buffett's. Price abruptly replied, "No. The mindset is similar. But Buffett is different. He can identify businesses with very unique franchises. We're not good at that. We're not. We look for value."[15]

Value investors search for value. They identify, evaluate, and buy shares of companies as if they were purchasing the entire company, not just its shares. While this approach has proven to be very effective over the years, few investors have been able to put it into practice. The challenge has always been—and continues to be—on execution. Staying consistent with this approach requires a great deal of focus, patience, and emotional discipline. With share prices and markets gyrating wildly, Wall Street analysts upgrading and downgrading stocks frequently, and market gurus of one sort or another forecasting the next correction, staying the course remains a constant challenge. Within all this clutter and chaos, the value investor must maintain his or her purchasing discipline, completely motivated by a robust mental framework.

Value investors are interested in purchasing shares of companies that they believe have a big enough discount to fair value, in order to generate adequate returns in two to three years. Given that companies with low valuations are generally "out-of-favor" or contrarian plays, this investment approach requires detailed, fundamental business and financial analysis to assess properly the risk/reward profiles of each potential investment. The value investor's framework for considering investment opportunities is summarized throughout the following five key questions:

1. Is this a good business run by smart people?
2. What is this company worth?
3. How attractive is the price for this company, and what should I pay for it?
4. How realistic is the most effective catalyst?
5. What is my margin of safety at my purchase price?

These criteria, aptly called the "Five Keys" are a compilation of the teachings of highly successful and well-known value investors.

---

[14]*The Dallas Morning News,* Michael Price Speaks His Mind, December 15, 1996.
[15]*The Dallas Morning News,* Michael Price Speaks His Mind, December 15, 1996.

EXHIBIT 1.3   The Five Keys of Value Framework.

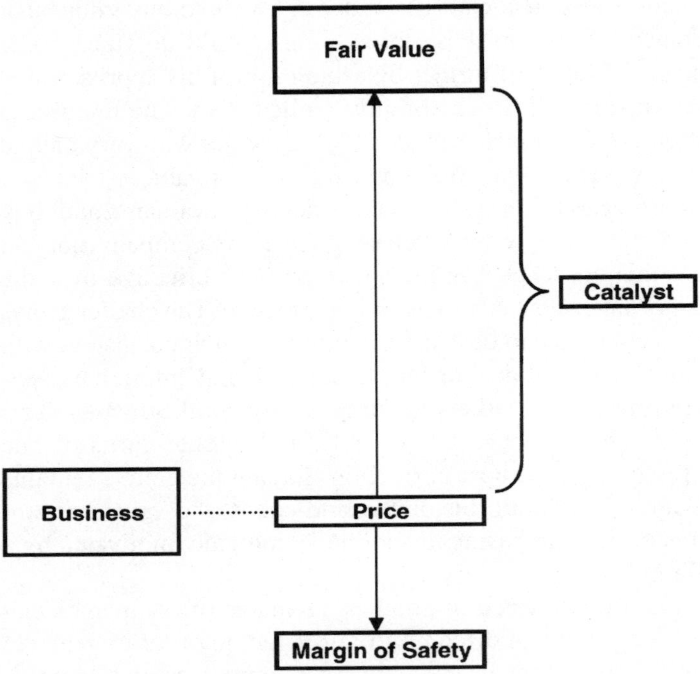

```
                  ┌─────────────────┐
                  │   Fair Value    │
                  └─────────────────┘
                           ▲    ┐
                           │     ⎰
                           │        ┌──────────┐
                           │       ⎱│ Catalyst │
                           │        └──────────┘
                           │     ⎱
  ┌────────────┐           │    ┘
  │  Business  │┈┈┈┈┈┈┈┌─────────────────┐
  └────────────┘       │      Price      │
                       └─────────────────┘
                           │
                           ▼
                  ┌──────────────────┐
                  │ Margin of Safety │
                  └──────────────────┘
```

Chapters 2 through 5 go into more detail on each of these five assessment levers, by defining each and explaining how they are used. First, in business assessment, the value investor focuses on a full range of relevant business and industry issues that affect the value of the enterprise. This may include items such as quality of earnings, product lines, market sizes, management teams, and the sustainability of competitive positioning within the industry.

Second, value investors perform fair value assessments that allow them to establish a range of prices that would determine the fair value of the company, based on measures such as normalized free cash flow, break-up, take-out, and/or asset values. Exit valuation assessment provides a rational "fair value" target price, and indicates the upside opportunity from the current stock price.

Third, price assessment allows the individual to understand fully the price at which the stock market is currently valuing the company. In this analysis, the investor takes several factors into account by essentially answering the question: Why is the company afforded its current low valuation? For example, a company with an attractive valuation at first glance may not prove to be so appealing after a proper assessment of its accounting strategy or its competitive position relative to its peers. The price of its shares may be cheap for permanent reasons. Price assessment also provides the reasonable price that one would pay for the company.

Fourth, catalyst identification and effectiveness bridges the gap between the current asking price and what value investors think the company is worth based on their exit valuation assessment. The key here lies in making sure that the catalyst identified to "unlock" value in the company is very likely to occur. However, not all catalysts are equal—they vary in degree of potency. Therefore, the level of effectiveness is critical. Potential effective catalysts may include the breakup of the company, a divestiture, new management, or an ongoing internal catalyst, such as a company's culture.

In cases where the catalyst is delayed or ineffective, the value investor's margin of safety assessment, prior to the purchase, becomes all the more critical. Buying shares with a margin of safety is essentially owning shares cheap enough that the price paid is heavily supported by the underlying economics of the business, asset values, cash on the balance sheet, etc. If a company's stock trades below this "margin of safety" price level for a length of time, it would be reasonable to believe that the company is more likely to be sold to a strategic or financial buyer, broken up, or liquidated, etc., to realize its true intrinsic value—thus making such shares safer to own.

PUTTING IT ALL TOGETHER: REVISITING VARIAN ASSOCIATES

In the company's Form 8-K, filed on August 21, 1998, Varian Associates announced a detailed plan to reorganize the company's core businesses in health care systems, semiconductor equipment, and instruments, breaking up into three separate public companies. Under the plan, the filing indicated that Varian would seek a tax-free spin-off to shareholders of two of the three businesses. I took note as the U.S. Securities and Exchange Commission (SEC) filing went to describe each business segment:[16]

Varian Medical Systems' business is organized around two major product lines—radiation oncology equipment for treating cancer and x-ray tubes for various diagnostic uses. With plants in California, Utah, Illinois, and South Carolina, in addition to production centers in England, France,

---

[16]Varian Associates 8-K filed on August 21, 1998 to the U.S. Securities and Exchange Commission.

Switzerland, and Finland, it had fiscal 1997 sales of $472 million. With over 3,500 systems in service, the business ranks as the world's largest supplier of radiotherapy equipment, as well as the leading supplier of x-ray tubes for original equipment and replacement use.

Varian's (officially known as Varian, Inc.) instruments business is a major manufacturer of analytical and research instrumentation for industrial and scientific applications. Its activities also include a line of vacuum pumps and leak detection equipment, as well as a state-of-the-art circuit board manufacturing center. These ventures posted combined 1997 sales of $527 million and included factories in Arizona, California, Colorado, and Massachusetts, along with plants in Australia, Italy, and The Netherlands.

Varian Semiconductor Equipment Associates makes and services ion implantation systems, a key step in the chip manufacturing process. Operating manufacturing and R&D facilities at two Massachusetts locations, and in Japan and Korea, the company's 1997 sales totaled $424 million. This operation is the world's leading supplier of ion implant systems, with over 2,500 systems shipped to chip manufacturers worldwide.

The filing went on to note that "the company's overall results are also often inordinately influenced by factors in a single area, such as the volatility of the semiconductor industry where the current down-cycle has helped to push its stock price as much as 50% or more below its historical high."[17]

As I later learned through industry-related Web sites, each of Varian's business segments were leaders in their markets. The medical systems business was the world's largest provider of integrated oncology systems. The instruments division was a major supplier of analytical and research instrumentation for chemical analysis, and the semiconductor equipment business was the world's number one manufacturer of a particular type of machine to make semiconductors.

On the day of the announcement of the company spin-offs, the share price of Varian jumped 19%, from $36 to $43 per share. I was not discouraged by the fact that I may have missed a great buying opportunity. I knew that it would take a year to get the tax-free ruling and complete the reorganization. During these long intervals, experience told me that the market would most likely behave irrationally from time to time. I would get my opportunity to purchase shares in the company when the margin of safety was higher. Never chase a stock.

I proceeded to gather sections of Varian's most recent filings with the U.S. Securities and Exchange Commission to search for the value of the enterprise. Management's Discussion & Analysis (MD&A) section provided very useful information. Specifically, it improved my understanding *behind* Varian's numbers. It gave me an understanding of why they were what they were and what

[17]Varian Associates 8-K filed on August 21, 1998 to the U.S. Securities and Exchange Commission.

they are likely to be. The MD&A is often the most critical filing value that investors read. It can be found in a company's annual report and 10-Ks. After critiquing the company's most recent filings with the SEC, Value Line, and the company's Web site, as well as its competitors', I generated my own assessment of the enterprise by employing the five levers.

I liked the businesses and the management teams...   After taking a closer look at the company's margins compared to its peers, normalized returns, and cash flows, my initial indication was that Varian was in good businesses run by top-notch management teams. In addition, I noticed that each of the three business segments had stellar growth prospects. Medical systems, for example, were likely to benefit from an aging population. The instruments division was expected to grow based on increased interest and funding for genomic research, and the semiconductor segment was due for a rebound given the cyclical nature of the business.

By now I clearly liked the businesses and noticed in the latest proxy statement that the chairman of Varian Associates owned over 2% of the company. This signaled to me that the likelihood of management's interest to create shareholder value was similar to that of shareholders, given their personal investment in the business.

From my vantage point, the company was worth at least $55 per share... I analyzed the company using three different metrics: sum-of-the-parts, historical valuations, and on a deal basis (i.e., what an acquirer would pay for the business). On a sum-of-the-parts basis, I used three different multiples: enterprise value to earnings before interest, tax depreciation, and amortization; enterprise value to free cash flow; and price to earnings. I used these same valuations and looked back historically to gain a perspective as to the valuation range that the market had been willing to value this company. To come to a transaction deal value, I relied on the notes I had been keeping that announced deals in various industries. I valued the company on a deal basis using an enterprise-value-to-cash-flow basis, as well as an enterprise-value-to-revenue basis. Compiling such a list over time is one discipline that this book strongly urges value investors to practice. These are the values that were generated: $56 on a conservative sum-of-the-parts analysis, $52 on historical values, and $58 on a transaction basis—i.e., what a potential buyer might be willing to pay for the enterprise. In aggregate, I arrived to a value of $55 per share.

These valuations did not take into account favorable or adverse changes in the economic environment. My objective was to get to a reasonable value for the business based on the information that was available in the fall of 1998.

I wanted to own the company at a 40 percent discount to fair value and limited downside... As for price, simple arithmetic indicated that if I wanted a 40-percent discount or more for what I deemed to be fair value for the company at the time, $33 per share would be the best price. There was another reason why purchasing Varian in the low 30s would make sense: such a price would provide ample safety levels. I calculated my safety level for Varian's shares to be $29 per share. This value was based on what I deemed to be Varian's replacement cost for the franchise and a valuation level that would make sense for the management team to take the company private. In this calculation, I used 5.5 times enterprise value to pre-tax and interest cash flow based on the similar deals I looked at in the medical device and analytical instrument areas. Given Varian's market position, balance sheet strength, and outlook, I reasoned that such a multiple would be a very attractive price to pay for this small conglomerate. Such valuation generated $860 of equity value, and dividing that number by the number of shares outstanding generated a $29 stock price. Chapter 3 provides greater detail as to how these assessment tools are used.

In addition to that assessment, the analysis indicated that purchasing the company's shares in the low 30s would equal the value of only two divisions, meaning that the entire semiconductor equipment business would cost nothing.

This is where art meets science. I could have waited to buy Varian at $29, an ideal valuation. But my perspective on the value of the company, based on the other metrics I used, indicated that a price of $29 would have been a result of an unbelievable opportunity in the market or impairment in the assets of the firm, with the latter situation requiring a reevaluation of the business.

Breaking up the company was the best way to create shareholder value... At this point in my analysis, I liked the company and was comfortable with my price of $33, based on the level of safety and the discount to fair value it provided. The final question was "How is it going to get to fair value?" The catalyst of breaking up the company was sure to occur; I needed to get some comfort level with the degree of its potency. Not all catalysts are created equal.

The reasons that the management team gave for breaking up the company in the months that followed confirmed my assessment that this was a classic value-unlocking opportunity, which the management team exploited. I have often referred back to this filing as a benchmark for other breakup opportunities. The board of directors of Varian Associates approved the breakup of the company and highlighted the following six key reasons in the company's 8-K filing to the U.S. Securities and Exchange Commission.[18]

Reasons given for the breakup of Varian Associates   Management Focus: Varian Associates' three businesses have different dynamics and business cycles, serve different marketplaces and customer bases, are subject to different competitive forces, and must be managed with different long-term and short-term strategies and goals.[19] Varian Associates believes that separating its businesses into independent public companies, each with its own management team and board of directors, is necessary to address current and future management issues and considerations that result from operating these diverse businesses within a single company. The separation will enable the management of each business to manage that business, and to adopt and implement strategies for that business, solely with regard to the needs and objectives of that business. In addition, as a result of the separation, the management of each business will be able to devote its full attention to managing that business.

Capital Structure: Varian Associates believes that the breakup of the company will allow each of the companies to organize its capital structure and allocate its resources to support the very different needs and goals of the particular business. The stock buy-back program can be discontinued, or dividends eliminated, freeing cash for acquisition and growth opportunities for Varian and Varian Medical Systems, and permitting Varian Semiconductor Equipment to conserve cash for use in the cyclical downturns in its industry.[20] Capital borrowings can be tailored to the specific needs of the various business units. Each business will be able to allocate its resources without considering the needs of the other businesses.

Attracting and Retaining Key Employees: Varian Associates' management believes that the ability to attract and retain key personnel is fundamental to furthering the technology required to maintain a leadership

---

[18]Reasons for breakup is drawn from Varian Associates' 8-K filed on 03/08/1999 to the U.S. Securities and Exchange Commission.

[19]Varian Associates is listed as "Varian" in the company's 8-K filed on 03/08/1999 to the U.S. Securities and Exchange Commission.

[20]Varian Instruments is listed as "IB," Varian Medical Systems is listed as "VMS," and Varian Semiconductor Equipment is listed as "VSEA."

position in its business. In particular, under the old corporate structure, Varian Associates had been unable to offer equity-based compensation linked specifically to the performance of each separate business. The breakup would enable each company to establish focused, equity-based compensation programs, allowing each section of the company the opportunity to attract better management and to retain key personnel.

Acquisition Activities: Varian Associates believes that growth through acquisition is an important ingredient of the future success of Varian and Varian Medical Systems. Such acquisitions and growth would be financed in part through the issuance of capital stock. It is expected that the breakup will increase the availability of equity, as well as decrease the cost of raising equity capital. Varian Associates' management believes that, as a result of the breakup, each company will have a more attractive currency, its stock, through which to make acquisitions.

Investor Understanding: Debt and equity investors and securities analysts should be able to evaluate better the financial performance of each company and their respective strategies, thereby enhancing the likelihood that each will achieve appropriate market recognition. The stock of each of the three companies will also appeal to investors with differing investment objectives and risk tolerance, and will allow potential investors to focus their investments more directly to the areas of their primary interest.

Cost Savings: Each company should be able to rationalize better its organizational structure after the breakup. Accordingly, the administrative and organizational costs of each company, taken together, should be reduced from the aggregate levels experienced by Varian Associates prior to the breakup.

Varian Associates and the Five Keys of Value framework:

- **Business:** Excellent company with strong market positions, and management teams with a great outlook.

- **Value:** Fair value at $55 per share.

- **Price:** At $33, buying at a 40% discount to fair value.

- **Catalyst:** Breaking up the company.

- **Margin of Safety:** Downside is 12% with a 67% upside potential, getting an entire division for nothing.

BUSINESS AND INDUSTRY ASSESSMENT

> "We try to find companies that have the most consistent earnings streams, companies that are very predictable, companies that are in industries that lend themselves to predictability, that we believe can generate good, consistent profits in the future."[1]
>
> *John W. Rogers, Jr.*

BUYING BUSINESSES VERSUS SPECULATING ON STOCKS

Value investors buy businesses, not stocks. In order to do this effectively, these investors must employ an intellectual framework in which to make these decisions. Hand in hand with the critical analysis of a company, the most successful value investors apply a healthy dose of emotional discipline to their investing behavior. This book introduces an investment framework called the Five Keys of Value, providing a glimpse into the thoughtful and patient consideration involved in value investing. It is a framework based on the teachings of Michael Price, Warren Buffett, and other well-respected investors. The five keys are easily broken up into the following: business, price, and value assessment, catalyst identification, and margin of safety.

---

[1]Sincere, M., *101 Investment Lessons from the Wizards of Wall Street* (Franklin Lakes: Career Press, 1999, p. 41).

This chapter focuses on the first lever: business assessment. Here we answer the simple, but necessary question: Is this a good business?

Buying a business is an investment; trading stocks is not. The difference is clear. Value investors believe that as stockholders, they are owners of the corporation with rights and privileges. Speculators of stocks seem to believe that shares of companies are pieces of paper to be traded back and forth among market participants, regardless of the underlying assets associated with the securities.

Investors in businesses base their investment decisions on the economics of the business, the price they are paying relative to the value they are getting. Market speculators make decisions based on their predictions of the behavior of others—buy if the stock "behaves" well and sell if it does not. Surprisingly, some professional stock market participants who speculate on the price movement trade in an out of stocks quite well. It works for them. For most of us, however, such market psychology games are beyond our competence level.

For the value investor, buying a publicly traded business is no different than buying a private company or a home. The thought processes are very similar. Individuals interested in purchasing a home are not interested in "trading" the property. Most individuals intend to buy and hold, or sell five to seven years later. These potential owners take their time, spend countless hours researching potential prospects in the newspaper and on the Internet, and follow up on recommendations from real estate agents. Thorough homework is done. Long-term value investors believe that this level of care should also hold true for events in the public markets.

EXHIBIT 2.1   Buying businesses vs. stocks.

Factors for Buying a Business	Factors for Trading Stocks
Earnings and cash flows	Market psychology
Management	Technical trends of charts
Products and markets	Investor sentiment
Competitive advantage	Moving averages
Fair/Intrinsic value	Relative strength indicators
Margin of safety	Price momentum
Catalysts	Investment theme

EXHIBIT 2.2 Purchasing a stock vs. buying a home.

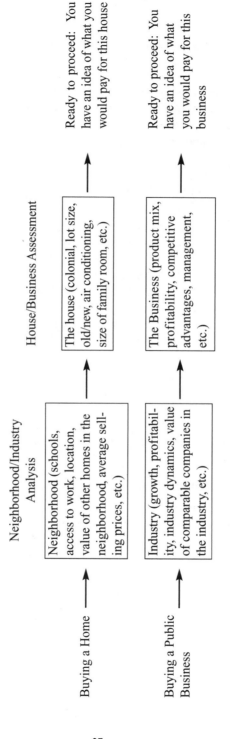

Neighborhood/Industry Analysis

House/Business Assessment

Buying a Home →

Neighborhood (schools, access to work, location, value of other homes in the neighborhood, average selling prices, etc.)

→ The house (colonial, lot size, old/new, air conditioning, size of family room, etc.)

→ Ready to proceed: You have an idea of what you would pay for this house

Buying a Public Business →

Industry (growth, profitability, industry dynamics, value of comparable companies in the industry, etc.)

→ The Business (product mix, profitability, competitive advantages, management, etc.)

→ Ready to proceed: You have an idea of what you would pay for this business

UNDERSTANDING THE BUSINESS

There are three understandings that value investors possess as they attempt to understand a business: they know where to get the best information to make the proper assessment, they know the approach to employ based on the business they are assessing, and they have the tools to dig deep into the SEC filings and financial statements of the business to minimize risk. Appendix A provides a list of tools you can use.

Without exception, understanding and knowing how to read the financial statements with the SEC filings is absolutely critical to any investor. "Whether you are a disciple of Ben Graham, a value investor, or a growth or momentum investor," Michael Price points out that, "you can agree that a stock's price must relate to its financials." Price goes on to say that "a sound understanding of how to read the basic financials should keep investors focused and thereby avoid costly mistakes…"[2]

There are several scholarly books that are written in great detail about how to analyze financial statements. Benjamin Graham's book, *The Interpretation of Financial Statements* is a classic. The following discussion on financial statements gives a general overview. The emphasis here is on the use of these statements.

GETTING THE MOST OUT OF THE ANNUAL REPORT AND FORM 10-K

The annual report is compiled for the benefit of several different types of readers, including investors, lenders, customers, etc. Investors can obtain a company's annual report through the company's Web site. There are a few sections to the annual report:

1.   The picture presentations
2.   Letter to shareholders
3.   The MD&A (Management's Discussion and Analysis)
4.   Financial statements
5.   Footnotes
6.   Other information

The most important part of the annual report is the Management's Discussion and Analysis (MD&A). In this section, simply speaking, management discusses and analyzes the company's performance. The MD&A is

---

[2]Graham, B. *The Interpretation of Financial Statements,* Introduction by Michael Price (New York: HarperBusiness, 1998).

required by the SEC, and therefore, entails information without the fluff. The MD&A is required to offer honest discussions that cover three areas:

1. The company's results from operations
2. The company's financial position
3. The past and future conditions and uncertainties that may materially affect the business

The picture presentation segment of the annual report comprises the areas of the business that the company would like to highlight. These often include information on the company's operations, financial status, and products. The letter to shareholders is a note from the top management. This is the section where the management is allowed to be the most optimistic about the future. In doing so, the management team often makes very vague comments about the business. The financial statement section is comprised of historical income, cash flow, and balance sheet statements. The footnotes support these statements. More often than not, the footnotes are extremely informative and contain as much relevant data as the financial statements do. These footnotes often include such information as accounting methods, commitments, long-term liabilities and the due dates on these same liabilities, inventory components, and other key disclosures. In fact, the footnotes are often management's hiding place of choice for adverse comments.

The financial reports summarize each material transaction or change in the form of numbers. Often, the same or similar transaction can be reported with various methods among companies. Because there is no one standard, companies are required to disclose the type of material transaction method they are using. This includes using inventory methods such as LIFO or FIFO and depreciation methods, etc. One particular footnote investors often look at is Note One, as the vast majority of companies list the methods they use in the first note. The annual report also includes information on the reporting of each division of the company (if there are more than one), a five-year summary of operations, and quarterly figures.

Most audit reports, sitting amongst the annual reports, read the same. The third paragraph is the most important because it contains the auditor's opinion. Auditors may express a "clean," "qualified," or "adverse" opinion, or they may "disclaim" and express no opinion at all. A negative opinion states that the auditors do not believe the financial statements are "fairly presented." Such opinion will often require the auditors to list the factors that led to this opinion.

The Form 10-K.   The Form 10-K contains similar information as found in the annual report. The 10-K is often regarded as a more complete source of information because this form is required by the SEC to include detailed information regarding the business. This form can be found on a company's and the SEC's Web sites.

The Form 10-K is presented in four different parts, and each part is divided further into individual items. Part I describes the company's business, including further information on the different segments of the company, such as domestic vs. foreign operations, product lines, etc. This part also describes the company's property and provides any legal proceedings in which the company is involved. Finally, this section discusses any matters that have been voted on by the shareholders. Part II describes the performance of the company's common stock, a five-year summary of financial data, management's discussion of the company's financial condition, changes that have occurred in the financial condition, and the results of operations. This part of the 10-K concludes by providing a set of financial statements, supplementary data, auditor's report, and any changes in accounting principles and disagreement with the auditors. Part III lists the board of directors and executive officers; compensation of executives and securities owned by them and major stockholders; and information relating to transactions between the company and the management, its subsidiaries, and major shareholders. The final part, Part IV, includes exhibits, financial statement schedules, and reports on Form 8-K.

The Form 8-K.   This form can be a very important filing, since it reports circumstances that are of material importance to shareholders and crucial to the SEC. These events must be reported within 15 days of occurrence; some are required to be reported earlier—as early as within 5 days of the event. Some of these events include changes in control of the firm, such as pending mergers, acquisitions, and dispositions of assets; court filings regarding bankruptcy or receivership; changes in the firm's accountants; other matters that would affect the future direction of the company; resignation of directors; and preliminary financial forecasts regarding business transactions or a change in the company's fiscal year.

The proxy statement.   The proxy statement contains information that must be provided to stockholders before they vote on company matters. It also provides information about salaries and the number of shares owned by the board of directors.

Getting what you need out of financial statements.   Financial statements are the most important source of information enabling investors to evaluate the economics of the business and the financial health of the company. The financial statements include a company's income statement, statement of cash flows, and balance sheet. There are three critical understandings that many value investors acknowledge when reading financial statements.

First, they realize that sometimes adjustments are required. These adjustments can be mandatory adjustments, such as converting all earnings-per-share numbers to a fully diluted basis; situational adjustments, which are on a case-by-case basis, to properly reflect the underlying economics of the business; and judgmental adjustments, which are based on the investor's own experience about a particular company or industry.[3]

Secondly, investors are prepared to analyze the numbers to understand how they affect the firm's value. This often refers to obtaining evidence on a firm's earnings power and cash flow strength.

Finally, value investors look for "red flags." Value analysts assess the degree to which the accounting of a company resembles the underlying economic reality of an enterprise. Red flags are those items that the investor determines must require further explanation. Red flags can also be abnormalities in a company's accounting as compared to its peers or other generally accepted standards of practice.

Let's briefly explain each statement. The income statement reports revenues and expenses incurred over a specific time period. The income statement is important because it provides value investors with information that allows them to gauge the prospects of a company's future earnings. Needless to say, predicting the future of earnings helps investors to value the company. It is with this statement that the investor is able to grasp a given company's earnings power—the strength and quality of income a company is expected to earn. Generally speaking, the more income noted, the stronger the earnings power. "Since the future is largely unpredictable," writes Ben Graham, "we are usually compelled to take either the current and past earnings as a guide, and to use these figures as a base in making a reasonable estimate of the future earnings."[4]

The cash flow statement originated after the dissatisfaction of many investors with reported earnings as a measure of a company's performance.

---

[3]Cottle, S., Murray, R., Block, F. *Graham and Dodd's Security Analysis,* Fifth Edition (New York: McGraw-Hill, 1988, p. 136).

[4]Graham, B. *The Interpretation of Financial Statements* (New York: HarperBusiness, 1998, p. 57).

As you will see in Chapter 3, one of the problems with reported earnings is that the final figure is affected by the accounting methods used and may not be indicative of underlying cash flows. Net income is not cash. The primary purpose of the statement of cash flows is to report information about a company's cash receipts and cash payments during a period.

There are three specific areas of information that the cash flow statement provides: 1) the sources of cash during a period, 2) uses of cash during a period, and 3) change in cash balance during a period. While a critical understanding of cash flows provides evidence of cash receipts and payments, it cannot be used to provide insight into future cash flows. The cash flow statement must be considered in combination with the balance sheet and income statement to predict future cash flows.

Value investors analyze a company's cash flows because it gives them insight into the quality of the company's earnings by linking the income statement to the balance sheet. In addition, analyzing the cash flow statement can give clues as to the strength of the underpinnings of the enterprise. For example, it is here that a dividend-conscious investor can determine the strength and security of internally generated cash flows that the company can use to pay its dividends. Cash flow analysis also gives investors clues as to the capital requirements needed to sustain the growth of the business. It can also raise red flags when the enterprise is likely to run out of cash or have problems meeting financial obligations. Clearly, cash flows are the lifeblood of the company.

There are three sections to the statement of cash flows:

1. Operating activities include the daily transactions involving the sale of products, and the results from providing services to customers. This could include the cash receipts from the sale of goods or services and the cash payments to suppliers to purchase inventory.

2. Investing activities include lending money, collecting on those loans, or buying and selling assets.

3. Financial activities include obtaining cash from creditors, repaying the amounts, and providing them with dividends.

These three segments are each very important. The most important, however, is the cash flow from operating activities, as it involves the sale of goods and services—the viability of the company. If it is clear that the cash flow from operations is not the primary source of cash, the company may be headed for trouble. The more the operating cash flow contributes to the overall cash need, the better.

The balance sheet reveals the financial condition of a company at a particular point in time. Most companies have a December fiscal year end. The balance sheet also provides information about the resources owned by the company, its obligations to outsiders, and the amounts to which the shareowners are entitled. Essentially, the balance sheet summarizes what the company owns and compares it to what the company owes to outsiders and investors. The balance sheet always balances between assets and liabilities plus equity. The assets in a balance sheet are the economic resources that are expected to generate future benefits to the company.

The balance sheet groups the assets of a firm in three categories: current assets; property, plant, & equipment; and intangible assets. Current assets primarily include cash and other assets that the company can convert into cash in less than one year. Companies use current assets to replenish, on an ongoing basis, the operations of the company. The most important current assets are cash, short-term investments that the company might have, receivables, and inventories.

Property, plant, & equipment relates to those assets with long depreciation schedules. Depreciation is a method of allocating the cost of an asset over its productive life. Accumulated depreciation is the total amount of depreciation expense that has been recorded. When PP&E is recorded on the balance sheet, it is done so after depreciation is deducted.

Intangible assets are basically rights that the company possesses. These assets have no physical substance. They may include trademarks, patents, franchises, etc. This right is very valuable in some cases. For example, patents give companies the right to profit from a product for 17 years thereafter, without interference or infringement by others.

Liabilities are obligations of a company to outsiders. There are two types of liabilities: current and long term. Current liabilities include those liabilities that are usually payable within one year. Long-term liabilities are those that will become due after one year.

Stockholders' equity is the shareholders' interest in the company. It is not cash. If the company is short on funds, it cannot get cash from the stockholders' equity account. Equity is on the liabilities side of the balance sheet, not on the assets side. It represents stockowners' claims against existing assets. The money in the stockholders' equity account has already been spent. The stockholders' equity includes the retained earnings account, which is the cumulative net income or losses, less any dividends distributed. This is a pool of earnings. However, the retained earnings balance provides no indication of the amount of cash the company possesses. It only represents the funds the company has reinvested in the operations of the company, as opposed to making distributions to shareholders in the form of dividends.

The balance sheet provides the independent value investor with the tools with which to make sound judgments on the financial health of the company. However, it does have limitations. For example, most assets are shown at their original costs. The exceptions are receivables, and short-term and long-term investments. This can be a problem for a company that purchased land 50 years ago, but cannot appreciate the value of the property to current values.

Understanding and using the balance sheet is a very important endeavor for any value investor—one that investors take pride in doing and executing. In addition to analyzing the financial statements, many value investors often rely on other sources of information that they trust and have proven useful over time. One of the most widely used sources for financial and business data on companies is the *Value Line Investment Survey.*

THE VALUE LINE INVESTMENT SURVEY: A "MUST HAVE" FOR THE VALUE INVESTOR

Value Line is a leading investment service that Ben Graham continually refers to in his many books, and it is the same service that his protégé Warren Buffet uses today. The publication is one of the most widely used research sources in the investment community and is very affordable for individual investors as well—a rare combination.

What is so attractive about *Value Line* is the fashion in which the data is organized. When investors pick up the one-page report on a company, they can immediately make a very good decision about whether or not a particular company warrants further research. When asked to reflect on how he uses the *Value Line,* Warren Buffett said the following: "We get incredible value out of it—because it gives us the quickest way to review a huge number of key factors that tell us whether we're basically interested in a company. It also gives us a good way…of periodically keeping up to date. *Value Line* covers 1,700 or so stocks…and reviews each of them every 13 weeks. So it's a good way to make sure you haven't overlooked something…the snapshot it represents is an enormously efficient way for us to garner information about various businesses…We're not looking for opinion, we're looking for facts. But I have yet to see a better way—including fooling around on the Internet or anything—that gives me the information about a company…I don't know of any other system that's as good. "[5]

[5]*Outstanding Investor Digest,* "Berkshire Hathaway's Warren Buffett & Charlie Munger," September 24, 1998, p. 41.

Like all other sources, investors use *Value Line* differently among themselves. Everyone has his or her own way of assessing the information. There are a couple of areas that many value investors focus on before pursuing further research. First is the most obvious—the stock chart. While value investors are not chartists, by any means, the chart is hard to ignore. Here the investor can delve into the shareholder value, creating records of the company for over 10 years, and gaining other data, such as how the stock performed during the past recession, stock splits, etc.

Second, a value investor may jump down to the bottom, far-right-most corner of the page to find the company's financial strength. Here companies are given a grade from "A++" for the highest grade of financially sound companies, to "C" for the weakest businesses. As a rule of thumb, some value investors are interested in companies with a "B+" or better, unless the investment is a special situation. The more tools and experience investors have to understand and analyze complex situations, the more they may consider lower-ranking companies.

Thirdly, the value investor may then take a look at the description of the business and the brief commentary. With knowledge of the company's stock price history and financial footing, the investor can better understand the description of the business and interpret the analyst's comments on the company's challenges and opportunities ahead.

Finally, eyeballing key historical statistics and *Value Line*'s projections on the company's sales, gross margins, earnings per share, return on equity, etc., gives the investor a sense of the company's economic value.

The other areas that may prove helpful are the company's capital structure, the current balance sheet, rates of change in sales and earnings, institutional and insider buys and sells, and the footnotes as to how the numbers were calculated.

USING WALL STREET RESEARCH

The vast majority of Wall Street research is great for getting facts. Value investors use the research from these firms because they are rich with factual information, such as the competitive dynamics in a particular industry, market shares among incumbents, financial performance, etc. The most valuable research is the industry or company initiation reports. In fact, some of these are collectibles. They are widely used and referred to, particularly for those investors who are new to a particular industry or company. For them, these reports are invaluable.

Wall Street research, however, is hard to come by for the individual investor. Fortunately, the advantages of having access to this research stream are not as critical for the long-term value investor. Professional investors in the value community use Wall Street research to gain a large amount of factual information for a given company or industry in a quick and orderly fashion. With the onset of the Internet and the continued popularity for companies and industry trade organizations to post information about their companies and industries on the World Wide Web, gaining first-rate facts on a company is becoming less of a hurdle for individuals. Value analysts are not concerned with getting special or superior information. Rather, their focus is on using the information that is already disseminated in a superior way. Not surprisingly, it all comes down to the level of analysis.

THREE APPROACHES TO ANALYZING A BUSINESS

The value investor analyzes a business by assessing a company's current strategies and track record. Value investors buy facts, not dreams. At the heart of any business analysis is the company's strategy. Whether an investor is value or growth-oriented, the strategy that a particular company employs is critical to the investor's assessment about the value of the enterprise. Strategy is about making trade-offs. It is about a company's choosing certain activities in order to deliver a unique mix of value to its stakeholders.[6] In the process of choosing activities, companies use resources in an attempt to deliver this value. Business assessment entails analyzing the trade-offs management has made in their effort to deliver the value that is expected.

There are several ways investors approach companies; many have their own customized ways. This book examines three approaches that investors might employ to understand the economics of a particular business: the vertical assessment approach, the ROE decomposition approach, and the cash-flow-based approach. The vertical approach is primarily strategy based. ROE decomposition is a combination of strategy and ratio analysis, and the cash flow trend approach is pure ratios.

VERTICAL ASSESSMENT APPROACH

The Vertical Assessment Approach is based on a company's income statement. There are six specific tools the value investor uses for a typical

---

[6]Porter, M. *Harvard Business Review,* "What is Strategy?" November–December 1996, p. 61.

EXHIBIT 2.3   Vertical assessment approach diagram.

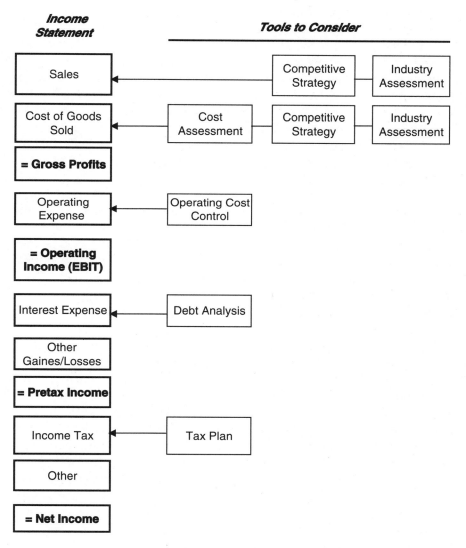

non-service-oriented company. They include the 1) industry analysis, 2) competitive position analysis, 3) manufacturing, 4) operating, 5) tax strategy assessment, and 6) debt analysis.

The use of a common-size statement is the most popular way of performing a vertical analysis. A common-size statement is an income statement that shows all items as a percentage of sales as well as in dollar form. A common-size analysis is useful when investors are comparing the income statements of different companies in the same industry. One useful purpose of using common-size analysis is to get an idea as to which area on the income statement one should focus on. The value analyst tries to uncover the strength and consistency of a company's margins, and how they might change.

At the top of the income statement is the sales figure. Sales or revenues are the money the company gets for the services or the products sold to the buyer. While sales are sometimes defined differently from company to company, the sales figure is generally recorded when the product or service has been delivered. How a company recognizes its revenue is a very critical part of vertical analysis; value investors look to the footnotes labeled "revenue recognition" for clarification. The method that a company uses to recognize its sales often determines the strategies it chooses to obtain profitability.

To obtain a better grasp of what drives sales, the value investor uses industry analysis techniques to assess the company's competitive position. There are several techniques that one can use. It ultimately depends on the users. Some prefer to look at industries based on their particular strengths, weaknesses, opportunities, and threats, better known as SWOT analysis. Others look to their own personal knowledge and experiences of the industry, or draw from contacts they may have in the industry, to give them guidance. Many value investors keep a table of industry contacts that they call upon to help them understand a particular sector of the marketplace. For example, it is very common for analysts to call their local physicians to get the latest news on medical devices, and then to incorporate this knowledge into the analysis.

One of the industry tools that has been well received among investors is the industry framework developed by Professor Michael E. Porter. He writes about this framework extensively in his book, *Competitive Strategy.* What makes the Porter framework particularly useful is that it is widely used among a variety of investors of different styles. His framework assesses five different "forces" that drive industry profitability. The forces include the threat of new entrants, the threat of substitute products, the bargaining power of buyers, the bargaining power of suppliers, and the degree of rivalry among competitors.

These forces are important in doing vertical assessment because of the impact they have on sales—they have an impact on volume and price. The threat of new entrants, for example, affects price. Therefore, if the barriers to entry in a given industry are low, the likelihood of new competitors' entering is very high, particularly if the industry enjoys desirable profit margins. In such a case, new entrants are more likely to enter the industry at a lower price point, thereby potentially driving industry prices and profitability downward. Substitute products can also have an adverse impact on price. The degree of this threat depends on how the competing products perform and the customer's willingness to substitute.

The bargaining power of buyers is a function of how sensitive they are to changes in price and the number of options they have. This dynamic can influence the price and volume of an industry. Profitability is often low in an industry where buyers or customers are extremely price sensitive and have several options. Supplier power is very similar. The bargaining power of suppliers is nonexistent, unless they are few in number, or what they supply is of critical importance to the buyer of the company or to the customer. The rivalry of industry participants can be fierce and may lead to the destabilization of pricing, and ultimately, of industry profitability.

These five forces have different degrees of impact from one industry to another. They are important to the value investor because of the impact they have on a company's unit volume, price, and cost to produce goods. These factors are the fundamental beginnings of business assessment. Sales, or top-line growth, is a function of volume and price, and profitability is based on the relationship between the price of each product and the cost incurred to make it.

Using Porter's framework to assess the industry, the three potential strategies that companies can employ to outperform their competitors are cost leadership, differentiation, and focus. Porter warns that there is a trade-off in resources that is required: "Effectively implementing any of these generic strategies usually requires total commitment and supporting organizational arrangements that are diluted if there is more than one primary target."[7] Whether competing on price or differentiation, a company having a focused strategy is preferred by most investors for these very reasons.

---

[7]Porter, M. *Competitive Strategy* (New York: Free Press A Division of Macmillan, Inc., 1980, p. 35).

Many companies become unfocused and diversified through a series of management's ill-advised acquisitions. Peter Lynch called such actions "diworseifications," and recommended that investors avoid such companies.[8] However, there are few exceptions to the diworseifications strategy, Lynch admits. Buffett's Berkshire Hathaway, for example, has been able to perform well, despite acquiring companies as diverse as candy stores to newspapers. It boils down to management.

After gaining a thorough understanding of industry dynamics and how a particular company competes for profits, one can better assess the other areas of the vertical analysis approach in their proper context.

Cost assessment: The objective here is to focus on the cost variables that have the greatest impact on a company's low-cost competitive advantage. Cost of goods sold (COGS) is the cost incurred to make the product. There can be a number of variables that affect cost. The three main components of COGS are manufacturing overhead, direct materials, and direct labor costs. Manufacturing overhead costs include such things as indirect materials, labor, utility costs, the factory building, etc. Direct materials costs relate to the components of the product. Direct labor is labor that actually "touches" the product during its creation, such as in the case of assembly line workers.

Operating cost control: Assessing a company's operating cost controls includes looking at the trend of expenses as a percent of sales over time. Operating expenses include selling and general administration expenses. Selling expenses are those expenses associated with the selling of the goods and services. Administration expenses include those costs linked to running the company. The operating expenses are often determined by the competitive strategy being implemented by the company, and how it chooses to manage its overhead. Interest expense is the interest charge incurred as a result of debt burden.

Not all debt is bad. A certain amount of debt on a company's balance sheet is good, because it can prevent management from making costly mistakes, i.e., implementing a diworseification strategy. Academics refer to this benefit as "the discipline of debt." There is a "right" amount of debt that a company can have to avoid financial distress, operate under ample disciplinary constraints, and maximize its returns. When considering debt analysis of a company, the value investor uses two primary tools: interest coverage and debt-to-total-capitalization ratios.

[8]Lynch, P. *One Up One Wall Street* (New York: Penguin Books, 1989, p. 146).

The interest coverage that is often used shows the cash that is generated by the operations of the company for every dollar that is required to pay interest. Favorable ratios among companies depend on the industry. Analysts typically look to leaders of industry to assess what the most appropriate ratio ought to be for a given company. However, among most industries, a ratio of one means that the company may be at risk of not making its interest payments. A reasonable debt-to-capitalization ratio is also based on the particular industry in question.

Other gains and losses in the vertical approach include changes in asset values due to transactions that are not related to the operations of the business.

Income tax expense often determines the investment returns to shareholders. Companies concentrate ample resources, trying to reduce tax expenses. As a result, a firm's tax planning may change from time to time. The footnotes in the annual report or 10-K should provide clarification on a company's tax plans. From these notes the value investor can get a deeper understanding of the company's tax planning, its financial impact, and the sustainability of it.

A good business using the vertical analysis approach: There are a few variables that would signal a good business using the vertical approach. Some of the best businesses are simple ones. If the drivers of the company's sales—ones that typically affect unit volume and price—are secure and are not threatened, the company can deliver consistent earnings to its shareholders by focusing on one particular strategy that it executes very well.

ROE DECOMPOSITION APPROACH

The return on equity (ROE) of a company is a result of the company's competitive position in its industry, the operating strategies it employs, and the financial flexibility it possesses. The ROE approach, better known as the "duPont Model," highlights how profitably management has been able to allocate the firm's resources.

Return on sales (ROS) indicates the amount of profits a company is able to keep for each dollar that the company takes in from the sale of goods and services. Asset turnover shows the amount of revenues the company is able to generate for each dollar of assets committed. Return on sales multiplied by asset turnover generates return on assets (ROA). This return metric indicates the amount of profit the company is able to generate for every dollar invested. Financial leverage shows investors how many dollars of assets the firm can use for every dollar of equity.

The analysis of a firm's specific intent has been the way to examine the components of expected ROE. Return on equity is a relative metric. Focusing

EXHIBIT 2.4   ROE decomposition.

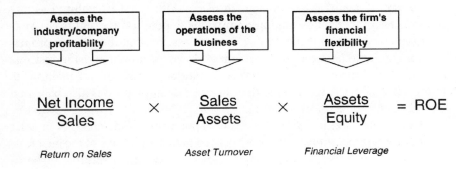

$$\underbrace{\frac{\text{Net Income}}{\text{Sales}}}_{\textit{Return on Sales}} \times \underbrace{\frac{\text{Sales}}{\text{Assets}}}_{\textit{Asset Turnover}} \times \underbrace{\frac{\text{Assets}}{\text{Equity}}}_{\textit{Financial Leverage}} = \text{ROE}$$

on a company's current ROE in isolation can lead to poor business assessment. One must examine the competitive environment to ascertain a firm's current ROE sustainability. Companies and industries are dynamic; they are in constant change.

There are three areas of strategy that can help one obtain a better understanding of a company. These strategies include a firm's corporate strategy, operations strategy, and financial strategy. Combined, these three strategies give the value investor clues as to the direction and level of the firm's future profitability.

A good business using the ROE decomposition approach: Good businesses consistently produce ROEs greater than their equity cost of capital. To do so, companies must have real sustainable competitive advantages or compete in industries with high entry barriers. In the long term, companies who generate ROEs significantly above their cost of capital will attract new entrants that will compete for those returns and drive it down.[9] Good businesses also operate in industries where competitors have—although in varying degrees— high returns as well. The benefit of using ROE decomposition is that the value analyst is able to see how the management of the company in question is allocating the company's resources to generate such ROEs. Good businesses also allocate resources in low-risk areas that generate adequate returns.

CASH-FLOW-BASED APPROACH
Value investors look at cash flows to assess a business. It is the most commonly used technique. One reason for this is that the cash flow approach provides insight into the quality of a company's earnings.

---

[9]Palepu, K., Bernard, V., Healy, P. *Business Analysis & Valuation Using Financial Statements* (Cincinnati: South-Western Publishing Co., 1996, p. 4-3).

The term "cash flow" is widely used and has a number of definitions in the investment community, even among value investors. There are three definitions that are perhaps most common: net cash flows, cash flows from operating activities, and discounted cash flows. [10]

Net cash flows are calculated by taking a company's net income and adding or subtracting noncash items. This is sometimes referred to as cash earnings. The intent of net cash flow is to show the cash that the company generates. This calculation is well liked among investors, with one caveat, however. The problem is that it assumes that a business's working capital accounts do not change over time. As a result of this failure, many investors look to cash flow from operating activities, which includes the change in assets and liabilities, as well as net cash flows.

The final type of cash flow is the discounted cash flows method (DCF), which is the sum of future cash flows discounted to the present. DCF is used—among other reasons—because it takes into account the time value of money. The discounted cash flows method is generally used as a valuation tool, and less as a business "assessment" tool.

The best set of cash flows the value analyst considers are those straight from the company's SEC filings. The cash flow statement from the financial statements has three sections. First, the cash flow from operations is the amount of cash the company earned after paying for the cost it incurred to create the goods and services for the customer. Second, the cash flow from investing activities is the cash received from buy and sell transactions and cash outlays for capital expenditure requirements. Third, cash flow from financing activities is the amount of cash raised from the debt and equity markets.

Value investors typically refer to a free cash flow number as their assessment of a firm based on the cash flow method. Free cash flow can be defined as a company's net income plus noncash items, such as depreciation and amortization, minus mandatory or promised outlays of cash, such as capital expenditures.

Using the cash flow trend approach, investors try to probe into the following key questions: What is the relative strength of the company's internal cash flow compared to its peers? Can the company continue to meet its short-term financial obligations without reducing the firm's financial flexibility? What is the trend and use of free cash flow? What type of external financing does the company rely on, and does it affect the company's risk profile?

---

[10]Higgins, R. *Analysis for Financial Management,* Fourth Edition (Chicago: Irwin, 1995, p. 20).

A good business using the cash-flow-based approach: A good business generates strong and consistent free cash flows that can be distributed to shareholders in the form of a dividend, a share repurchase, or by other means. A good company is a good business run by good managers who are able to make prudent decisions on the best use of free cash flows. All other analysis, whether it is on the industry or the company's operations, has to be focused on the company's ability to sustain or improve its free cash flow trends.

BUSINESS-QUALITY RED FLAGS

There are several key red flags that value investors look for when evaluating the earnings quality of a company. The following are the 15 common red flags; and, if identified, should warrant a closer look:

1. There is a difference between the company's accounting policy with other companies in the same industry such as how revenue is recognized. Changes in the accounting policies are usually found in the footnotes or the 8-K filing.
2. Management's incentive package is purely based on increasing earnings per share and has the discretion over accounting treatment. Management's incentives can be found in the company's 10-K and proxy statements.
3. There are unjustified changes in estimates, accounting, or financial policies in the 8-K or recent filings.
4. There are special business arrangements and deal structures to achieve accounting objectives, such as earnings growth. Special structures can be found in nearly all of the filings. A good starting point is the 10-K.
5. The Letter to Shareholders does not adequately disclose the company's business strategy and its economic consequences. The Letter to Shareholders can be found in the company's annual report.
6. The management was not complete in addressing the prior year's poor performance in the MD&A. The Management's Discussion and Analysis (MD&A) can be found in the 10-K or annual report.
7. There are changes in accounting. Look at the footnotes in the most recent filings.
8. There are unexplained transactions that helped earnings. Scrutinize the footnotes to uncover uncertainties.

9.   There is an abnormally high increase in inventory relative to sales growth. Review the latest income statement, as well as the balance sheet.

10. There is an abnormally high increase in accounts receivable relative to sales. Take a look at the income statement and balance sheet.

11. Net income is growing faster than cash flow from operations. Take a look at the most recent statements of cash flow and income.

12. There is an unexpected and large write-off or charge-off. See most recent news on the company, as well as the 8-K.

13. There is a large fourth-quarter adjustment. Take a look at the annual report or 10-K.

14. The company is lending money to customers or has a significant equity stake in its customers. Take a look at the 10-K.

15. The company changes expense calculations or any other material items that can enhance earnings. See the 8-K or the footnotes in the annual report or most recent 10-Q.

ASSESSING MANAGEMENT

Management of companies are expected to act and think like owners of the company. This is what value investors require. Assessing the quality of management is more of an art form than a science, and often investors add their personal touch to this analysis. For some professional investors, seeing the CEO eye to eye is a must, while others are more content with a telephone conversation. However, most individuals often do not have the luxury of visiting with a company's CEO. Warren Buffett, however, provides individual investors some guidance about ways to assess management.

His advice is to read the annual reports of the company and compare them from one year to the next. Go back as far as possible to determine whether management lived up to the promises made. Buffett also suggests that investors compare a company's annual reports to its competitors' reports.[11] Management credibility is extremely important. And the best way that managers can earn credibility over time is to deliver on their promises. Value investors typically assess past promises by reviewing management's past letters to shareholders and analyzing the financial statements.

---

[11]Hagstrom, R. *The Warren Buffett Portfolio* (New York: John Wiley & Sons, 1999, p. 96).

In analyzing the financial statements, some investors employ an economic value added (EVA) approach to assign management's ability to make decisions. EVA simply assesses if current management was able to generate excess returns with the capital they've invested above the cost of their capital. EVA is a company's after-tax operating income minus its cost of capital. The formula is as follows: EVA = After-Tax Operating Income − (cost of capital × capital employed). Economic value added is appealing because it takes into account management's ability to make prudent capital allocation decisions; it can be used to compensate management and can be used as an incentive tool.[12]

ASSESSING A BUSINESS: HERMAN MILLER, INC.

On January 28, 1999, Herman Miller, Inc announced that its third quarter earnings, which shareholders expected to increase, would not be achieved due to a short fall in order trends. The company also indicated that it was seeing weaknesses across its product line both in the United States and in foreign markets. Given this outlook, Herman Miller announced that it was in the process of reducing costs through a variety of cost-cutting measures.

Wall Street was swift to react—eliminating 33% of the firm's value in seven trading days. After getting used to 14 consecutive quarters of excellent quarterly results, investors wanted out. The party was over. The significant drop in market value caught the attention of many value investors, including myself.

I got the latest *Value Line* report on the company, and I liked what I read. Herman Miller was in a very profitable business, had strong financials, and had good long-term prospects. After re-reading the reasons for the short fall in the company's stock price, I deemed the situation was worthy of further research. I gathered the company's latest 10-K, 10-Q, annual report, proxy statements and information from the company's Web site. I did the same for two of Herman Miller's competitors.

With pages of the company's SEC filings on hand, I assessed Herman Miller two different ways: with the cash flow-based and the ROE decomposition approach. What I found was that the company generated consistent free cash flows with strong returns of shareholders' equity.

To get a firm grasp of what the analysis meant, I first looked at the industry and competitive dynamics. One revelation was that the industry

[12]Higgins, R. *Analysis for Financial Management* (Chicago: Irwin, 1995) Fourth Edition, p. 302.

EXHIBIT 2.5   Herman Miller Free Cash Flow & ROE Decomposition.

	1995	1996	1997	1998	1999E
Net income	$32	$57	$85	$128	$140
Non-cash items	40	45	48	51	50
Less capital expenditures	63	54	55	74	80
Free cash flow	$9	$48	$78	$105	$110
Return on sales	3%	4%	6%	8%	8%
Asset turnover	1.8x	1.9x	2.1x	2.1x	1.9x
ROA	5%	8%	12%	16%	15%
Leverage	2.0x	2.3x	2.4x	3.2x	3.5x
ROE	11%	19%	29%	50%	53%

Herman Miller is in was not as cyclical as I had thought. With over 17 years of growth, the industry had only 1 year of negative growth. In fact, the contract office furniture industry had grown at 1.3 times the rate of the U.S. economy.

There were several factors that drove this growth rate, such as growth in corporate profits and white-collar employment as the overall economy shifted to a more service-oriented, secular environment. As the industry was growing, Herman Miller was gaining share. In 1995, its industry markets share was 9 percent and had climbed to 11 percent two years later.

ASSESSING HERMAN MILLER'S MANAGEMENT

Given the company's announcement, I reasoned that any shortfall in any one of these factors would be the one that management was well prepared for and knew what to do about. In fact, the management team was swift to outline specific plans to reduce costs and soften the impact of a potential slowdown.

I looked carefully at the most recent Management's Discussion and Analysis to get a firm understanding of management's ambitions and judgment. It begins with customary provisions, then goes into the corporate culture of continuously seeking to increase shareholder value. Herman Miller uses the EVA methodology.

Excerpt form Herman Miller's 1998 Form 10-K

Let us begin our overview by stating that we had another record-setting year at Herman Miller, Inc. We set records in "Economic Value Added" (EVA), net sales, new orders, net income, earnings per share, cash flow from operating activities, and cash returned to shareholders.

If you have been following our company for the past few years, you will remember that two years ago we adopted EVA as our measurement tool to determine whether or not we had created value for both our external shareholders and our employee-owners. Extensive independent market research has shown that EVA more closely correlates with shareholder value than any other performance measure.

Simply put, EVA is what remains of profits after tax once a charge for the capital employed in the business is deducted. As an operating discipline, the main advantage of EVA is that it focuses management's attention on the balance sheet as well as on the income statement. Our company is, in effect, competing for scarce capital resources. Management's task is to put this scarce resource to work and earn the best possible return for our shareholders. This means investing in projects that earn a return greater than the cost of the funds sourced from our investors. As long as we are making investments that earn a return higher than the cost of capital, then our investors should earn a return in excess of their expectations.[13]

Here, the management team signals to me that they do think like owners, and they have the proper incentives in place to increase value for shareholders. The company also took the liberty of sharing with the investment community how they calculate their EVA results for the company. This information is very important because it allows value investors to follow the progress and predict the possible outcomes of future economic value added results. Professional value analysts and those who have access to the management team can use this data to determine answers to critical questions.

[13]Herman Miller, Inc., May 30, 1998 Form 10-K, p. 10.

EXHIBIT 2.6   Herman Miller's Economic Value Added.

(In Thousands)	1998	1997	1996
Operating income	$208,295	$130,683	$74,935
Adjust for: Divestiture/patent litigation		14,500	16,535
Interest expense on noncapitalized leases	4,166	4,500	4,316
Goodwill amortization	6,161	4,725	4,115
Other	13,765	5,093	3,071
Increase in reserves	1,290	18,649	6,548
Capitalized design and research	2,101	2,819	1,984
Adjusted operating profit	235,778	180,969	111,504
Cash taxes	−90,703	−72,091	−34,561
Net operating profit after taxes	145,075	108,878	76,943
Weighted-average capital employed	606,018	617,727	605,438
Weighted-average cost of capital	11%	11%	11%
Cost of capital	66,662	67,950	66,598
Economic value added	$78,413	$40,928	$10,345

Source: Company Documents

Herman Miller generated $78.4 million of EVA that year while their EVA increased 91.5 percent. The following continues with an explanation as to why the company had been so fortunate over the past year. In this part of the MD&A, investors take note of these key drivers to get a firm grasp of what drives shareholder value in the business. The management also gives their insight into the industry. Value investors tend to scrutinize management's judgment in this section because here they make forward-thinking statements about their industry.

Excerpt form Herman Miller's 1998 Form 10-K

We took EVA a step further by linking our incentive-based compensation to it. All of our executive incentive compensation plans as well as all of our employee gain-sharing programs at each of the business units have been linked to this measure. Using EVA-based plans shifts the focus from budget performance to long-term continuous improvements in shareholder value. The EVA target is raised each year by an improvement factor, so that increasingly higher EVA targets must be attained in order to earn the same level of incentive pay. Our Board of Directors has set the EVA improvement factor for a period of three years.

This year, we decided to present our results to you by discussing what changes in our business have driven our EVA improvement. We believe this is important because EVA is utilized not only to measure our results, but also to evaluate potential business opportunities. In addition, we hope you will get a clearer picture of what will drive future improvements in both net income and in EVA and ultimately the value of your investment in our company. Let's begin by reviewing our EVA results.[14]

---

[14]Herman Miller, Inc., May 30, 1998 Form 10-K, p. 11.

3

PRICE AND VALUE ASSESSMENTS

"The successful promoter using value investing understands why others do what they do, then takes advantage of it."[1]

Martin J. Whitman

IF A STOCK IS PRICED AT **$20** PER SHARE, what does it mean for value investors? If Company A and Company B both have share prices of $20, which company has the share price that could be considered cheap and which other one would be considered expensive? Ultimately, there are a number of factors that must be evaluated before the stock price can be assessed. Share prices cannot be looked at in a vacuum.

To understand price, investors must first understand the business in which the *price* is represented, and the metric used to value the enterprise. Chapter 2 outlines ways in which investors can accomplish the first task of understanding the business. This chapter focuses on how to interpret price and determine value. This is where the rubber meets the road. After obtaining all the facts about a company and determining whether it is a good business, value investors assess the price that the market is offering for the company, and set their own value.

[1]Whitman, M. *Value Investing: A Balanced Approach* (New York: John Wiley & Sons, 1999, p. 19).

As for Company A and Company B, the $20 price tag can be "expensive" for one company, using a certain metric, and "cheap" using another. A metric can include the price-to-earnings ratio, price-to-book value, etc. The objective in the game of investing is to buy low and sell high. Clearly, investors can only understand price if they understand the tools and metrics that a rational buyer for the enterprise would use when evaluating the business at a later date.

TO APPRECIATE PRICE IS TO UNDERSTAND VALUE

To understand price is the attempt to understand *how* prudent investors are valuing a company, and *why*. The metric used by this investor base to value a particular company, and those companies in its industry, is not difficult to obtain. Whatever way the company is being valued, the value investor takes a mental note of the tools used, while keeping in mind that a metric used to determine price today might not be the same one used tomorrow.

After identifying the metrics used, the next step is to understand why a particular company of interest is being afforded its valuation. This takes a little more digging to get the best answer. The reasons for a low valuation can range from a falloff in earnings to a lack of management credibility.

To properly assess the price of a company's stock, one has to be willing to uncover the necessary data points in order to understand fully the business and the value metrics that a rational buyer of the enterprise would be using in valuations. Essentially, you will need to see today what potential buyers of the enterprise will see tomorrow, and the metrics that they will use to measure it. Therefore, to understand and appreciate price, one has to understand valuation—they are yoked together.

When it comes to valuing an enterprise, how the valuation tools are used, and the types of tools available for investors to employ, vary greatly. Some prefer to rely on price-to-earnings ratios, and others base their decisions on discounted cash flows. Individuals may still differ on how these tools are actually used.

There is no absolute "right" way to use the various tools available to analyze businesses. The best way is the one that works for the individual investor; it is each individual that knows the specific strengths, weaknesses, and assumptions that go along with picking a tool.

For example, some investors spend time trying to estimate what the next three to four years will look like for a particular company. There are a variety of news services and research companies that publish the future earnings predictions of Wall Street analysts.

Investment analysts use these estimates to value companies. Value-minded investors, on the other hand, focus not on earnings that are too distant; rather, they concentrate on what earnings and cash flows are today.

ASSESSING VALUE: TOOLS TO CONSIDER

To get to a company's fair value, the value investor triangulates a valuation. Triangulation involves using three of the best valuation tools for that particular business. There are no perfect valuation tools. They all have defects. There are three broad categories of tools that a value investor uses to value a company. They are comparison based, asset based, and transaction based.

In each of these approaches, using "multiples" is the most common tool that investors use to value companies, as they are easy to understand and calculate. The casual observer often misuses this tool because of its presumed simplicity. The value investor understands that behind the multiple are often complex assumptions that are linked to the economics of the business.

There are different types of valuation tools. Some are comparison based, whereby the value of the enterprise is based on the valuation of other similar companies. There is an asset-based valuation, which focuses on the intrinsic value of the enterprise. Transaction-based valuation tools assess the worth of a business based on what other companies have been sold for in the market place.

Value investors do not use every tool in these tool sets. In fact, the use of some is more controversial than others. However, like any well-stocked toolbox, there are certain situations in which some tools are much more appropriate than others. What follows is a discussion on the most applicable way to use a selected group of these tools, and reasons one might consider not doing so. It is up to the individual investor to understand the pros and cons of each and when to use them effectively.

COMPARISON-BASED TOOLS

Comparison-based tools compare one company to another company of similar likeness. In the comparison-based valuation toolbox, value investors possess many different valuation tools that they can call upon to determine the value of an enterprise. The most common tools are price-to-earnings (P/E); price-to-book (P/B); enterprise value to earnings before interest, tax depreciation and amortization (EV/EBITDA); and price to sales (P/S) or enterprise value to revenues (EV/R). This discussion starts with the most commonly used valuation metric of them all: the price-to-earnings ratio.

Price-to-earnings.   The price-to-earnings ratio, or P/E, is one of the easiest ratios to use when valuing a company because the variables needed are readily available. The P/E ratio is defined as the stock price divided by the earnings per share.

Despite its ease of use, there are several ways that P/E ratios can be computed. While the numerator can stay constant, the denominator can vary. For example, earnings per share can range from the past twelve-month earnings, last fiscal-year earnings, to forward-looking earnings.

The most common way to use P/E ratios is to find a few companies that are very similar to the particular company in question. These similar companies are often called comparable or "twin" companies. The objective is to get a relative sense of the value of the enterprise based on the current value of the company's peers. Finding good twins may be a problem because no two companies are completely alike. They may have a different product mix, financial leverage, etc.

The P/E ratio of one firm compared to another can be difficult for a few reasons. For example, companies may have different ways of growing; one firm may grow organically, while the other may have grown through acquisitions. In addition, they may have different accounting methods, which, as discussed earlier, may have a wide impact on earnings and the range of the P/E ratio.

There are many variables that affect P/E ratio ranges, as this ratio can vary from industry to industry, higher growth to lower growth, good management to not-so-good management. Investors try to make up for this by buying companies with P/Es relative to a twin company with a similar risk/reward profile.

The relative P/E ratios are used to assess the P/E ratio of a company in relation to the market. One can compute relative P/E by taking the company's current P/E and the current P/E of the stock market. The relative P/E metric is used two different ways. Some use the firms' relative P/E and compare it to the historical trends. For example, if a company's stock has had historically a 10-percent discount to the overall market P/E, and now it is trading at a 25-percent discount, the stock would presumably be cheap. The other way that investors use this metric is to compute a relative P/E ratio as it relates to its sector-average P/E. Value investors use this relative valuation technique on occasion, and most often reluctantly. They prefer to look for absolute and not relative performance. For example, if the overall market were expensive, value investors would perhaps rather keep their investment dollars in cash than buy overpriced securities with significant downside risk.

One shortcoming with using the P/E ratio is that it cannot be used to value firms with negative earnings. Some on Wall Street simply change the numerator to include the expected future earnings, say in five years. Using distant future earnings is very common in the industry. These earnings can be obtained using *Value Line Investment Survey* or other investment services. This approach, however, is very difficult because in order to do it correctly, one would have to project the five-year earnings for all comparable companies. Value investors shy away from making such future projections on unprofitable businesses. As Warren Buffet says, "Valuation is counting cash, not hopes or dreams."[2]

While price-to-earnings is perhaps the most widely used metric to value the equity of a firm, it is also one that possesses fundamental limitations, and can severely limit the ability to assess a firm's economic value. There are four primary concerns that relate to the use of earnings. First, the accounting used can have too much of an impact on earnings among similar firms. For example, twin companies in the same industry, selling the same products with the same margins, can have different earnings if management uses different accounting procedures, such as in regard to inventory usage (LIFO or FIFO), depreciation schedules (straight-line or accelerated), or treatment of prior mergers (purchasing accounting or pooling of interest). Such accounting changes rarely impact other valuation tools such as those based on cash flows.

Another concern with using earnings is the fact that it excludes both business and financial risks. Simply put, two firms' earning $1.00 in earnings says nothing about their individual businesses and financial health. One may have too much leverage, and the other may not generate enough cash to finance its operations.

The earnings number is not a "cash" number. This fact leads to the third concern: earnings exclude required investments to keep the business operating and growing. Investments such as capital investments are excluded in the earnings calculation. Capital expenditures are critical because significant outlays should be taken into account when assessing the economic value of an enterprise. While depreciation expenses are included in the earnings number, they are a noncash item; they thereby

---

[2]Cunningham, L. *The Essays of Warren Buffet for Corporate America* (New York: Cardozo Law School, 2001, p. 22).

reduce the economic value of the enterprise. Value investors often add back depreciation and deduct capital expenditures as an ingredient to obtain a firm's economic pulse.

Yet, with these well-known concerns on hand, the P/E ratio is still the preferred choice for many investors because of its ease of use. For value investors, however, it is just one tool out of many because of these weaknesses. Therefore, P/E valuation may be used with some investments and not with others. It primarily depends on the economics of the individual company.

The P/E ratio is best used among investors when evaluating financially sound companies with no near-term (in one to three years) capital expenditure requirements on the horizon. However, prior research shows that earnings do not drive stock prices, as one would expect, and that the stock market on a long-term basis focuses on management's impact on the cash flow growth rather than pure accounting earnings.[3]

Price-to-book.   Price-to-book, or P/B, is defined as the price per share divided by the book value per share. The numerator is easy to obtain; the denominator, or book value per share, can be a bit trickier. The reason is that if there are several classes of a company's stock, such as common and preferred, you might have a situation of comparing apples to oranges. In an attempt to resolve this potential problem, some investors often do not include equity that is from preferred stock, choosing to use only common stock in calculating book value of equity.

The other issue with the book value per share relates to figuring out which book value to use. Companies release an updated book value of firms once every three months. Some investors use an average book value over the past three quarters, or the book value from the latest annual report in their calculation of P/B. Many investors use the latest reported book value if there have been significant changes in the firm's balance sheet. Since companies often reflect seasonal changes that may overstate or understate book values, and quarterly reports that need not be audited, many investors prefer the book value from the annual report.

The P/B ratio is one of Wall Street's favorites metrics. Like the price-to-earnings ratio, P/B remains very easy to understand and use. This valuation tool gives investors a sound measure of value, which can be compared to the market value.

[3]Copeland, T., Koller, T., Murrin, J. *Valuation: Measuring and Managing the Value of Companies* (John Wiley & Sons, Inc., 1991, p. 81).

Book value, net worth, and shareowners' equity value are essentially the same. Another "equity" value indicator, called "market capitalization," is the public market valuation of a company's equity share count multiplied by the stock price. This equity value is an indication of what the market expects from the company, based on cash flows and earnings. The book value of the equity on the company's balance sheet is the total assets of the firm, minus its liabilities. The market's expectation plays a significant role in determining the market value of the equity. On the other hand, accounting plays a significant role in setting the book value of assets.

Specifically, the book value of assets is the price paid for the assets, reduced by depreciation over time. Likewise, the book value of liabilities reflects the liabilities when they were first obtained. The difference between the book value and the market equity value is that book value is often based on a historical cost, and the latter is the "up-to-date" assessment of the value of the assets minus liabilities.

P/B is also attractive to some investors because one can value companies with negative earnings—a feature that the well-liked P/E ratio fails to deliver. While P/B is not effective in valuing companies with negative book values, it still is an overwhelmingly useful tool by some investors, as companies with negative book values are few. Unfortunately, like other seemingly simple tools, the P/B valuation metric is generally misused with investors using rules of thumb to guide their decision making. Specifically, many novice investors view companies selling below book value as an indication of undervalued opportunities, and those companies selling above book value as a warning of overvaluation.

This leads us to explore the failings of P/B. Book values are severely affected by the accounting decisions on items that management has room to change, such as depreciation. The value investor might look carefully into the depreciation methods of a company and compare them to others in its industry. The critical failing here is that P/B is useless if legitimate treatment of depreciation is different among firms in an industry. Therefore, investors using P/B without taking a very close look at items such as depreciation would be misled. The other critical failing is that as the economy becomes more technology and service oriented, the less P/B becomes valuable as a tool. Specifically, the tangible assets of companies in the technology and service sectors are insignificant. Ideas and human capital, while difficult to quantify, are much more important assets for these market sectors.

The handling of options is another concern with the book value assessment. Companies with various amounts of options outstanding can be wrongly assessed as being undervalued or overvalued. In some cases, companies with a great number of options outstanding can appear to be undervalued, since the market value in the numerator appears lower due to the unrealized level of options in the company. The value investor typically adds the market value of the options to the market value of the equity before calculating the P/B ratio.

When comparing book values across firms, the value investor also takes into account stock buyback programs and recent acquisitions the company may have had, in order to assess it properly. When companies buy back their own stock, the book value of the equity declines by the amount of the repurchase. This is what happens when a company pays a cash dividend. In fact, some regard stock buybacks as just another form of a dividend. However, buybacks have historically been larger in dollar amount than dividends, and therefore have had a larger impact on a firm's book equity.

The price-to-book ratio has a special relationship to the approach one takes in analyzing a business. The relationship is perhaps strongest with the ROE (return on equity) decomposition approach. In fact, the return on equity has a significant impact on the price-to-book ratio. For example, a drop in ROE typically has an indirect, adverse impact on P/B ratios as the book value falls. Like other multiple-based valuation tools, everything should be received in its proper context. Every industry has its own definition of what constitutes a high and a low P/B value ratio. The reason for the variety of P/B levels among companies in the same industry is straightforward. They differ because they all have their own risk, growth, and return on equity profiles.

Some investors believe that the strong relationship between ROE and price-to-book value gives some of the best clues to uncover undervalued companies. Companies with high ROE should trade at high price-to-book value multiples and vice versa. Companies in which value investors are most interested are those with a high ROE, and are valued in the marketplace with low P/B value ratios.

On an excess cash flow return basis, the price-to-book value ratio is influenced by the cost of equity to the firm. Historically, a higher cost of equity generates a lower P/B value ratio. The key here is excess equity return above one's cost for that equity. Therefore, a company with a high ROE, less cost of equity, will garner a higher price-to-book value ratio. High ROE with a low cost of equity is optimal. Said differently, the P/B ratio should increase if the spread between ROE and the cost of equity increases.

Compared to other multiple-based valuation metrics, the P/B value ratio is more dynamic than most, because of its relationship with ROE. The rationale is that given the way a firm's ROE changes over time, so should the P/B value of the enterprise change as well. For example, companies that do a good job with their corporate strategies to increase return on share-owner's equity have historically been rewarded a higher valuation than firms whose corporate strategy isn't effective.

EV/EBITDA.   Enterprise value to earnings before interest, tax, deprecia-tion, and amortization (EV/EBITDA) is a very popular method among many value investors to value companies. To understand the best way EV/EBITDA can be used, one must start at its formation, by understanding the numerator and denominator.

The advantage of using enterprise value in the numerator is very appealing to many investors as an alternative method, since price-to-earnings and price-to-book values are primarily equity valuations, and not "firm" valuation tools. While these are good tools to use to value a business, value investors also try to gauge the intrinsic worth of a com-pany by examining the entire firm—the company's enterprise value. This is done by taking the company's market value, adding its total debt, and then subtracting the cash. Including a control premium, this is the value that a private or strategic buyer of the enterprise would pay for the company.

The treatment of cash is what often confuses new users of this tool. There are two simple reasons why cash is excluded. First, the value of a firm is the value of its equity and its debt. By taking out the cash, the for-mula is essentially using a "net" debt number—debt less the cash, or absolute debt. The other reason is more complex. Interest income is not included in the EBITDA number. Often, this interest income involves returns from idle cash. Therefore, since this interest income is not included in the EBITDA calculation in the denominator, then it should be taken out of the numerator as well.

Public and private equity investors favor this valuation tool for a number of reasons. First, this multiple can be used across a wide vari-ety of firms with negative or depressed earnings. Second, given the dif-ferences in depreciation among companies, EBITDA adds back the depreciation to compare the operating-cash-generating strength of similar companies.

As with other valuation metrics, there are many shortcomings with using the EV/EBITDA multiple. For example, it doesn't allow one to assess the value of a holding company. Also, this valuation tool is not good for companies that have equity stakes in other companies. First, if the equity holding is one of a minority interest, the EBITDA does not reflect the income from the holding; the numerator—the enterprise value—however, would include the value of the equity stake in marketable securities. This creates a higher enterprise value, which can be misleading. Second, if the company has a majority holding, EV/EBITDA still falls short. In such cases, the denominator would include all of the income from the holding company, but the numerator would only carry part of the equity, thereby making the multiple appear to be too low. In such cases, the investor would be required to strip out the earning contributions from the numerator and denominator, and value the holdings separately.

The EV/EBITDA multiple follows the same rules as any other comparable multiple. One advantage over other multiples, however, is that EBITDA multiples can be compared with those in the private markets. As will be noted later, this is a significant benefit for investors who look to private and public deal transactions in valuing a company.

However, EBITDA has some very strong adversaries. "The one figure we regard as utter nonsense," says Warren Buffett, "is so-called EBITDA...Any business with significant fixed assets almost always has a concomitant requirement that major cash be reinvested simply to stay in the same place competitively in terms of unit sales. Therefore, to look at some figure that is stated before those cash requirements is absolutely *folly*. But that hasn't stopped EBITDA from being misused by lots of people to sell all manner of merchandise for years and years."[4]

According to *Moody's* June 2000 report on the subject, leverage buyout companies promoted the concept in the 1980s. Since depreciation and amortization are noncash items, it can be used to pay down the company's debt burden. Users of EBITDA, however, went too far and began applying the tool to a wide range of companies with a variety of financial situations.

The use of EBITDA has been too widespread, and many investors—including value-oriented ones—forget about the pitfalls of using such a

---

[4]*Outstanding Investor Digest,* "Berkshire Hathaway's Warren Buffett & Charlie Munger," September 28, 1998.

EXHIBIT 3.1 EBITDA and income statement comparison.

EBITDA	*Income Statement*
Sales	Sales
Cost of Goods Sold	Cost of Goods Sold
= Gross Profits	**= Gross Profits**
Operating Expense	Operating Expense
= Operating Income (EBIT)	**= Operating Income (EBIT)**
	Interest Expense
Add back D&A	Other Gaines/Losses
	= Pretax Income
	Income Tax
	Other
= EBITDA	**= Net Income**

tool. See Appendix C for a more detailed look at shortcomings of EBITDA. Below are the critical failings of using EBITDA according to *Moody's*. The findings illustrated in this chapter are used with permission of *Moody's*.

MOODY'S TEN CRITICAL FAILINGS OF EBITDA AS THE PRINCIPAL DETERMINANT OF CASH FLOW[5]

1. EBITDA ignores changes in working capital and overstates cash flow in periods of working capital growth.

2. EBITDA can be a misleading measure of liquidity.

3. EBITDA does not consider the amount of required reinvestment—especially for companies with short-lived assets.

4. EBITDA says nothing about the quality of earnings.

5. EBITDA is an inadequate stand-alone measure for comparing acquisition multiples.

6. EBITDA ignores distinctions in the quality of cash flow resulting from differing accounting policies—NOT all revenues are cash.

7. EBITDA is not a common denominator for cross-border accounting conventions.

8. EBITDA offers limited protection when used in indenture covenants.

9. EBITDA can drift from the realm of reality.

10. EBITDA is not well suited for the analysis of many industries because it ignores their unique attributes.

With the proper perspective on the failings of EBITDA on hand, the investor can begin to apply the EV/EBITDA tool with the proper level of caution. The best way is to focus on three variables: tax rate, depreciation and amortization, and capital expenditures. Regarding the tax rate, value investors often regard companies with lower tax rates as companies who deserve a higher EV/EBITDA multiple, as opposed to those with higher tax rates. Likewise, they view companies who derive a greater portion of the EBITDA from depreciation and amortization as companies of a lesser quality and believe that these companies should warrant a lower multiple. Finally, the value investor focuses on capital

[5]Stumpp, P., Marshella, T., Rowan, M., McCreary, R., Coppola, M. *"Putting EBITDA in Perspective: Ten Critical Failings of EBITDA as the Principal Determinant of Cash Flow"* (New York: Moody's Investor Service, June 2000).

expenditures and concludes that companies using a greater portion of EBITDA for capital expenditures deserve a lower multiple. In addition, that investment in capital expenditures has to generate a return above the company's cost of capital.

Given these variables, the prudent investor believes that this multiple is best used for those companies that have already omitted the majority of capital expenditure needs, and for comparable companies that use various depreciation methods.

As *Moody's* points out, EBITDA does have some merits, if used properly. Specifically, EBITDA remains a legitimate tool for analyzing companies that are not generating earnings in the bottoms of their cycles. Breaking down its components into EBIT, Depreciation, and Amortization best assesses EBITDA. The greater the percentage of EBIT in EBITDA, the stronger the underlying cash flow. EBITDA is a better measurement for companies whose assets have longer lives.

Top-Line Multiples: EV/Revenue and Price/Sales.   Enterprise value to revenue is calculated by taking the firm value, which includes the firm's debt and equity, and dividing it by revenues. The current equity market value, which is the stock price multiplied by the shares outstanding divided by the revenues, gives us the price-to-sales ratio, or P/S.

The revenue multiple is a very basic tool that values companies based on their sales or revenues. Companies that trade at a relatively high EV/R or P/S multiple are considered, and those that trade at lower multiples are more attractively priced. But like other simple tools, revenue multiples are often misused.

Enterprise value to revenues is used similarly to price to sales. In the very rare occasion when value investors use revenue-based multiples, they prefer using EV/R because it values the entire firm. Price to sales values the equity portion of a company. In general, the reason why most daring investors like to use revenue multiples is that they are not influenced by accounting decisions that can plague other valuation tools such as the P/E or EV/EBITDA multiples. For example, accounting decisions such as depreciation schedules, accounting for acquisition, inventory, etc., do not impact revenue valuation.

There have been, from time to time, companies that have used suspect accounting methods to record sales, but such cases are rare. Being exempt from a company's accounting decisions makes the EV/R and P/S multiples less volatile than, say, the P/E multiple; therefore, many investors believe that they are more aligned with the trends in the value of the firm, as opposed to the fluctuations of the stock price. This "steadiness" feature adds another advantage to EV/R and P/S, making them valuable in looking at firms with negative earnings or negative EBITDA.

Some investors prefer the EV/R ratio to the P/S multiple, because it is an assessment of firm valuation based on revenues. P/S is fundamentally not consistent. Specifically, in P/S, the numerator uses the value of only the equity of the firm; the denominator uses the revenues generated by the entire firm.

The premise of EV/R is that since we are using the revenues of the entire firm in the denominator, we must remain consistent and use the entire value of the firm as well. As a result, when using P/S, a company is seen as being undervalued despite the fact that it may have too much debt on its balance sheet. Therefore, when comparing one company to another, P/S ignores the amount of debt a company has on its balance sheet—which is an important element in determining firm value.

The disadvantages of EV/R and P/S are their heavy emphasis on future top-line growth—almost exclusively. For example, investors often pay a high multiple for a company that is showing strong sales growth despite the fact that it is losing money or going into lower-margin businesses. Some investors call this "hurt" growth. Firm value is based on cash flow and earnings. Not revenues. The EV/R tool ignores this fundamental premise. The belief in using EV/R is that cash flow and earnings will be produced at some point in the future.

If an investor decides to use EV/R or P/S, it is done in concert with an assessment of the firm's industry growth dynamics, the company's competitive positioning, and profit margins—all of which are discussed in Chapter 2. The two analyses go hand in hand. The objective is to eliminate the opportunity for hurt growth and assess whether higher revenues are indeed likely to create shareholder value by taking advantage of scale.

Other Enterprise Value metrics.   There are other variations to EV/EBITDA used by investors. There is EV/EBIT, EV/EBITDA-Capital expenditures, and EV/Cash Flow. These multiplies have the same characteristics as EV/EBITDA, but with more variables included in the denominator like EBITDA-CAPEX, free cash flow, EBIT, etc., with the exception of the EV/EBIT ratio, which does not add back depreciation. EV/EBIT is often used in industries where capital expenditures are typically for maintenance purposes and are close to depreciation and amortization expenses.

The PEG Ratio.   Many on Wall Street use PEG ratios to value a company. Most value investors do not use PEG ratios. It is discussed here to give some arguments as to why this is so. PEG ratios are a common tool and therefore warrant discussing. The PEG ratio is basically a firm's P/E ratio divided by the expected growth rate. For example, a company with a P/E ratio of 30 and a growth rate of 15% would have a PEG ratio of 2. The key to the PEG ratio is that the growth rate used in the denominator is the growth rate of earnings. Some on Wall Street actually use this ratio to identify undervalued companies. When the ratio is less than 1, these speculators believe it means that the company is "cheap."

While there are some good reasons to use this metric, the value investor chooses not to for a number of strong reasons. Some of the not-so-good reasons include the fact that there are too many variations for PEG ratios. In the numerator, the P/E ratio can range from current calendar or fiscal year P/E to forward P/E. The denominator can range from the growth rate of the current fiscal year to a compound annual growth rate over a certain time frame, let's say, five years. Some practitioners of PEG use forward-looking PE ratios. They would say, "This company is trading at 15 times on next year's earnings and growing at 20% per year. It's undervalued!" This practice can be misleading. When investors use the PEG ratio this way, they are double counting the growth of the company. Using a forward-looking P/E in the numerator already takes into account the growth prospects of the company.

Several investors on Wall Street compare PEG ratios among industry groups. If a company has a high ratio relative to the group, it is deemed overvalued, and vice versa. This practice also has faults. For example, most avid users of PEG apply it to value technology-related companies that show evidence of promising growth. However, there are different forms of growth. Let us take a deeper look to understand the differences. The key here is a firm's level of retained earnings. If two companies have the same growth rate with one paying out a large part of its earnings in the form of dividends, the dividend-paying company would have a more desirable growth characteristic than the one with 100% of earnings reinvested in the company.

Comparing PEG ratios works only when companies have the same growth characteristic and risks associated with that growth. The casual user of PEG may be convinced that if differences in growth among firms were not heavily considered in the PEG ratio, then the PEG ratio is worthless. It would therefore be reduced to the P/E ratio. Finding twin growth characteristic companies is very difficult, and therefore, severely limits the use of PEG ratios.

The results from the comparative use of PEG ratios within an industry can be misguiding. For example, a few companies with very optimistic growth rates for the future, who are therefore more risky, will look very inexpensive because PEG becomes more attractive as a firm's projection becomes more risky. Also, companies with subpar returns to shareholders will have more attractive PEG ratios than firms with a higher ROE.

Many proponents of PEG argue that PEG is very easy to use, the variables are readily available, and it is a very common valuation tool in the investment community. This is true, but should not be the sole reason why one chooses it to value a company. At a minimum, it should be used with other tools—and with extreme caution. The best way to use PEG—if at all—is to find the absolute perfect twin company with similar earnings risk, growth prospects and type, and retained earnings characteristics.

ASSET-BASED TOOLS

Asset-based valuation tools are not based on the valuation of twin companies. They are based on the value that a particular company generates—its intrinsic value. The focus is on the assets of the firm. There are many ways to value an asset. The discussion below addresses one of the best ways of valuing the assets of an enterprise.

Discounted Cash Flows.   Discounted cash flow (DCF) is a very common valuation tool in the investment community, taking into account a company's cash flows and the factors affecting its growth rate. Specifically, this is taking the cash flows generated by the company and discounting them back. The discount rate depends partly on the company's cost of capital and the rate available for a risk-free investment at the time. Any minor changes in these variables, such as changes in interest rates and cash flow projections, will have a noticeable impact on the firm value.

Discounted cash flow becomes a very useful tool for valuing the assets of a firm. At its core, it values companies without using market price quotations, and incorporates the time value of money. DCF helps investors focus on their returns on invested capital by simply forcing them to think through the following question: If I invest these funds today, how much will I get back in the future, and how will I be compensated for taking this risk?

There are three variables that one must consider when using the DCF valuation—the cash flow, the discount rate, and time. The value of a firm is the discounted value of a company's free cash flow. A simple free cash flow can be computed by starting with a company's net income, adding back depreciation and amortization, and subtracting capital expenditures. The free cash flow formula that is simple and easy to compute is as follows:

$$\begin{aligned}
&\text{Net Income} \\
+\ &\text{Depreciation} \\
+\ &\text{Amortization} \\
-\ &\text{Capital Expenditures} \\
\hline
=\ &\text{Free Cash Flow}
\end{aligned}$$

The discount rate one uses is based on the level of risk that is associated with the cash flows. Warren Buffet, however, uses one single rate regardless of the enterprise: "...In order to calculate intrinsic value, you take those cash flows that you expect to be generated and you discount them back to their present value—in our case, at the long-term Treasury rate. And that discount rate doesn't pay you as high a rate as it *needs* to. But you can use the resulting present value figure that you get by discounting your cash flows back at the long-term Treasury rate as a common yardstick just to have a standard of measurement across all businesses. And if the company is investing wisely, then even though the cash flows from those heavy expenditures would be discounted back more years, the resulting growth in future cash development should *offset* that. If it doesn't, then the company wasn't investing it wisely."[6]

When asked why he does not use different discount rates for different businesses given the changes in their risk profiles, Buffett answers: "We don't worry about risk in the traditional way—for example, in the way you're taught at Wharton. It's a good question, believe me. If we could see the future of every business perfectly, it wouldn't make any difference to us whether the money came from running street cars or selling software because all of the cash that came out—which is all we're measuring—between now and Judgment Day would spend the same to us."[7]

Investors use a weighted average cost of capital (WACC) as their discount rate because it is the overall expected return from the entire enterprise. Those investors who use WACC calculate a company's weighted average cost of capital by observing two parts—debt and equity. Investors try to weight the significance of each according to the specific situation. All sources of capital from these two parts are included, such as bonds, tra-

[6]*Outstanding Investor Digest,* "Berkshire Hathaway's Warren Buffett & Charlie Munger," September 28, 1998.

[7]*Outstanding Investor Digest,* "Berkshire Hathaway's Warren Buffett & Charlie Munger," September 28, 1998.

ditional bank debt, and common stock. The cost of capital is calculated with the following formula:

$$WACC = E/Cap \times Ec + D/Cap \times Dc \times (1 - Tr)$$

Where:

E = the equity market value of the enterprise

D = the debt market value of the enterprise

Cap = capitalization, which is E + D

Ec = cost of equity, which is the returns shareholders require from the company

Dc = cost of debt, which is the returns lenders require from the company

E/Cap = equity financing as a percentage of capitalization

D/Cap = debt financing as a percentage of capitalization

Tr = the company's tax rate

Users of DCF must also determine the time horizon or the expected life of cash flows. Many investors use a five- to seven-year time frame when determining the value of an enterprise using the DCF approach. Three years is too short because the DCF valuation then becomes more like a cash flow multiple, and years beyond ten are too long given the dynamic nature of American enterprise—the business is more likely to be different in a decade.

Like other tools mentioned earlier, there are once again pros and cons for using DCF. Discounted cash flow is a stronger tool then P/E and many others, due to a variety of factors. The strongest reason is that P/E uses earnings per share in the denominator, and "earnings per share ignores the effects of many natural or contrived peculiarities of accounting. It can therefore lead, or allow, mangers to make choices that destroy value in the long term, often without the short-term share price movement they hoped for...Accounting earnings are useful for valuation only when earnings is a good proxy for the expected long-term cash flow of the company. Not all companies generate the same cash flow for each dollar of earnings, however, so earnings approaches are generally only useful for first-cut value approximations."[8]

There are also many issues regarding the challenges in using DCF, including the difficulty of getting to an appropriate discount rate. Also, the

---

[8]Copeland, T., Koller, T., Murrin, J. *Valuation: Measuring and Managing the Value of Companies,* pp. 73, 74 (John Wiley & Sons, Inc.).

vast majority of the value in a DCF analysis is in the distant years. The other concerns are more practical. DCF does not work well in very common situations, such as when analyzing cyclical companies, companies who are acquisitive, companies undergoing a corporate restructuring, and companies with hidden or underutilized assets.

The problem with using DCF when analyzing cyclical companies— companies that have sales fluctuating in cycles, typically with the economy—is that the investor's bias and ability to predict the bottom and top portions of the cycle becomes too much of a factor in the DCF assessment. Otherwise, a smoothing effect on cash flows would have to be employed, thereby distorting the economic realities of the business.

Using DCF on companies using a growth-through-acquisition strategy can also be problematic, as it may lead to a false, low valuation. The management teams of companies that acquire other companies as a means of growth usually do so because they believe in the savings that are likely to be captured by the business combination. The problem with using DCF is that the management's ability to capture those savings is paramount to the value of the business and the DCF calculation. In addition, the investor using DCF would have to adjust his or her discount rate to incorporate the new business risks given the acquisition.

Similarly, companies undergoing massive change or restructuring would reap a low valuation under DCF. As discussed in Chapter 4, companies undergoing restructuring can be great opportunities for value investors. DCF, however, is not the best way to value these types of opportunities because the proper discount rate and cash flow to use is often unknown. Companies undergoing restructuring undertake an ongoing process. As such, it can change a company's capital structure or management; it can divest assets, spin-off divisions, etc., all of which change the future cash flows and the risk of the enterprise. Therefore, discounting a company's future cash flows would be very difficult given its unpredictability.

Finally, one of the specialties of value investors is searching for hidden treasure within companies to "uncover" hidden assets that are being underutilized by the firm. Unfortunately, DCF is not the best tool to use for such endeavors. In such situations, DCF would only be able to value realized assets or assets that produce cash flows. For example, assets such as idle but valuable land or unutilized licensing agreements would be valued at nothing under DCF. At best, DCF could perhaps be used in conjunction with other tools, but not alone because it is simply inadequate.

The discounted cash flow method of valuing companies is not a new tool. Rather, it is one that has stood the test of time. Value investors use DCF when the cash flows of the enterprise are not too cyclical, and it can be assumed that they will have relatively the same risk profile in the forecasted future of five to seven years.

Sum-of-the-parts.   The sum-of-the-parts method is essential for carving the business in different parts, which may require different tools to evaluate each. For example, if one were to value General Electric Company, several metrics would be needed because the investor would value GE's appliance business differently than their financial service or NBC division. The Form 10-K is typically the place investors start in order to get a sense of the best ways to segment a company's businesses. With the segment information from the 10-K or the annual report, the value investor can begin to understand the economics of each of the businesses within a particular company.

In Varian Associates' 1997 10-K, for example, the section entitled "Industry Segments" lists the company's three business divisions, and includes information pertaining to each of the division's sales, pretax earnings, assets, capital expenditures, and depreciation. With this information on hand, the value investor can proceed with a customized approach to valuing the company as a whole.

TRANSACTION-BASED TOOL

The transaction-based tool relies on the values that the acquired company places on a firm's assets. The applications of the tools are less rigid, essentially using the same valuation metrics that buyers of business have used in the general market. These metrics can include EV/cash flow, P/S, DCF, etc. It all depends on the data that is available. The only requirement is that the value investor searches aggressively for prior transactions of similar businesses. Ample information can be found on business news wires on the Internet, financial TV programs, or in the newspaper.

More often then not, the valuation multiple that was paid is not clearly stated and has to be determined by the investor. For example, if one hears on CNBC that company X is buying company Y for $700 million, the investor would have to look at the prior and next years' estimates for revenues, earnings, etc., to get an appropriate multiple to use.

VALUING HERMAN MILLER

With Herman Miller's stock price at $17 per share in February of 1999, I assessed the business and concluded that the company was a good business in an attractive industry being run by smart people, as described in Chapter 2. The next step was to figure out how much the company was worth and if the current price of $17 provided enough of a discount.

My first objective was to understand the *price* of the company. I calculated the company's enterprise value, which incorporates important variables such as the company's stock price, market capitalization, information on the company's debt and cash position, and the value of the firm.

After calculating the market capitalization and enterprise values, my next objective was to determine the earnings and free cash flow for the company.

I then looked at Herman Miller's EBITDA because the transactions that had been announced provided enough data to calculate the size of the transaction on an EBITDA basis. This calculation would prove helpful in calculating the value of the enterprise.

Putting everything together, I got a sense as to where the company was trading relative to my own assessment of the value of the enterprise.

Finally, I used three different valuation techniques to triangulate a valuation of the company—discounted cash flow, historical price-to-earnings ratios, and private-market valuation. Using the free cash flow number in my DCF calculation, I came to a valuation of $2.6 billion for the equity value of the company. With a historical P/E fair value multiple of 14x, I arrived at a value of $1.9 billion. Finally, I relied on past business combinations in the industry to provide a valuation range for what I thought the business would

EXHIBIT 3.2 Herman Miller enterprise value calculation.

Stock Price	$17
Shares Outstanding	85
Market Capitalization	$1,445
Plus Debt	166
Less Cash	115
Enterprise Value	$1,496

EXHIBIT 3.3   Herman Miller free cash flow calculation.

	1998 Reported	Next year's estimate
Revenues	$1,719	$1,800
Net Income	128	135
Add: D&A	51	62
Cash Flow	$179	$197
Less: Cap Ex.	74	100
Free Cash Flow	$105	$97

EXHIBIT 3.4   Herman Miller EBITDA and EBITDA less Cap. Ex. calculations.

	1998 Reported	Next year's estimate
Operating Income (EBIT)	$208	$222
Add: D&A	51	62
EBITDA	$259	$284
Less: Cap Ex.	74	100
EBITDA-Cap. Ex	$185	$184

be worth to a potential buyer. I used a multiple of EBITDA because it was one of the best comparable valuation tool at the time, to assess the value of the enterprise. The following shows the calculation.

Combined, the three tools generated a value of $26, which is the price where I began to exit my investment in Herman Miller 18 months later.

EXHIBIT 3.5   Herman Miller valuation.

	1998 Reported	Next year's estimate
P/E	11.3x	10.7x
EV/Revenues	0.9x	0.8x
EV/Free Cash Flow	14.2x	15.4x
EV/EBITDA-Cap. Ex.	8.1x	8.1x
EV/EBITDA	5.8x	5.3x

EXHIBIT 3.6   Take-out valuation.

Next year's EBITDA	$284
A multiple a buyer would pay	8.0x
Firm Value to buyer	$2,272.0
Less: Debt	166
Plus: Cash	115
Equity Worth	$2,221

EXHIBIT 3.7   Herman Miller triangulating a value.

	Value
P/E Valuation Tool	$1,870
DCF Tool	2,550
Take-out Evaluation	2,221
Simple Average	$2,214
Shares Outstanding	85
Implied Worth of Stock	$26.04

EXHIBIT 3.8   Herman Miller Consolidated Income Statement

	05/30/98	05/31/97	06/01/96
(In Thousands, Except Per Share Data)			
NET SALES	$1,718,595	$1,495,885	$1,283,931
COST OF SALES	1,079,756	961,961	848,985
GROSS MARGIN	$638,839	$533,924	$434,946
Operating Expenses:			
Selling, general, and administrative	396,698	359,601	316,024
Design and research	33,846	29,140	27,472
Patent litigation settlement	—	—	16,515
Loss on divestiture	—	14,500	—
TOTAL OPERATING EXPENSES	$430,544	$403,241	$360,011
OPERATING INCOME	$208,295	$130,683	$74,935
Other Expenses:			
Interest expense	(8,300)	(8,843)	(7,910)
Interest income	(11,262)	(8,926)	(6,804)
Loss on foreign exchange	270	1,687	1,614
Other, net	1,456	3,196	2,119
NET OTHER EXPENSES	($1,236)	$4,800	$4,839
INCOME BEFORE INCOME TAXES	209,531	125,883	70,096
Income Taxes	81,200	51,485	24,150
NET INCOME	$128,331	$74,398	$45,946
EARNINGS PER SHARE—BASIC	$1.42	$0.79	$0.46
EARNINGS PER SHARE—DILUTED	$1.39	$0.77	$0.46

EXHIBIT 3.9 Herman Miller Consolidated Cash Flows

	05/30/98	05/31/97	06/01/96
(In Thousands)			
Cash Flows from Operating Activities:			
Net Income	$128,331	$74,398	$45,946
Adjustments to reconcile net income to net cash provided by operating activities	140,392	143,772	78,512
NET CASH PROVIDED BY OPERATING ACTIVITIES	$268,723	$218,170	$124,458
Cash Flows from Investing Activities:			
Notes receivable repayments	561,923	449,405	455,973
Notes receivable issued	(544,182)	(460,956)	(454,261)
Property and equipment additions	(73,561)	(54,470)	(54,429)
Proceeds from sales of property and equipment	870	5,336	13,486
Net cash paid for acquisitions	(4,076)	(9,743)	(5,101)
Other, net	(7,102)	1,548	(212)
NET CASH USED FOR INVESTING ACTIVITIES	($66,128)	($68,880)	($44,544)
Cash Flows from Financing Activities:			
Short-term debt borrowings	192,808	236,627	517,862
Short-term debt repayments	(189,619)	(239,417)	(579,613)
Long-term debt borrowings	—	—	270,985
Long-term debt repayments	(70)	(186)	(222,772)
Dividends paid	(13,516)	(12,463)	(13,015)
Common stock issued	18,529	11,989	12,203
Common stock repurchased and retired	(201,982)	(97,962)	(25,101)
Capital lease obligation repayments	(172)	(116)	(250)
NET CASH USED FOR FINANCING ACTIVITIES	($193,959)	($101,528)	($39,701)
Effect of Exchange Rate Changes on Cash and Cash Equivalents	519	1,346	352
NET INCREASE IN CASH AND CASH EQUIVALENTS	$9,155	$49,108	$40,565
Cash and Cash Equivalents, Beginning of Year	106,161	57,053	16,488
CASH AND CASH EQUIVALENTS, END OF YEAR	$115,316	$106,161	$57,053

EXHIBIT 3.10   Herman Miller Consolidated Balance Sheet

(In Thousands, Except Share and Per Share Data)	05/30/98	05/31/97
ASSETS		
Current Assets:		
Cash and cash equivalents	$115,316	$106,161
Accounts receivable, less allowances of $13,792 in 1998		
and $12,943 in 1997	192,384	179,242
Inventories	47,657	53,877
Prepaid expenses and other	44,778	46,584
TOTAL CURRENT ASSETS	$400,135	$385,864
Property and Equipment:		
Land and improvements	27,279	26,936
Buildings and improvements	156,605	156,002
Machinery and equipment	364,817	346,653
Construction in progress	47,171	25,991
TOTAL PROPERTY AND EQUIPMENT	$595,872	$555,582
Less accumulated depreciation	305,208	290,355
NET PROPERTY AND EQUIPMENT	$290,664	$265,227
Notes Receivable, less allowances of $8,430 in 1998		
and $8,489 in 1997	27,522	47,431
Other Assets	66,025	57,065
TOTAL ASSETS	$784,346	$755,587
LIABILITIES and SHAREHOLDERS' EQUITY		
Current Liabilities:		
Unfunded checks	35,241	25,730
Current portion of long-term debt	10,203	173
Notes payable	19,542	17,109
Accounts payable	92,241	76,975
Accrued liabilities	221,105	165,624
TOTAL CURRENT LIABILITIES	$378,332	$285,611
Long-Term Debt, less current portion above	100,910	110,087
Other Liabilities	74,102	72,827
TOTAL LIABILITIES	$553,344	$468,525
Shareholders' Equity:		
Preferred stock, no par value (10,000,000 shares		
authorized, none issued)	—	—
Common stock, $.20 par value (120,000,000 shares		
authorized, 86,986,957 and 46,030,822 shares issued		
and outstanding in 1998 and 1997)	17,397	9,207
Additional paid-in capital	—	—
Retained earnings	227,464	292,237
Cumulative translation adjustment	(9,360)	(10,863)
Key executive stock programs	(4,499)	(3,519)
TOTAL SHAREHOLDERS' EQUITY	$231,002	$287,062
TOTAL LIABILITIES AND SHAREHOLDERS' EQUITY	$784,346	$755,587

CATALYST IDENTIFICATION AND EFFECTIVENESS

"Dramatic change is required. Unlock the value, or let someone else do it for you."[1]

Michael F. Price

CATALYST DEFINED

Investors define the word "catalyst" differently. Some view catalysts as one-time events, such as a spin-off or a merger. Others have a broader definition of this, which would include events or a series of events that affect change. *The American Heritage Dictionary* defines catalyst as "one that precipitates a process or event..."[2] A *process* is an ongoing series of activities. An *event* takes the conventional thinking of a catalyst, which is shorter in duration than a process or a "one-time" occurrence. Whether an investor's definition of a catalyst is traditional or broader based, what is certain is that all catalysts are expected to ignite change—a difference that ultimately will increase the value of an enterprise.

Value investor Seth Klarman explains why many value investors rely on identifying these sorts of situations: "Value investors are always on the look

---

[1]*Fortune,* "Michael Price: The Scariest S.O.B. on Wall Street," December 9, 1996.

[2]*The American Heritage Dictionary,* Second College Edition (Boston: Houghton Mifflin, p. 247), 1985.

out for catalysts. While buying assets at a discount from underlying value is the defining characteristic of value investing, the partial or total realization of underlying value through a catalyst is an important means of generating profits. Furthermore, the presence of a catalyst serves to reduce risk."[3]

Not all catalysts are cut from the same cloth. There are "firm value" catalysts and "stock" catalysts. Firm value catalysts include such business transactions as a company merger or acquisition. Stock catalysts drive the share price of a company without improving the value of the firm. Events that drive stock price appreciation without having an impact on a company's value are not "real" catalysts, but only perceived changes or anticipation of changes that never come to fruition. One example of such perceived catalysts are stock splits. Stock splits basically change the number of shares in a company but have no real effect on the cash flow, growth, or profitability of the firm.

The only impact that stock splits have is that they encourage stock ownership for the general public, given the reduced price per share. The perception is that the company is cheaper. The stock price may be lower, but not the price that one is paying for the actual value of the enterprise. This action, undoubtedly, served historically to increase the shareholder base.

Other "stock" catalysts can include what traders on Wall Street call "sector rotation." This occurs when large investors, particularly institutions and big mutual funds, sell stocks in one industry to buy stocks in another industry.

This book, however, focuses on firm value catalysts—events that take place that increase the value of the company, regardless of how its stock reacts. The belief is that eventually the market will realize the value that has been created, transferred, or unlocked by such an event and deem it a worthy catalyst.

The following discussion refers to catalysts in the broader sense. It includes the many definitions of catalysts from the value investment community, as well as the views of CEOs and managers who execute these events.

There are different combinations of catalysts, which may vary in type and in length of time for them to become effective. These events can be internally generated or externally induced. Length of duration refers to the time period in which the actual catalyst takes place. Some catalysts are one-time events, such as with an asset sale or a merger. Catalysts can also be defined as events stemming from both inside the organization and from external factors. "There are a number of forces that help bring security prices into line with underlying value. Management prerogatives such as

---

[3]Klarman, S., *Margin of Safety* (New York: HarperBusiness, 1991, p. 164).

share issuance or repurchases, subsidiary spin-offs, recapitalizations, and, as a last resort, liquidation or sale of the business all can serve to narrow the gap between price and value,"[4] explains Seth Klarman.

Some catalysts provide a shorter or more immediate impact, as well as a variety of ongoing benefits. For example, as detailed in Chapter 1, the breakup of Varian Associates had a real and positive impact that went beyond savings from a reduced corporate structure. As the management of the company explained, the reorganization allowed a series of longer-lasting events to occur, and accomplished a number of set objectives. The change improved the culture of each new company, as management became more focused. In turn, the companies were better able to provide specific incentives for their employees. The breakup also gave each independent company the chance to raise its own capital and make its own capital allocation decisions—all of which can have longer-term benefits.

Exhibit 4.1 illustrates the many combinations of catalysts.

POTENTIAL CATALYSTS

As the exhibit below illustrates, there are externally and internally driven catalysts. The following are a few examples of these two types of catalysts.

EXHIBIT 4.1   Catalyst matrix.

	One-time event; Short term in duration	Ongoing, a series of events; Longer term in duration
External	Industrywide: for example, M&A activity	Cyclical industry coming off of its trough
Internal	Asset sale, spin-off share repurchase	Effective organizational change: new operational and/or corporate strategies

[4]Klarman, S., *Margin of Safety* (New York: HarperBusiness, 1991, p. 101).

INTERNAL CATALYSTS

New management can be installed.   New management or a change in the focus of existing management can prove to be a potent catalyst—one that endures. New managers can take on a number of initiatives to drive shareholder value, such as cost reductions, reorganizations, divestitures, etc.

The company can employ a new corporate strategy.   Value seekers keep an eye open for changes in a company's corporate strategy. While these changes are subtle and often hard to detect from an outsider's perspective, changes in a company's industry position, product focus, etc., are often proven to be strong and meaningful catalysts for long-term shareholder value creation.

Investors trying to identify change must identify what the new corporate strategies are trying to influence. There are many targets at which corporate strategies can take aim. One must focus on the impact that such strategies might have on growth and profitability. In Michael Porter's book, *Competitive Strategy,* he makes the case that firms often make trade-offs between revenue growth by implementing a low-cost strategy with higher margins through differentiated products.[5] For example, when companies raise the prices of their goods and services, they may improve profit margins. However, due to the higher price for each product, they are likely to suffer on volume. Companies often choose between focusing on either volume or price to spur exceptional revenue growth. Price leadership often requires a company to possess superior products or services, while volume leadership requires exceptional operational efficiencies to give the firm cost advantages. Such actions, with all else being equal, will drive revenue growth, and ultimately earnings.

Investors often look at a sales-to-capital ratio as a tool to help analyze such revenue growth prospects. The investor calculates this ratio by taking the sales figure, available on the income statement, and dividing by the firm's capital, found on the balance sheet. A higher sales/capital ratio limits the need for the company to plow back cash to finance growth, thereby increasing cash flows and ultimately the value of the enterprise. If this ratio increases, the investment returns on the company's capital also increase.

Unfortunately, such successful strategic catalysts are often short-lived. Studies have shown that if a company receives high returns from the use of one strategy, competitors will mostly likely imitate it and reduce the strat-

---

[5]Porter, M., *Competitive Strategy* (New York: The Free Press, 1980, pp. 35–36).

egy's profitability. The best opportunity for such a catalyst, based on superior strategy, is for a company in a high-barrier industry or a firm with a business plan that requires significant resources and experience to imitate. This situation would give the company and its shareholders enough time to benefit from such strategies.

Not all corporate strategies are geared towards obtaining revenue growth. Income or cash flow growth often arise from accelerated capital allocations in higher-return areas of the firm. However, greater allocation in these areas is usually at the expense of the company's cash flows. If these allocations are going to more risky areas, such a move, they could also increase a firm's cost of capital, thereby reducing the firm's value.

Many investors often focus first on the impact that investment decisions have had on a company's overall cost of capital, in order to gauge their potential returns. The objective is to identify capital that is being allocated to more profitable areas of the firm, which are not likely to increase the company's cost of capital or the risk profile of the enterprise. When the growth in profitability is driven by an increase in capital funding, and there is minimal impact on a firm's cost of capital, then the firm value obviously increases. Investors understand that if the increase in profitability is based on the company's entering new, riskier ventures than its core business, it is very likely that the increase in the company's cost of capital will offset the benefits from an increase in profitability.

Companies can also implement new product strategies.   The threat to a company's operations lies in the risk to its cash flow. One factor that has an impact on cash flow is the level of "stickiness" found with the company's products and services. When referring to a business, "stickiness" essentially means the ability to draw in repeat customers. The more choices the customer has for products, the more risky the firm's operations and cash flow are. This leads to a higher cost of capital and a lower valuation for the firm. Value investors watch for potential catalysts that will reduce operating risk by making the company's products and services stickier. Advertising is often a company's method of choice to accomplish this goal.

Improved operational efficiencies can also be a catalyst.   New operating strategies based on efficiencies can be strong and lasting catalysts to increase the value of a company. It is clear that the more valuable a firm is in a given industry, the higher the profit margins. Therefore, if a company can increase its operating margins relative to its peers, it can generate greater value for its shareholders.

A company can accomplish this task in several ways, from improving the culture of the firm to changing the operational procedures. Investors often target companies with low margins relative to their industry counterparts, because these companies will benefit most from this type of catalyst.

Cutting costs is one of management's favorites. The most common method of choice by management to improve operational efficiency is to cut costs. General cost cuts are potential catalysts only if they are not from sources that are likely to contribute to operating income and future growth. Often, companies reduce costs by cutting back on research and training, even though this may be sacrificing their future growth potential. Such cost cutting is not prudent, and will often be a detriment to the company in the long term.

Value can come from a number of sources, such as a firm's technology, people, products, training, etc. Cutting costs as a sole means to drive firm value can be a dangerous game. In fact, cost cutting is often promised as a means to justify value-destroying decisions by management. Take acquisitions for example. Companies often overpay for companies and offer cost-cutting opportunities to pacify shareholders. Unfortunately, rarely are such promises delivered. Investors are very aware of this. Value investors know that the bigger the cost-cutting promise, the deeper an investor must look at qualifying real prospects. It is often a signal that something is being overvalued, or someone is overpaying.

The truth of the matter is that it is more difficult for companies to separate resources that do not contribute to tangible benefits from those that do contribute. With this in mind, the value investor spends time going through the details of the cost-cutting strategies outlined by the management team. Again, the bigger the promise, the greater the skepticism.

Investors often view a new financial strategy as a potential catalyst. One way a firm can increase profitability is to reduce delicately its cost of capital. While there are several ways that a company can accomplish this objective, a change in a firm's financial strategy is often a catalyst for increased profitability and firm value. The cost of a firm's capital is a combination of the cost of the company's debt and equity financing. The value of a firm is often determined by the cash flows generated by the company, discounted back to the present at a cost of capital. Typically, a reduction in a company's cost of capital will increase the value of a firm. To reduce a firm's cost of capital, management will often change the levels of debt and equity on the balance sheet. Debt is much cheaper than equity, as the lender bears less risk than the equity holders. Therefore, a company with relatively more debt will reduce its cost of capital and increase its firm value.

However, too much debt could cripple a company and push it into financial distress. As the cost of capital decreases, the value of the enterprise will only increase if the higher debt levels do not affect the cash flows of the firm. This is a delicate balance that value investors must assess carefully.

A sustained tax rate reduction can be a potent catalyst.   The value of a company is based on its after-tax free cash flows. A clean and meaningful reduction of taxes—that can be sustained—can be a potent catalyst to spur firm value appreciation. Clearly, there are certain tax rules that management cannot—and should not—avoid. However, there are certain initiatives that can be implemented to help reduce the tax burden. These include multinational companies moving income around to take advantage of optimal tax environments, acquiring operating losses from other companies so they can use them to shield future income, or using complex risk management procedures to reduce the company's average tax rate. Risk management systems often smooth out income over time to help a company limit its exposure to high margin tax rates.

Value investors, in general, are skeptical of tax strategies to increase firm value. However, if companies can sustain such efficiencies over time, investors would have to reward management, given the increase in cash that has been retained for the benefit of shareholders.

Reducing working capital can free up cash.   The noncash working capital in a company is the difference between the noncash current assets and the nondebt portion of current liabilities. This typically includes inventory and accounts receivable less accounts payable. Working capital could be used as a catalyst, since any cash tied up in working capital cannot be put to use in other areas of the company—areas that can generate higher returns. Needless to say, increasing working capital is a cash outflow, and it can only increase firm value if the investments in working capital are decreased.

Companies often point to working capital as an opportunity to increase shareholder value because it is very straightforward. In reality, however, it is trickier than most companies would have investors believe. Any setbacks making improvements in working capital could affect the company's future growth and operating income. This is due to the fact that companies often maintain inventory and provide credit to their customers as encouragement to buy more goods and services. If the company is too aggressive in reducing working capital, it may, in effect, cause lost sales and ultimately the reduction of the company's value.

When considering the potency level of working capital as a potential catalyst, the value investor assesses the potential risk that the company may lose sales in an attempt to reduce investments in working capital. The value investor also looks at the company's use of technology and inventory management systems to facilitate a reduction, which may have a positive impact on firm value.

Reducing capital investments to create value is very tricky. Capital reduction is often a catalyst used to increase firm value, if the company is able to reduce its net capital expenditures on existing assets. The net capital investments made by companies—the difference between the company's capital expenditures and depreciation—is cash coming out of the company that reduces the cash flow to the firm. This cash is typically used to fund future growth opportunities, while maintaining other assets in the company.

Using capital expenditures as a means to increase firm value must be done in a delicate manner. While a company might generate cash inflows by reducing investments in existing assets, which can generate value for shareholders, it also risks reducing the life span of these assets. Conversely, if a company invests all of its capital on existing assets, there may be no free cash flow—a move that may impair firm value. Finding the right level of capital expenditure requirements is the first step towards assessing whether or not reducing it to generate cash in order to invest elsewhere is likely to drive share price appreciation.

Share buybacks are one of investors' favorite catalysts. At times, one catalyst leads to another. There are catalysts aimed at closing a value gap between the current share price of a company and the implied value of the enterprise. Needless to say, it is when a company's stock price trades at a significant discount to a firm's fair value that value investors mostly search for catalysts. The most common catalyst, and certainly less complicated in terms of execution, is the stock repurchase.

The stock repurchase can be done in virtually any publicly traded company; it is often up to the management team to realize the opportunity—the value gap between their company's share price and its worth—to ignite a share buyback program. It is very hard to anticipate such a decision by management, and hence to benefit fully from such a decision. Announcements of share repurchase programs often produce an immediate increase in a company's stock price.

Company share repurchase is one of the most common tools that management uses to create shareholder value, as it essentially returns cash to shareholders. As a result, it is no wonder that investors like to see share repurchase programs: "We spend a lot of time on both large and small reorganizations," says Michael Price. "Often when we own these stocks, they're selling well below break-up value and well below book, so most of the time it makes sense for them to buy their own common. We like to see the sale of an asset for a profit, and have the company take money and buy stock back..."[6]

A company usually buys back its own shares in three different ways: a) via an open market repurchase; b) through a privately negotiated buyback; and c) by way of a repurchased tender offer. In a tender offer, the company often communicates to the public the number of shares desired for purchase, the price it is willing to pay, and the period during which the offer is in effect. Open market buybacks are more common. In an open market repurchase, the company is not required to inform the market of its activities. However, the company will make public its share repurchase plans. Privately negotiated buybacks typically involve buying shares from a large shareholder through direct negotiations with the company. Among the three ways that companies might repurchase their shares, private negotiations are the least common.

There are six primary reasons why companies buy back their own stock: 1) to reduce the company's dividend cash outflow without reducing the dividend itself; 2) to signal to the stock market that the company's stock is undervalued; 3) to increase earnings per share; 4) to change the company's capital structure; 5) to buy the shares of a big seller of the stock; and 6) to give current shareholders a tax-friendly cash distribution.[7]

Cash distribution is a very common objective for management teams. However, one of the issues that investors focus on is that companies buying back their own stock must pay a premium above the market price. The risk is that the company may overpay for its own security, thereby transferring wealth from the long-term shareholders of the company to the selling shareholders. Value investors view a buyback as an acquisition made by the company; the price has to be right.

The company's management team may also repurchase shares in an effort to reduce cash dividends. The money saved through the reduction in

---

[6]*Barron's,* "A Man for All Markets," March 11, 1985.

[7]*Journal of Applied Corporate Finance,* "Common Stock Repurchase: What Do They Really Accomplish," by Larry Dann, University of Oregon, 1983, pp. 72–79.

dividends is expected to be far greater than the funds spent to redeem the shares. This should indicate to the market that compared to paying a dividend, repurchasing stock is a better investment and could generate shareholder wealth over time.

"Signaling" can be a very potent catalyst as well. Since the company is willing to spend cash to repurchase its own shares, it shows that the management team has high confidence in the business and that its share price is undervalued. Signaling such confidence often leads to higher share prices.

Repurchasing shares often leads to an increase in earnings per share. Increasing earnings per share is many times best achieved when the company uses new debt to finance the repurchase. This action increases not only earnings, but may also increase a firm's ROE. Return on equity could increase due to the change in the firm's capital structure.

The final reason for a share repurchase is to buy the shares of a large shareholder who is looking for liquidity. This action could be advantageous, particularly if the purchase is from a shareholder who wishes to reduce a company's proven value creation plans.

Spin-offs and equity carve-outs can be a good way to spur a company's share price. "A spin-off is a tax-free transaction in which a parent corporation transfers the business to be spun off to a new subsidiary and then pays a special dividend to its shareholders consisting of the shares of the new subsidiary. After the spin-off, the new firm is a separate, publicly traded company with a shareholder base identical to that of the parent corporation. The shareholders of the parent company receive the shares of the subsidiary on a pro rata basis, without paying any additional consideration or incurring any tax liability."[8] An equity carve-out often occurs prior to a spin-off, with an equity carve-out only allowing for a small part of the division to be offered to the public. The main difference between an equity carve-out and a spin-off is that a carve-out raises cash for the parent company, and spin-offs do not.

There are four key qualities of a spin-off. First, spin-offs can help companies refocus on their primary core competencies by allowing them to separate business divisions that do not fit strategically, operationally, or financially with the parent company. Second, shareholders, because of the valuation differences created between the spun-off company and the parent company, often cheer such actions. For example, a slow-growth, low-margin conglomerate

[8]Cornell, J., *Spin-off to Pay-off* (New York: McGraw-Hill, 1998, p. 3).

that has a fast-growing, high-margin division, may be a good candidate for a spin-off, due to the potential valuation differences. In addition, companies with several divisions and complex structures are hard to value, and are often valued at a significant discount to the values of their parts. Spinning off divisions is often a remedy that eliminates this conglomerate discount.

Third, the spun-off company also has an opportunity to create shareholder value by giving it a new corporate structure. New spun-off companies typically possess very focused management teams who are given strong incentives to generate shareholder value. The fourth quality, and perhaps the most financially sound reason for a spin-off, is the tax advantage. The parent company and the recipient shareholders are not taxed, despite the fact that the parent company recognizes a financial gain, as if it had sold assets. Additionally, the recipient shareholders are not taxed, even though they receive dividend income.

When contemplating investing in a spin-off or equity carve-out, the value investor assesses the business, the value-unlocking opportunities of the enterprise, and the management team. Like in other investments, these attributes are essential to understanding the value opportunities of the enterprise. In addition, the value investor focuses on issues that are related to such reorganizations, including changes in accounting, debt allocation, and separation issues like the relationship that the spun-off company will have with the parent company, and regulatory approval prospects.

There are four primary reasons why a company would consider using the spin-off catalyst to spur stock price appreciation. First, a division with its own equity base and shareholders may be better able to raise equity financing as an independent unit. A second reason for a spin-off may be that it is due to regulatory requirements. This reason for a spin off could come from the Federal Trade Commission and the Department of Justice asking a company to sell or spin-off a division to get regulatory approval of a bigger transaction. The company may spin off a division in order to receive a better credit rating as well. The final reason for a spin-off is the possibility that the division under consideration may not fit well with the parent company's corporate strategy.

Split-offs.   A split-off is similar to a spin-off. The difference is that in a split-off, investors must choose which company they would like to own, the parent or the new company, but not both. If investors wish to own the shares of the subsidiary, they must swap their shares of the parent for shares of the new company. The parent company often offers a price incentive for the new company in an attempt to encourage shareholders to exchange their parent company stock for the subsidiary's stock. The parent company is eager to do this because this is, in effect, a stock buyback for the parent company. The key difference between a share repurchase program and a split-off is that instead of using cash to repurchase stock, the split-off process allows the parent company to use the newly created stock as currency. Value investors focus on the quality of the two businesses, their values, and the price at which these investors would own the shares—factoring in any incentive from the parent company.

Asset Sale: An asset sale is only part of the value creation. The other half is the use of the proceeds.   Sales of assets of a company are usually a good sign of value being unlocked. Assets in a company represent the investments that have already been made, which generate the current operating income for the firm. Typically, if these assets generate investment returns less than the company's cost of capital, or what they could potentially generate, then they are the most potential candidates for sale.

There are ways that an investor might evaluate the level of value that an asset sale could have. To achieve this end, value investors take the present value of the expected cash flow that the company might have received if the assets were not sold, and compare it to the cash received from the sale of the asset itself. If the cash received from the sale of assets were less than the present value of the expected cash flows, then the sale of assets would have a negative impact on shareholder value. If the cash received were greater than the present value of the cash flow, such sale would increase value for shareholders. If the proceeds from the asset sale were equal to the present value of the expected cash flow, then the asset sale would have no real value to shareowners.

The use of the cash received from the sale of assets can also be a catalyst. There are typically three uses for the cash received. First, the company can invest the cash in the stock market. Secondly, the company can invest the cash in other areas of the company, which might produce a higher return for the company. Finally, as a less risky alternative, the company might share the proceeds of the asset sale with shareholders by repurchasing stock or issuing a dividend.

Worth more dead than alive: full or partial liquidations are often a potent catalyst.   After consistently earning a return on capital that is far less than its cost of capital, a full or partial liquidation would be a potent catalyst. Liquidation would stop the investment in business projects that destroy value, and return the funds to shareholders. A complete or a partial liquidation might perhaps be the best way to increase firm value for those companies in poor, value-destroying businesses. Liquidating would be a catalyst if the stock price of the company trades well below its liquidating value—a value that is computed as the net worth of tangible assets to the firm.

EXTERNAL CATALYSTS

The presence of shareholder activists.   Shareholder activists can range from individual investors to institutional investors, or can come from the ranks of a foundation or public pension fund. Their objectives may stem from corporate activism, relating to issues of corporate governance or to company policy concerns regarding the environment. The presence of an activist is often a catalyst for change. Even if the specific battle with management is lost, other potentially catalytic events are often initiated as a result.

For example, a public bout with management may encourage discussions inside the organization about the concerns of shareholders. The media may also look into the issues publicly revealed by dissented shareholders. Whether to accomplish specific goals or to ignite other peripheral actions, corporate activists may employ several methods to achieve their goals. These methods include proxy fights, letter-writing campaigns, filling shareholder resolutions, and using the media as a public forum. While many activists can agitate the management of companies, the value investor has a keen interest in those activists who are focused on increasing a firm's value by encouraging some sort of catalytic event to take place.

Activists typically propose very specific recommendations for the company's management team, such as corporate and financial management strategies to increase the value of the firm. Actions taken by activists to improve corporate governance often include recommendations to increase the number of outside directors, establish a separate audit unit, or combat excessive executive compensation.

Shareholder activists often target a company to minimize the effect of control mechanisms, such as antitakeover provisions, set up by management to limit the influence of dissident shareholders. Antitakeover measures can lower a company's stock price, especially during periods of underperformance by the management of companies in a consolidating industry. The most common antitakeover tactic is the use of the poison pill. This essentially makes a company's stock less attractive to any would-be acquirer. It is a strategy that makes a company's stock less desirable to those interested in a hostile takeover. Unfortunately, the poison pill has perhaps been one of management's greatest victories in the fight for corporate control with limited accountability. This tactic helps to keep low-performing management teams and board members intact, and continues to frustrate many investors who strongly believe in management accountability.

"This is a free market system. When you own stocks, you should have the right to decide what happens to that business," says Michael Price. He goes on to say, "And the boards of directors should protect the shareholders, not the managements. Even though the shareholders vote for them, boards are really the management's chums. Managements nominate the boards, more often than the boards do the managements. Unfortunate, but that's what we've got..."[9]

"In retrospect," says shareholder activist Carl Icahn, "I think I should have done everything in my power to fight the 'poison pill' and other deterrents that have been fostered by entrenched managements during the past decade. I would have liked to be the one to lead such a legislative charge, but I am not politically astute. In the final analysis, I'm only a guy who loves investing..."[10]

In addition to the likes of Price and Icahn, institutional investors such as The California Public Employees' Retirement System (CalPERS) have a very determined and public role as shareholder activists. In fact, every year, CalPERS produces a list of companies that require some level of shareholder activism. This list is widely followed by value investors.

To come up with the list, CalPERS uses three criteria for its company selection: companies who have had poor three-year returns based on their stock prices, companies who allocate their capital inefficiently, and those with inadequate corporate governance structures. "Shareowners collectively have the power to direct the course of corporations. The potential impact of this power is staggering. Through shareowner action, economic wealth can either be created or destroyed. In CalPERS' view, the responsibility that results from this power must be exercised responsibly."[11]

Industry merger activity can also be effective.   Merger activity in an industry can prove to be a catalyst since it generally provides metrics to value other companies in the same industry. What determines the impact of merger activity in a particular industry is that the valuation of other industry participants is often found in the reasons for such activity.

---

[9]*Barron's,* "A Man for All Markets," March 11, 1985.
[10]*Fortune,* "Icahn Fights Back," August 14, 2000.
[11]CalPERS: Shareowner Action, *http://www.calpers-governance.org/alert/default.asp*, January 2002.

There are several reasons why companies merge with one another. The five key reasons for merger activity that the value investor focuses on include taking advantage of scale economies, diversification, exploiting debt capacity, tax benefits, and closing a valuation gap or a pure financial investment by another company. Regarding valuation gaps, companies often buy entities based on certain valuation gaps in the marketplace. This gap is often the difference between the public and private valuation of an enterprise. The difference in valuation is often a direct result of high-quality assets that are mismanaged or misunderstood in the marketplace, and are then seen differently by a prospective buyer.

Investors' abilities to identify potential candidates can be very useful as they assess a potential investment. A good acquisition target might be a firm that is doing a poor job managing its assets or one that has assets that are too complicated to be properly valued by the general market. For example, companies that have several business units often trade at a deep discount to their after-tax sum-of-the-parts valuation. Such assets often make good acquisition candidates, especially if the acquirer can gain value by simply liquidating the business post merger.

Taking advantage of real or perceived scale economies is another common reason why companies merge. Economies of scale effectively reduce a company's cost of doing business over time, and thereby increase profit margins, and ultimately, the value of the firm. Companies often look for targets in their industry peer group with whom they can benefit from increased scale in production, sales and marketing, research and development, and distribution.

With diversification, whether by product or market, companies look to make acquisitions that they believe will increase value for their shareholders. Unfortunately, diversification in and of itself does not create shareholder value, as evidenced by the fact that companies with multiple business lines often trade at a "conglomerate" discount to the sum of the parts. The reason for this discount is that shareholders can diversify on their own by purchasing shares of various companies and holding them in a portfolio. "Forced" diversification is not particularly appealing when competitive advantages and profitability are not being realized because of it. In addition, conglomerates often do not have the "best of breed" businesses—but a hand full of weaker companies.

The financial structure of an enterprise can also play a role in an acquirer's reasoning. Exploiting a target's debt capacity, for example, is a viable reason for acquisition. An underlevered company with unused debt capacity is often a target because of the borrowing capabilities available to help finance the acquisition. Also, an increase in the debt capacity will help lower the combined company's cost of capital, and in turn, will boost firm value.

Having substantial tax benefits can play a role in the process as well. The value investor is particularly interested in the benefits relating to net operating loss carry forwards and the handling of depreciation. Both of these items have a positive impact on the cash flow of the buyer, since they can potentially lower one's tax rate. After-tax free cash flows increase, and obviously, so does the firm's value.

Time: the silent external catalyst.   The end of a temporary, negative catalyst—an adverse event or series of events, such as high resin costs for packaging companies or low oil prices for oil-related companies—can also prompt value enhancement. In such cases, *time* is often the best catalyst, as the many economic, political, or financial factors work their way through the system to change the company's course. Time can only be a catalyst if nothing out of the ordinary has occurred and the cyclical or seasonal pattern is well defined. Value investors try to take advantage of such situations, since they have a propensity to be longer-term oriented.

In summary, all of these possibilities are unique to the particular acquisition target. Therefore, the value investor focuses on the distinctive nature of each merger activity in a given industry, in an attempt to come to a rational justification as to why other industry players may be the next target, and deserving of higher valuations.

MANAGEMENT UNLOCKING VALUE AT THERMO ELECTRON CORPORATION

In the fall of 1998, I began reading about a very diverse conglomerate called Thermo Electron. At the time, Thermo was a leader in the manufacturing of monitoring, analytical, and biomedical instrumentation devices. The company also had good market positions in a number of other areas, such as paper recycling, mammography systems, alternative-energy systems, hair-removal products, etc. The company provided a wide array of services that included industrial outsourcing and environmental-liability management, laser communications, and the like. All in all, the company competed in over 15 industries and had majority equity stakes in over 20 publicly traded companies. Thermo was geographically diversified as well, with operations in 22 countries. Fifty-six percent of revenues were in the

EXHIBIT 4.1a   Old structure.

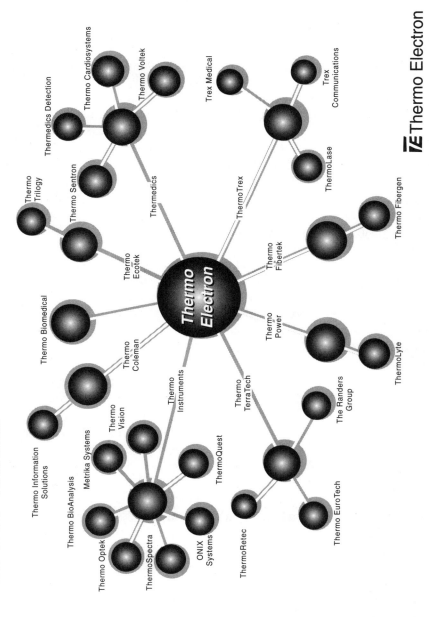

United States, with 30 percent coming from Europe, 10 percent from Asia, and 4 percent from Latin America.

The company's prior growth strategy was twofold: the acquisition and the commercialization of technology-based devices. The company had made approximately $1.8 billion in acquisitions since 1995 in order to enter new markets or increase its product breadth. Thermo's commercialization strategy consisted of developing a particular technology, forming a company around that technology, selling a minority interest of the subsidiary to the public equity markets, and realizing the cash proceeds from such sales. This was an ingenious strategy that worked very well in the past for several reasons. Perhaps the most recognizable benefit was the fact that this strategy allowed Thermo to become a multifaceted company with a rare mix of mature and high-growth businesses, supported by an extraordinarily strong balance sheet. It was one of a kind, and the market rewarded the company with a very high market valuation.

After reading the annual reports on all of the subsidiaries and a few of the company's key competitors, I liked most of the businesses in which they were involved. My conclusion was based on a vertical cash flow analysis of Thermo's core businesses. It was clear from the beginning that Thermo was a very profitable company with strong free cash flows, despite the fact that they had come down a bit from the prior year. The company had a leading position in nearly all of the markets in which they competed. Its strategy seemed to have produced a winning franchise.

I continued to probe further to gain an understanding of why there was a drop in margins and cash flow, given the industry's growth and the company's market share. Further analysis revealed that in recent years, Thermo's strategy became overextended, and the company began to lose focus as it strayed away from its core investments in analytical and biomedical devices. Additionally, as I began to look closely at the company, it was revealed that Thermo was experiencing a slowdown in revenue and earnings growth due to the weakness in the semiconductor equipment market, softness in the industrial markets, a strong U.S. dollar, and an Asian economic crisis. A quick estimate indicated that 20 percent to 30 percent of Thermo's subsidiaries were not contributing to operating income.

Thermo Electron was very inexpensive and was trading in the marketplace at private-market valuations both on a free cash flow basis as well as on a sum-of-the-parts basis. The company's stock was trading at around $14 per share. My assessment of what the company was worth was around $30 per share, based on take-out valuations, price-to-normalized earnings, and on a free cash flow basis. Thermo had a strong and underleveraged balance sheet. The management teams in the various divisions were strong, and each section of the company possessed seasoned operators. After comparing the company's operating numbers over a seven-year period with their competitors', I was very comfortable with management's ability to run the business. I calculated my margin of safety—a concept discussed in Chapter 5—to be in the neighborhood of $10.50, based on a valuation that included what I believed was a high probability that the company would either be taken private, sold, or easily financed. This thinking was based on the company's free cash flow generation and debt capacity, and having such transactions financed by selling the company's assets.

The reasons not to pursue this opportunity—which I considered—were the fact that Thermo was undergoing extreme competitive pressures within its core business line, and the fact that the semiconductor industry upon which Thermo relied heavily was in decline, particularly in Asia. The company's unique corporate structure added to the potential challenges as well.

Using the Five Keys, my final assessment could be summarized by the following:

- I liked the business, the industry, and the performance of the managers.

- I liked the current price of $14 per share.

- I thought that the company was worth at least $30 that day, generating an upside potential of 114 percent.

- My downside was 25 percent, but I was convinced that such a risk was warranted given the fact that at such a price, the company would have been taken private or sold.

The only "key," which had not been identified at that point, was a potent catalyst. I had done some work to come up with several options that management could take to close the valuation gap; however, we were not current shareholders. I waited for almost four months and almost forgot about Thermo Electron.

Then on March 15th, 1999, the company announced that it had appointed a new CEO to oversee the day-to-day operations of the company. The new CEO had been an outside director of the company for two years. He was replacing the founder of the company.

We became owners of the company that very day.

With the catalyst—a new CEO in place—we believed that an aggressive restructuring plan would more likely take place, and that a CEO from the outside would be more able to initiate bold plans in order to create shareholder value. By the time we had finished our purchase of the company's

EXHIBIT 4.2 Value line page. Reprinted with permission from *Value Line.*

THERMO ELECTRON NYSE-TWO

RECENT PRICE	**13**	
P/E RATIO	**13.4**	(Trailing: 14.4 / Median: 23.0)
RELATIVE P/E RATIO	**0.90**	
DIV'D YLD	**Nil**	

TIMELINESS	**4**	Lowered 11/5/99
SAFETY	**3**	New 7/27/90
TECHNICAL	**3**	Raised 7/30/99
BETA 1.20	(1.00 = Market)	

High: 6.1 11.2
Low: 3.8 5.7

2002-04 PROJECTIONS

	Price	Gain	Ann'l Total Return
High	30	(+130%)	23%
Low	19	(+45%)	10%

Insider Decisions

	D	J	F	M	A	M	J	J	A
to Buy	0	0	0	2	0	0	3	0	1
Options	0	0	0	0	0	0	0	0	0
to Sell	0	0	0	2	0	0	1	0	0

Institutional Decisions

	4Q1998	1Q1999	2Q1999
to Buy	112	109	108
to Sell	172	147	140
Hld'g(000)	104168	101354	104923

Percent shares traded: 12.0 / 8.0 / 4.0

LEGENDS
14.0 x "Cash Flow" p sh
···· Relative Price Strength
3-for-2 split 11/86
3-for-2 split 10/93
3-for-2 split 5/95
3-for-2 split 6/96
Options: Yes
Shaded area indicates recession

Target Price Range 2002 | 2003 | 2004

% TOT. RETURN 9/99

	THIS STOCK	VL ARITH. INDEX
1 yr.	-10.8	22.4
3 yr.	-66.8	50.4
5 yr.	-34.0	107.6

© VALUE LINE PUB., INC.

	1983	1984	1985	1986	1987	1988	1989	1990	1991	1992	1993	1994	1995	1996	1997	1998	1999	2000	02-04
Sales per sh A	3.97	5.11	5.43	5.64	6.61	8.51	9.47	9.97	9.23	10.38	11.59	13.82	16.75	19.55	22.35	24.40	28.30	29.05	31.25
"Cash Flow" per sh	.15	.32	.36	.39	.49	.53	.61	.74	.81	.98	1.10	1.44	1.71	2.04	2.36	2.10	2.00	2.35	2.50
Earnings per sh ABE	.00	.13	.20	.25	.30	.34	.40	.49	.55	.64	.70	.82	.99	1.22	1.41	1.01	.95	1.05	1.45
Div'ds Decl'd per sh	--	--	--	--	--	--	--	--	--	--	--	--	--	--	--	--	Nil	Nil	Nil
Cap'l Spending per sh	.10	.14	.14	.15	.19	.34	.33	.35	.38	.66	.52	.52	.48	.83	.70	.93	1.00	1.05	1.15
Book Value per sh C	1.73	1.83	2.08	2.48	2.79	3.09	3.44	4.33	5.51	6.05	7.96	8.63	9.86	11.70	12.55	14.18	12.45	12.25	12.20
Common Shs Outst'g D	45.81	45.95	48.90	58.83	58.00	58.81	61.16	71.01	87.27	91.46	107.82	114.72	131.78	149.98	159.21	158.49	158.10	160.00	166.00
Avg Ann'l P/E Ratio	NMF	NMF	14.5	14.7	21.5	14.7	20.4	17.7	20.3	19.6	24.5	22.6	26.8	31.4	25.8	28.6	Bold figures are Value Line estimates		16.5
Relative P/E Ratio	NMF	1.63	1.45	1.51	1.44	1.22	1.54	1.31	1.30	1.19	1.45	1.48	1.79	1.97	1.51	1.49			1.10
Avg Ann'l Div'd Yield	--	--	--	--	--	--	--	--	--	--	--	--	--	--	--	--			Nil
Sales ($mill) A							579.0	708.0	805.5	949.0	1249.7	1585.4	2207.4	2932.6	3558.3	3867.6	4475	4650	5200
Operating Margin							5.6%	7.8%	9.2%	10.8%	13.3%	15.3%	15.1%	15.2%	15.2%	13.9%	12.0%	13.0%	13.5%
Depreciation ($mill)							12.7	18.8	23.4	29.2	42.4	62.3	85.0	115.2	135.7	162.3	175	180	210
Net Profit ($mill)							24.6	33.9	47.1	60.6	76.6	103.4	140.1	190.8	239.3	170.0	155	170	240
Income Tax Rate							25.6%	29.5%	31.4%	26.9%	25.5%	34.0%	33.0%	29.6%	35.8%	44.3%	44.5%	43.0%	43.0%
Net Profit Margin							4.3%	4.8%	5.8%	6.4%	6.1%	6.5%	6.3%	6.5%	6.7%	4.4%	3.5%	3.7%	4.6%
Working Cap'l ($mill)							262.4	240.7	465.2	503.3	828.2	1146.2	1306.4	2002.0	2218.6	2163.0	1800	1650	1500
Long-Term Debt ($mill)							172.1	210.0	255.0	494.2	847.5	1049.8	1116.0	1550.3	1742.9	2025.5	2150	1920	1900
Shr. Equity ($mill)							210.6	307.3	480.9	552.9	858.5	990.3	1299.8	1754.4	1997.9	2248.1	1970	1960	2150
Return on Total Cap'l							7.7%	7.9%	7.6%	6.9%	6.1%	6.1%	7.1%	6.6%	7.3%	4.9%	4.0%	4.5%	6.0%
Return on Shr. Equity							11.7%	11.0%	9.8%	11.0%	8.9%	10.4%	10.8%	10.9%	12.0%	7.6%	8.0%	8.5%	11.0%

CAPITAL STRUCTURE as of 7/3/99
Total Debt $2156 mill. Due in 5 Yrs $1300 mill.
LT Debt $1984 mill. LT Interest $115.0 mill.
LT Interest earned: 6.1x; Total interest cov.: 4.7x
Incl. $585.0 mill, 4.25% senior debenture, conv. to 15.5 mill. shares of common at $37.80, due 2003.
(50% of Cap'l)

Leases, Uncapitalized Annual rentals $83.8 mill.
Pension Liability None
Pfd Stock None
Common Stock 158,184,285 shs. (50% of Cap'l)
as of 7/30/99
MARKET CAP: $2.1 billion (Mid Cap)

CURRENT POSITION ($MILL)	1997	1998	7/3/99
Cash Assets	1522.7	1547.3	1068.1
Receivables	797.4	875.5	930.2
Inventory (FIFO)	543.6	599.7	646.0
Other	230.5	278.8	297.5
Current Assets	3094.2	3301.3	2941.8
Accts Payable	251.7	272.5	282.1
Debt Due	176.9	134.1	171.9
Other	663.6	731.7	785.5
Current Liab.	1092.2	1138.3	1239.5

ANNUAL RATES of change (per sh)	Past 10 Yrs.	Past 5 Yrs.	Est'd '96-'98 to '02-'04
Sales	12.5%	16.5%	5.5%
"Cash Flow"	16.5%	17.5%	3.5%
Earnings	15.0%	14.0%	3.0%
Dividends	--	--	Nil
Book Value	16.5%	14.5%	-.5%

Cal-endar	QUARTERLY SALES ($ mill) A				Full Year
	Mar.Per	Jun.Per	Sep.Per	Dec.Per	
1996	652.4	745.7	740.0	794.5	2932.6
1997	763.5	875.0	909.9	1009.9	3558.3
1998	944.2	947.8	977.2	998.4	3867.6
1999	1009.5	1092.0	1175	1198.5	4475
2000	1070	1100	1230	1250	4650

Cal-endar	EARNINGS PER SHARE A B				Full Year
	Mar.Per	Jun.Per	Sep.Per	Dec.Per	
1996	.28	.29	.32	.33	1.22
1997	.31	.34	.36	.40	1.41
1998	.23	.28	.27	.22	E1.01
1999	.18	.23	.25	.29	.95
2000	.20	.24	.29	.32	1.05

Cal-endar	QUARTERLY DIVIDENDS PAID				Full Year
	Mar.31	Jun.30	Sep.30	Dec.31	
1995					
1996	NO CASH DIVIDENDS				
1997	BEING PAID				
1998					
1999					

(A) Fiscal year ends on the Sat. nearest December 31st. (B) Primary through 1990, diluted thereafter. Next egs report due mid-February.

Excl. extraordinary item: '98, 24¢. Excl. non-recurring item: '98, d17¢.
(C) Includes intangibles. At 12/31/98: $1,915.6

million, $11.47/share. (D) In mill, adj. for stock splits. (E) 1998 earnings do not add due to changes in the diluted share base.

BUSINESS: Thermo Electron has abt. 20 public subsids, divided into seven segments: owns 85% of Thermo Instrument (analytic and env. instrs. and svcs.); 74% of Thermedics (biomed. mater., detection equip.); 86% of Thermo TerraTech (incineration, heat-treating equip.); 79% of Thermo Power (nat. gas engines, cooling sys.); 60% of Thermo Cardiosystems (heart assist dvcs.); 91% of Thermo Fibertek (paper recyc. equip.); 94% of Thermo Ecotek (indep. power plants). '98 R&D: 9.5% of sls. Depr. rate: 12.6% Has 23,600 empl. Putnam Invest. owns 5.4% of common; FMR Corp., 8.9%; Off. & dir., 5.3% (4/99 Proxy). Chairman & C.E.O.: Richard F. Syron. Inc.: DE. Addr.: 81 Wyman St., PO Box 9046, Waltham, MA 02254. Tel.: 781 622-1000. Internet: www.thermo.com.

Thermo Electron shares continue to fall. For years, this stock was considered an attractive vehicle for long-term growth. Shareholders have had high expectations, awarding TMO shares with an earnings multiple far exceeding the market multiple. Much like a venture-capital firm, Electron is an incubator of new business, typically in the instrumentation and environmental services industries. The company would support fledgling operations with the necessary startup capital until they were deemed ready to become independent entities. At that point, Electron would tap the equity market by spinning off these operations into publicly traded subsidiaries, often keeping a majority stake. Notably, these stock issuances resulted in gains that inflated the company's earnings. Meanwhile, TMO has been an aggressive acquirer of businesses, looking to inexpensive operations with strong, complementary technologies. For much of the past ten years, the company executed these two growth strategies with success. However, as the Thermo Electron Family grew in size, it became increasingly difficult to manage these forms of "artificial" top- and bottom-line growth. Soon enough, growth expectations far exceeded the company's potential. In 1998, when acquisition and spinoff opportunities failed to come about, TMO's growth prospects were called to question. And worse, it became clear the company had succumbed to the pressure of performing spinoffs as a way to enhance earnings, as evidenced by operating redundancies and underperforming units. **Investors should remain on the sidelines until Thermo Electron shares attain a favorable Timeliness rank.** Several upcoming developments are of interest. The company is currently reorganizing its corporate structure in the hopes of generating greater efficiencies. If management successfully improves margins, we should see a reversal in TMO's downward earnings trend. Recovering markets in Asia also may provide some upside to our estimates over the next several quarters. Finally, we look for Hewlett Packard's pending spinoff of its instruments business, Agilent Technologies, to provide investors with a good comparison for valuation.
John Martin
November 5, 1999

Company's Financial Strength	B++
Stock's Price Stability	40
Price Growth Persistence	75
Earnings Predictability	65

To subscribe call 1-800-833-0046.

EXHIBIT 4.3   Thermo Electron stock price compared to S&P and NASDAQ.

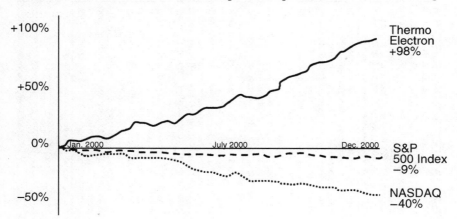

stock, we owned six percent of the company, totaling nearly 11 million shares—enough to get a CEO's attention.

After courting management for nearly one year, the new CEO launched an aggressive reorganization plan that surprised many of us. From Thermo Electron's 8-K filed with the SEC, what I read is illustrated in Appendix D.

In the final analysis, there were several externally and internally generated catalysts in place to close the valuation gap at the company. These catalysts included:

• A new and focused management team

• The presence of shareholder activists

• Industry growth in drug research

• New corporate and operation strategies to improve margins

• A proposed plan to complete two tax-free spin-off companies

• $1 billion worth of proceeds from asset sales and business divestitures

Needless to say, shareholders were pleased.

THE "MARGIN OF SAFETY" PRINCIPLE

> "Benjamin Graham has influenced many investors through his writings and teaching. The concept of "margin of safety" is perhaps his greatest and most enduring contribution to the investing profession"[1]
>
> *Joel Greenblatt*

WHAT IS MARGIN OF SAFETY?

In his book *The Intelligent Investor,* Benjamin Graham describes the concept of "margin of safety" as being an essential part of any true investment. He goes on to say that margin of safety is an element of investing that can be demonstrated quantitatively with sound rationale and from a historical perspective.[2]

His definition of margin of safety is essentially the gap between price and value. All else being equal, the wider the gap between the two, the greater the safety level. Graham also explains that the margin of safety is important because it can absorb mistakes in assessing the business or the fair value of the enterprise.

---

[1]Greenblatt, J. *You Can Be a Stock Market Genius* (New York: Simon & Schuster, 1997, p. 42).

[2]Graham, B. *The Intelligent Investor,* Fourth Edition (New York: Harper & Row, 1973, p. 283).

"The buyer of bargain issues places particular emphasis on the ability of the investment to withstand adverse developments. For in most such cases he has no real enthusiasm about the company's prospects…If these are bought on a bargain basis, even a moderate decline in the earning power need not prevent the investment from showing satisfactory results. The margin of safety will then have served its proper purpose."[3]

From its origin, the calculation of margin of safety was never related to the volatility of the stock price of a company. The focus of most value investors has always been based on the intrinsic worth of the company in question.

In the Five Keys of Value framework, the margin of safety key can be applied to several types of investment opportunities. The concept, however, works best with undervalued companies. The reasoning is simple—the margin of safety is always based on the price of the shares and their value. The price you pay helps to determine the safety of your investment, but not price alone. It is the difference between the price paid and the value of the enterprise that defines margin of safety. The best price relative to value is found in undervalued companies.

Even with a margin of safety, an investment can still go bad. This is not a failure of the concept of the margin of safety principle, as the concept only provides assurance that the odds are in the investors' favor that they will not lose money. However, it is not a guarantee that the investors will not lose money.

There are and have been many adjustments to Benjamin Graham's margin of safety concept in the modern era. The way that Benjamin Graham calculated margin of safety years back is different than how some calculate it today. It is the inclusion of the concept that is important in one's assessment of an opportunity, rather than the actual mechanics and particulars of the safety calculation. Some value investors use a variety of measures in determining a firm's safety levels. They are as keen on asset values as is on earnings and cash flow. They also use a variety of measures just in case one of them does not hold up—the objective is never to be caught off guard. Based on this criterion, these value investors look for several other different measures, such as break-up value, favorable dividend yield, and price-to-cash flow, as supporting casts to Graham's margin of safety concept. For example, if earnings fall short, one of the other

---

[3]Graham, B. *The Intelligent Investor,* Fourth Edition (New York: Harper & Row, 1973, p. 281).

measures is expected to limit the adverse impact to the firm's share price such as the firm's book value.

Buying companies with a margin of safety prevents owning companies with a high burden of proof to justify their stock valuations. When a stock trades at a high valuation level, the expectations are so great and often so specific that a slight disappointment or an adverse change in expectations could be catastrophic. Buying shares with ample safety means buying stocks with the lowest possible burden.

Value investors also believe that margin of safety should incorporate an investor's appetite for risk. The disparity of safety levels among investors is based on the amount of volatility they are willing to tolerate, the mistakes they are willing to accept, and perhaps the financial pain they are willing to endure.

Some of the adjustments to the margin of safety definition include more intangible values of an enterprise. The Five Keys of Value approaches the margin of safety discipline a bit differently. The Five Keys criterion looks at margin of safety as a *support* mechanism for a company's stock.

It essentially asks the question, "What is supporting the stock price at its current level?" or, "Why shouldn't the stock fall significantly from today's current price?" FKV's margin of safety is heavily conscious of what can go wrong, and not what the discount it is to fair value—the safety is thus purely based on the value of the assets.

QUANTITATIVE AND QUALITATIVE REASONING

The value investor often employs a combination of both qualitative and quantitative factors to arrive at a safety level for a particular stock. Quantitative factors can range from the analysis of liquidation values and the value of investment holdings. Qualitative factors might entail taking a look at the company's market position, brand strength, or reputation, etc.

QUANTITATIVE REASONING
According to books he has written, when Graham invested, his primary focus seemed to have been placed on asset values and margin of safety. By focusing on these two elements, he sought to prevent excessive losses by buying companies at "net-net values"—a price equal to the firm's current assets less all liabilities, giving very little value to property, plant, and equipment. Graham seemed to have cared very little about the companies and businesses themselves. His focus was almost purely quantitative.

At the core of analyzing a firm quantitatively is the assessment of the cash-generating possibilities of its assets. The analysis, as discussed in Chapter 2, deals with the specifics of the business and the dynamics of the industry in which the company operates.

Liquidation value. Based on their understanding of the industry, investors typically make certain decisions about the margin of safety valuation tool they will apply. If the company in question operates in a declining industry, the investor might use a liquidation value of the assets, given the fact that such assets would often prove to be of little or no use to others, especially if they are specific to a particular business.

The liquidation value of a company is different from the value of a self-sustaining, ongoing resource conversion company. A resource converter in a growing, profitable industry would command a higher valuation than its liquidation value because it has been effective in converting the company's resources into shareholder value. In a declining industry, however, the opposite is often true—the liquidation value is greater because the actual selling of assets is a better converter of the resources of the company than would be its operations. In calculating liquidation value, some value investors prefer a different approach, first calculating the asset value then subtracting the liabilities.

In calculating this number, some value investors take the value of cash and marketable securities. Marketable securities, assuming that they are short term, are valued at the face value at the time, which is essentially how the stock market values them—or they are valued at what is reported on the latest SEC documents. Then they would give a discount to other assets like plant, property and equipment, and inventory. Depending on the industry and the usefulness of the asset, discounts can range from 20 percent on generic goods, which can be used in other industries, to 80 percent for highly specific goods that are useful to a particular industry. Such a high discount is essentially scrap value for such assets. Items such as goodwill and other intangibles are excluded in the valuation process.

Replacement value. If the company in question is in a normal and stable industry, the value investor might choose to value the assets at replacement cost. The rationale is that if a competitor wanted to enter the industry, the suitor would either buy its way in or build its operations from the bottom up. Acquiring a company would require a certain premium over asset value. Building operations from scratch would require purchasing assets at more favorable price points. Therefore, it would make sense to use replacement cost valuation as a margin of safety metric for promising companies in stable industries.

Generally, the replacement cost assessment is very similar to liquidation; however, the former has more asset-specific adjustments. Like the liquidation method, cash and marketable securities are taken at book value. While it would be more accurate to use the actual market value of the securities owned by the company, this information is rarely available to outside shareholders. A concern that one might have by simply using the stated value of marketable investments made in a high-flying bull market would be whether or not the company should have written off a portion of past investments that failed, were failing, or were likely to fail—investments that were purchased during the Internet euphoria, for example.

After cash and these marketable securities, the value investor looks at a company's receivables. The receivables on the balance sheet are the first area requiring an adjustment, as they include provisions should customers become delinquent. If a company entering the industry wanted to build a similar level of receivables, that company would most likely have to incur higher debts in order to reach similar levels to a firm already operating in that market. As such, the replacement value for receivables should be adjusted to reflect this expected increase in delinquent customers.[4]

Value investors tend to look closely at the cost of inventory, because determining its replacement value depends more on specific issues related to a company. For example, if inventories are recorded at $80 million, but the company has had idle finished goods on hand for an excessive number of days, it would be fair to assume that a company that wishes to enter the business by purchasing said company, would not have to load up on so much inventory. Accordingly, the value investor would reduce the cost of inventory. There would be an increase in replacement costs in situations where the inventory on a company's books had the benefit of lower raw material costs. A new business owner would not be able to take advantage of such low costs.

For example, if a company makes plastic toys and has plenty of raw materials that were purchased when plastic prices were excessively low, a new business entrant may not have the same advantage if entering at a different time. The inventory "costs" would be higher than those reported on the balance sheet. Therefore, the value investor would increase the cost to replicate those inventories.

[4]Greenwald, B., Kahn, J., Sonkin, P., Biema, M. *Value Investing: From Graham to Buffett and Beyond* (New York: John Wiley & Sons, 2001, p. 56).

Other items under current assets, like prepaid expenses and deferred taxes, remain relatively at face value. Prepaid expenses are expenses paid in advance by a company, like a year's rent. A deferred tax number is a refund from the government; it has real value, and therefore does not require an adjustment. Fixed and noncurrent assets are a different matter, and are worthy of close attention. Unlike current assets, the adjustments in these areas can have a very significant impact on the asset value of the firm.

Property, plant, and equipment (PP&E) are often the largest noncurrent assets on the balance sheet. The value investor assesses each part of the PP&E to arrive at the best replacement value. The "property" part of the PP&E is often stated below replacement value given the fact that property, such as land and real estate, typically appreciates in value over time.

Depending on the actual "plant," this can either be assessed above or below its replacement cost. The disparities in cost can be very large for a couple of reasons. First, the depreciation schedule of the book value and its replacement cost may not resemble the economic value of the asset. For example, land can depreciate over several decades, while the value of the asset may have appreciated significantly over the same time period. Inflation can also have an adverse effect on the true value of the asset. The depreciation that is charged on the asset is based on a historical cost, which has no relevance to the value of what it is worth today. Therefore, income may be overstated due to using the lower, historical cost associated with the asset rather than the higher current market cost of such asset.[5]

The "E" is for "equipment" in PP&E, and is depreciated over its useful life. This figure often requires few adjustments. Equipment can include items such as machinery, tools, computers, etc. It is very difficult to determine what is exactly included in the equipment, given that it is lumped together with PP&E. Unless investors have an edge in the particular industry in which the business operates, i.e., they know about the industry with enough detail to understand what may be included in "equipment," most investors usually use the most conservative assessment of such items.

Moving on to goodwill, one can justify valuing it at zero, since it represents the markup for overpaid assets. The problem with tacking a zero value to goodwill is that it fails to give the complete picture of the financial environment. The fact that only tangible assets are calculated understates the value of an enterprise. [6]

[5]Greenwald, B., Kahn, J., Sonkin, P., Biema, M. *Value Investing: From Graham to Buffett and Beyond* (New York: John Wiley & Sons, 2001, p. 58).

[6]Copeland, Koller, Murrin, *Valuation: Measuring and Managing the Value of Companies* (New York: John Wiley & Sons, 1991, p. 215).

There are good reasons and not so good reasons to consider the value of goodwill in one's margin of safety analysis. Some value investors recognize that goodwill is a cost to new industry entrants for a company's intangible assets, such as its brand, firm culture, customer loyalty, reputation, etc. For example, Warren Buffett considers the value of intangibles, such as broadcast licenses and the particular brand of a soft drink, as a significant part of his analytical reasoning. Other investors, on the other hand, believe that such intangibles have very little or no margin of safety, and prefer to focus their analysis on tangible assets. [7]

It clearly takes some level of industry expertise on the part of the value analyst to adjust the goodwill appropriately. As a back-of-the-envelope way for assessing goodwill, some value investors often use a portion of goodwill, which can range from 10 percent to 60 percent of the value reported on the balance sheet. This is then adjusted again for the degree to which this intangible asset contributes to the value of the firm. A company with strong brand value, allowing it to sustain a strong market position with increasingly loyal customers, could garner a higher value for its goodwill than a firm that has lesser characteristics.

In general, the valuation of intangible assets of a firm is based on revenues. For example, if a brand name product garners a premium over a general brand, it is more valuable. During a sale, customers are more likely to pay a higher price for the branded product. Similarly, valuing licenses, copyrights, and trademarks is based on the corresponding revenues produced. In addition, these intangible assets can also be valued by using comparable valuation multiples for similar assets that have been sold in the past.

For example, valuing a media company with one star product—this could be a particular movie or program channel—would have to be done on a two-step basis. The first step would be to value the business without the star product. Next, value the portion of the star product's contribution. Obviously, this is not an exact science; common sense is paramount.

The debt portion of a firm plays a decisive role in the strength of its margin of safety. Having too much debt is often a red flag; any slight miscalculation of the asset value can be catastrophic to the value of the equity. We have seen it time and time again. As a rule of thumb, some value investors take a critical look at a company's debt, particularly if the financial strength is rated a B or less by *Value Line*. You should always do your own independent assessment of a company's debt, but *Value Line* is a good place to start.

---

[7]Klarman, S. A. *Margin of Safety* (New York: Harper Business, 1991, p. 93).

It is critical to assess the past obligations, long-term debt, and ongoing obligations of the firm in question. Ongoing obligations include those liabilities that are needed under normal business conditions. Some examples are items such as accounts payable, wage costs, accrued expenses, credit terms with suppliers with no interest, etc. These obligations are often listed under current liabilities and are due within one year. Generally speaking, the larger the liability—without being too excessive—the smaller the investment the company needs to make to finance its assets.

Value investors deduct these liabilities from the replacement asset value to get the replacement value of net assets. The objective is to assess the replacement value of a firm that is meaningful to shareholders. Using the replacement value of net assets, the value investor deducts from this number the next two categories of liabilities: any past obligations, and long-term debt. Past obligations include such items as old tax bills. Long-term debt is the formal debt that the company carries on its balance sheet. Subtracting it gets to the net asset value for equity holders.

Interpreting the replacement value.   Comparing asset value and the value of the company, as an ongoing resource converter, can give helpful insights into the company. Many value investors believe that if the asset value is greater than what the company is worth, then it can be assumed that it is a direct result of poor management or a bad industry. In this case, operating the company actually produces subpar returns, depleting the company's scarce resources.

If the asset value is approximately equal to the current valuation of the worth of the company, it signals to value investors that management is mediocre at best, and that there are no competitive advantages over the company's competitors.

Finally, if the asset value is less than the intrinsic worth of the company, the magnitude of the difference sends an important message to investors. In this situation, value investors determine that there is considerable strength in the firm's competitive advantage, or there exists a superior management team. Value investors believe that if they can purchase shares of a company below its asset value, they have a very good chance of making money in stock, or the company will be taken over by another company—i.e., an outside catalyst will emerge.

Book value assessment.   Some investors rely on the book value of a company to gain insight into what a company would be worth if it were liquidated. Needless to say, one would have to make the proper adjustments to use book value correctly in such instances. These adjustments often include changes in goodwill and inflation. For example, if a company has an asset on its balance sheet such as real estate, which has appreciated over the years, its book value would need to be adjusted accordingly in a liquidation analysis.

QUALITATIVE REASONING

One calculation of the value of a company is based on the discounted cash flows generated from its assets. Unfortunately, in actual analysis, some assets are not easily valued because they do not generate cash flow. Some tangible assets in this category may include certain real estate assets, patents, and other rights and licenses. The intangible assets might include reputation, brand name, etc.

Qualitative reasoning is essentially determining the value of these assets. Value investors tend not to rely too heavily on intangible assets because of the limited amount of intrinsic value that supports their price. The best way to value these assets is to use relative measures, despite the fact that it is extremely difficult to find a decent comparable asset.

"Take-private" valuation—a valuation based on what an investor reasonably thinks a company could be worth in a privately negotiated transaction—is the valuation used for making a case for a firm's safety levels. The rationale is that if a well-managed and sound publicly traded company trades at a price level that is attractive enough to another entity to raise capital to acquire the company, then that level is what investors can rely on as being the "floor" for the stock. Assuming that capitalism is alive and well, share prices of companies with excellent free cash flow do not fall to zero.

For example, if a company is trading in the public market at eight times firm value to free cash flow, when the private market is buying similar companies at five times firm value to free cash flow, then it is reasonable to assume that the price of the public company would hover above five times firm value. It is because of this public and private market valuation relationship that many value-orientated investors carefully monitor the actions of the private deal market to help establish a "floor" for certain publicly traded companies.

Getting something for free.   A "sum-of-the-parts" valuation can be useful in determining the safety level in a stock price. Value investors often separate companies by division, not because the particular company is breaking up, but rather to determine whether the current price is offering one or more of the pieces of the business for "free." In this scenario, one might take a company like General Electric and look at it on a sum-of-the-parts basis to determine whether the current price fully reflects the value of GE's various businesses. GE's share price would present attractive safety levels if its various parts were being valued conservatively and the prized NBC unit, for example, was being valued at nothing by the public markets. While one has to use some quantitative techniques to get to the numbers, it is one's qualitative abilities to properly assess the overall market environment, and the appropriate valuation tools and multiples needed to value each division, that will determine investment success.

Dividend yield factor.   Dividends can be a source of safety because of the yield generated for investors. As such, the value investor often compares this dividend with other possible investments with similar risk profiles. For example, if XYZ Company trades at $40 per share and has a $1.16 annual dividend, its yield would be 3 percent. With a stock price decline to $25 per share, a 5-percent yield would be generated. Assuming no deterioration in the company's cash flow, a 5-percent yield would be too generous in a normal market environment. Investors, particularly those who are income conscious, would adjust the yield accordingly by purchasing the company's shares. Dividend yields, while easily obtained, are seldom ever used as a sole factor in determining margin of safety levels of a given stock.

Historical perspective.   Historical interpretations of how a particular company has faired in the market can also be helpful in assessing the current value of a firm. This is not chart reading to guess the future direction of the stock. It is merely a historical account of what investors were willing to pay for the franchise in different economic markets. Taking this historical perspective of companies could prove beneficial to owners who are assessing what the buyers would be willing to pay for the enterprise. However, these types of exercises should be limited to those companies that are of a more cyclical nature in their business models.

RISK AND UNCERTAINTY

Understanding risk and uncertainty is an important part of assessing a company's margin of safety levels. It is important that investors know the difference between the two, how the difference can change or alter the way an opportunity is assessed, and the tools required to quantify properly the downside potential of any investment.

The difference between the two is that risk is quantifiable and uncertainty is not. There are many different categories of risks and uncertainties. In simple terms, taking on risk occurs when an investor is not sure what might happen among a list of scenarios. Taking on uncertainty occurs when an investor does not know what can happen with an unknown range of possible outcomes.

HOW TO APPROACH RISK

For the value investor, there are only two kinds of risk: general market risk, and basic business risk. The total risk relationship is as follows:

Total Investment Risk = Basic Business Risk + General Market Risk

Basic business risk is based on adverse events that can have a negative impact on a particular company and its share price. The margin of safety principle is heavily focused on reducing this type of specific risk. While the number of items that can cause basis business risk are many, they are all, however, quantifiable. They can be measured. These risks include an unsuccessful cost-cutting program by management, a failed new product, loss of market share, a failed deal transaction, etc.

General market risk is not specific to any company. It is based on more macro factors such as the economy, inflation, interest rates, etc. Investors cannot protect themselves entirely from this type of risk. It is part of being an investor in the public markets, and as a result, many value investors do not put too much effort into eliminating this type of risk. As is discussed in Chapter 8, diversification should be done cautiously if one is trying to reduce investment risk. In fact, the more one diversifies, the more one's portfolio will look like the broader market. However, the greater the resemblance the portfolio has to the general market, the greater the market risks.

While it is prudent to take some action towards limiting general market risk, it is a very normal aspect of investing and should not be the primary focus of one's strategy to reduce overall risk. Value investors, in general, refuse to spend time predicting economic trends or interpreting market sentiment. Time spent trying to predict the future is time not well spent. Focus on the basic business risk.

It is important to take advantage of general market risk. However, avoid trying to predict it. During the Asian and Latin American turmoil in 1998 when most investors were fearful of these events, I found significant value in companies that I typically would not own under normal circumstances. Prior to this upheaval, the market consistently overvalued many of these businesses. In late 1998, however, I found significant value being overlooked at FDX Corporation—the world's leader in overnight delivery. FedEx had a great business in a very favorable industry, driven by, among other things, low oil input costs at that time, and the increased need for its services. Below $22 per share, my assessment revealed that FedEx was trading at private-market valuations. Accordingly, I saw a tremendous opportunity to make a satisfactory return in FDX Corp due to the company's temporarily "depressed" valuations.

Further analysis indicated that at current price levels, I would not only be purchasing the U.S. operations at private-market valuation, but I would also be getting the international operations virtually for free. I also suspected that FDX Corp was sure to benefit from e-commerce in the long run. My exit valuation assessment indicated that the company had a fair value, excluding all growth expectations, of approximately $45 per share. Still, the company could trade for as much as $60 per share, given its growth opportunities. FDX Corp generated dependable cash flows and had a strong balance sheet. FedEx's share price traded for two months under my desired share price. Four months later, the market quickly realized the company's undervaluation and traded its stock well above $45 per share.

With a strong margin of safety due to the company's brand equity, cash generation, market share, balance sheet condition, etc., buying FDX Corp at private-equity valuations had minimal basic business risk—most of the risk that I identified was based on the general market. I did not try to predict when the general market risk would subside; I just knew it would at some point in time. It came sooner than I thought. Selling shares of the company at $42 per share implied a +68-percent gain when the market resumed its overvaluation of FDX's stock.

IDENTIFYING AND AVOIDING UNCERTAINTY
There are two types of uncertainty: situations with possible outcomes that are believed to be unknown by the general market, and situations with possible outcomes that are unknown to the investor.

General market uncertainty relates to rare occurrences in the broad market where there is real uncertainty about a particular event and its short-term implications. The events of September 11th are one example. More commonly, this type of uncertainty can also be company or industry specific. For example, in 1998 many of the hospital and nursing home companies, such as Columbia HCA, Quorum Healthcare, Beverly Enterprise, and Vencor, were being devalued in the marketplace in large part due to the uncertainty of new pay structures developed by lawmakers in Washington, D.C. During this time, some went bankrupt, others restructured themselves, and still others decided that their stock prices were so depressed that going private—when the management team goes out and borrows money to purchase all of the company's shares back from shareholders—was the best way to save the company. There are always uncertain events in the marketplace. In 2002, uncertainties with the accounting of many well-respected companies have caused their values to get decimated, practically overnight. The uncertainty resulted from whether or not a company's accounting could be trusted, specifically as it related to off-balance-sheet debt. Off-balance-sheet debt was a rather fashionable financing technique in the years prior.

An outcome that may be known by members of the general investment community, but not to the particular investor, also resembles uncertainty, because it essentially asks the investor the question: Are you the best owner for this company? Many investors find themselves in this situation. Often, people provide investors with what seems to be a great investment idea. The only problem is that the investors do not understand the business. This is not risk. It is uncertainty. Even if they were to purchase the share, they would be ill equipped to monitor their investment, because they would not know *what* to monitor.

The problem is that unlike risk, uncertainty cannot be measured. Remember that value investors buy businesses, not stocks. Who would buy a business that they did not understand? How would you value it? How do you know if you are paying a reasonable price for it? Therefore, whether the uncertainty stems from the general market or one's personal lack of understanding of a particular business, the value investor shuns investing in companies with uncertainty.

MAYTAG CORPORATION: FINDING A SAFETY LEVEL

In September of 1999, Maytag's share price had a spectacular fall. The stock price went from $65 per share to $30—down 54 percent in a matter of weeks. Not surprisingly, I began to search for value in the carnage. I was not an owner of the stock, but opportunity was calling my name. I took a look at the company's most recent *Value Line* and Form 10-K.

THE VALUE PROPOSITION

I liked what I read from my initial observation of the company—specifically, the company's strategy to create shareholder value. Maytag's return on equity was 31 percent in 1997, 51 percent in 1998, and 70 percent in 1999. Based on my knowledge of highly profitable industries, and given the fact that we were in a strong economic expansion period, this trend in Maytag's profitability

Excerpt from Maytag's 1998 Form 10-K

Net Sales: The Company's consolidated net sales for 1998 increased 19 percent compared to 1997. Net sales in 1998 included sales of G.S. Blodgett Corporation ("Blodgett"), a manufacturer of commercial cooking equipment, which was acquired by the Company on October 1, 1997. Excluding Blodgett, the Company's net sales increased 16 percent in 1998 compared to 1997.

Home appliances net sales increased 15 percent in 1998 compared to 1997. Net sales were up from the prior year due to the introduction of new products, including new lines of Maytag Neptune laundry products, Maytag refrigerators, Maytag cooking products, Hoover upright vacuum cleaners, and Hoover upright deep carpet cleaners. In addition, net sales were up from the prior year due to the volume associated with shipments to Sears, Roebuck and Co. in connection with the Company's agreement to begin selling the full line of Maytag brand major appliances through Sears stores in the United States beginning in February 1998. The Company's net sales also benefited from the significant volume growth in industry shipments of major appliances in 1998 compared to 1997.

Net sales of commercial appliances were up 84 percent from 1997. This net sales increase was primarily driven by a significant increase in the sales volume of Dixie-Narco enhanced capacity venders introduced in 1997 and the inclusion of Blodgett's results for a full year. Excluding Blodgett, net sales increased 48 percent from 1997.

International appliances net sales increased 5 percent in 1998 compared to 1997. The sales increase was primarily attributable to higher unit volume partially offset by price reductions on selected models in response to competitive conditions in China.

Gross Profit: The Company's consolidated gross profit as a percent of sales increased to 29 percent in 1998 from 27.5 percent in 1997.

Home appliances gross margins increased in 1998 compared to 1997, due to the increase in sales volume, favorable brand and product sales mix, lower raw material costs, and the absence of production start-up costs associated with the Company's new line of refrigerators which were incurred in 1997.

Commercial appliances gross margins increased in 1998 compared to 1997, due to the increase in sales volume, partially offset by inefficiencies from the reorganization of manufacturing operations at Blodgett.

International appliances gross margins decreased in 1998 compared to 1997 primarily from the decrease in selling prices on selected models.

The Company realized slightly lower raw material prices in 1998 compared to 1997 and expects raw material prices in 1999 to be approximately the same to slightly lower than 1998 levels.[8]

Net Income: Net income for 1998 was $281 million, or $2.99 diluted earnings per share, compared to net income of $180 million, or $1.84 diluted earnings per share in 1997. Net income and diluted earnings per share were impacted by special charges for the early retirement of debt in both years. The after-tax charges for the early retirement of debt were $5.9 million and $3.2 million for 1998 and 1997, respectively.[9]

was sure not to last. I knew that we were in the back nine with this run. I just did not know if we were in the eleventh hole or the seventeenth. Given the steep decline in the company's stock price, I determined that the company warranted a quick look. I downloaded the company's most recent annual report, Form 10-Q, and other SEC documents to understand the economics of the business, and began to look closely at the numbers.

After decomposing Maytag's ROE, there were three key strategies that were noteworthy and sparked my interest to pursue the idea further. The first item that piqued my interest was the company's manufacturing capabilities. Maytag employed manufacturing techniques, which allowed it to increase output with little increase in capital expenditures. The goal of this strategy was to get as much out of existing facilities without increasing capacity by needing to build more manufacturing plants. This strategy also eliminated waste and increased the quality of Maytag's products and its margins, by using the least amount of time and resources to manufacture each product.

Maytag also had a knack for keeping its pipeline full with innovative products, which would allow the company to maintain its market share,

---

[8]Maytag Corp., December 31, 1998, Form 10-K, p. 10.
[9]Maytag Corp., December 31, 1998, Form 10-K, p. 11.

particularly in the high-end market. It was clear that this company had a differentiation strategy—offering high-quality products for a premium price. While the company did have about 20 percent of its products in the low-end price range, its entire organization was geared towards innovation and producing the most differentiated products customers would be willing to buy. Lastly, the company made the most use of leveraging its brand value. It used its brand to gain access to channels and to expand its retail reach. This level of brand awareness is often a competitive advantage among industry participants.

The assessment of Maytag's strategies was confirmed after reading through the Form 10-K, *Value Line,* and searching through the company's Web site. The price I was willing to pay was $29 per share or lower. When I began working on the idea in 1999, the stock was trading well above my preferred purchase price. It was not until March of 2000 that I had the opportunity to own Maytag at what I thought was a reasonable price.

At that time I reassessed my rationale of buying the company. Once again I concluded that I liked the company's strategy; below $29, the company was trading at less than 8.5 times price-to-earnings on my estimate of $3.50 for the following year. I was comfortable paying a P/E of 8.5 times for Maytag. This number was much more conservative than the $3.80 to $4.00 range that Maytag's management team was expecting to earn. On a normalized earnings basis, or what I thought the company could earn in a normal economic environment, the P/E ratio was very attractive for a cyclical company. It was also cheap on an enterprise value and discounted cash flow basis.

Next, I assessed what the franchise was worth, using techniques discussed in Chapter 3. I triangulated a valuation and used a take-out, historical valuation assessment, and a discounted cash flow analysis with normalized growth rates. In the final analysis, I arrived at a value of $50 per share for Maytag at that time.

With a $29 buy price and a $50 value for the enterprise, I tried to identify the catalysts that would spur stock price appreciation. I came across several potential catalysts. The three most important included the realignment effort that the company was undergoing. The company had targeted about $100 million in savings from a cost-reduction program scheduled for the next 24 months. These cost savings would be derived from manufacturing improvements, cutbacks in general and administrative expenses, and business division consolidations. The other areas of savings would come from changes in working capital and stock repurchases. Another catalyst was the possibility of the economy's stabilizing or turning positive again. Finally, I

considered the possibility of an outright sale of Maytag as the likely catalytic event to take place if the share price continued to lag the overall market, based on the cash flow and balance sheet strength of the enterprise.

FINDING SAFETY

My next step was to assess my downside in the stock price, or my margin
of safety. To determine a safety level, I relied on an assessment of what I
thought it would cost to replace the entire company. The risk that I was trying to assess was where the stock would be if the economy did not turn
around. I was certain that at some point in the future it would; I did not
know when and what would support the stock price if the economy continued to languish—or got worse.

I reviewed the footnotes of the Form 10-K, filed with the SEC, to gauge
the economic values of the assets of the firm as if it were to be sold at
"bare-bones" valuations. Professional value investors run a very detailed
model when it comes to assessing a company's margin of safety. The following, however, is a back-of-the-envelope way of arriving at similar
results. All figures are based on numbers that are drawn from the company's 10-K and annual report.

Cash is cash, and cash equivalents are very liquid investments; therefore, they should be valued at full worth. Valuing accounts receivable is not
as straightforward. Receivables are trade debt—what is owed to the firm.
Before revenues are considered cash, they must be collected from accounts
receivable. The vast majority of companies monitor very closely the average time it takes to collect on these receivables. There are even professional
services that focus on retrieving cash from questionable accounts. Depending on the industry, I would typically use 60 percent to 90 percent of the
reported accounts receivable. Given Maytag's end markets and the predic-
tion that the country was most likely heading towards an economic decline,
I used a percentage near the lower end of the range.

Maytag reported inventory costs with the last-in, first-out (LIFO)
method for approximately 77 percent of its inventories. Costs for other
inventories have been determined principally by the first-in, first-out
(FIFO) method. Maytag has commoditylike inventories, i.e., steel, plas-
tics, etc., and therefore, I used a relatively high asset value of the
reported inventory.

Deferred income taxes reflect the expected future tax consequences of
temporary differences between the book carrying amounts and the tax basis
of assets and liabilities. This deferred tax benefit may be worth something to
a would-be acquirer of the company, but would most likely be worth nothing

otherwise. As for other assets, I used what I believed to be a fair percentage of reported value. For example, a prepaid pension and intangible pension assets are valued at zero. While they have some value, for this exercise I deemed it not significant to the going concern value of the enterprise.

Maytag states property, plant, and equipment on a cost basis. These assets are depreciated using a straight-line method to amortize the cost of the assets over their estimated economic useful lives. The company esti-mates the useful lives of these assets to be 15 to 45 years for buildings and improvements, and 5 to 20 years for machinery and equipment. Given the nature of the business, it was fair to assume that such assets would fetch a value close to reported book value.

In addition to obtaining a reasonable value for the assets of the firm, I also included the value of the seemingly secure dividend stream. With a cost of equity capital at around 8.5 percent, one can use the formula of div-idends/equity cost of capital to calculate the value of the dividend stream to equity holders. Maytag's dividend payout was expected to be $68 million that year. Thus, the value of the company's dividend stream to equity hold-

Exhibit 5.1   Simple Asset Value Calculation.

(000s)	Dec. 1999				Value
Cash and equivalents	$ 28,815	x	100%	= $	28,815
Accounts receivables	494,747	x	70%	=	346,323
Inventories	404,120	x	70%	=	282,884
PP&E	976,108	x	90%	=	878,497
Other assets	540,458	x	80%	=	432,366
Total current assets	$2,444,248				$1,968,886
Value of dividend stream					800,000
Less debt					641,278
Implied value					$2,127,608
Shares outstanding					90,000
Implied asset value per share					$24

ers was approximately $800 million. Based on this very simple calculation, I arrived at a safety level for the company of $2.1 billion or $24 per share.

I also looked at a private market assessment and historical valuation range for the company to gain a different perspective as to what my safety level might be. On a historical valuations basis, and given the cyclical nature of the business, I looked at the valuation ranges at which the company was trading during the last through periods. All in all, I was buying a very profitable and focused company at attractive valuations with a 72 percent upside potential and 17 percent downside, based on my fair value and margin of safety assessments. The risk/reward probability was in my favor.

RELYING ON MARGIN OF SAFETY

By the time of Maytag's annual meeting in May, I was an owner of the stock, and several catalysts were brewing in the company. Investing is a dynamic process that requires constant checks, updates, and constant scrutiny of the investment rationale.

After monitoring the company for one year, by October of 2000, I had sold the stock. I had come to realize that the investment no longer possessed potent catalysts. I had given the catalysts several quarters to show signs of progress, but they had not done so. While there had been spikes of optimism during this period, the fundamentals of the business never turned the corner, and the catalysts proved ineffective. Even what seemed to be an eminent sale of the company failed to materialize.

After analyzing the company's third-quarter report filed to the SEC and listening to management's conference call to shareholders, I came away with five reasons to sell our stake in Maytag. The first reason was related to pricing issues. My interpretation of the third-quarter financial press release was that the pricing environment—Maytag's ability to raise or maintain its high prices—was getting worse, and there were no signs that the company would be able to maintain the high prices for its products. This was great for consumers, but bad for the owners of the business. After I reviewed the financial results of two of Maytag's competitors, it was clear that the profit margins of Maytag were threatened. They were clearly getting hit hard on the pricing front. The entire industry was expected to be less profitable in 12 to 18 months. Therefore, I believed that it was unlikely that Maytag would be able to create shareholder value at current levels considering the steady drop in appliance prices.

The second issue related to volume. While the volume number the company reported was better than I had expected, particularly in their

North American division, the key segment of commercial appliances was down by a surprisingly stunning number of 13 percent.

The company also had distribution issues, which surfaced during this time period. One of Maytag's largest distributors decided to get out of the home appliance business, and other appliance distributors were rumored to follow. Additionally, another large distributor had announced a few weeks earlier that they were having problems with their growth plans. These events reduced my comfort level in Maytag's ability to reach the volume expectations and ultimate return on my investment.

The lower tax rate in the third-quarter press release was a surprise to me, as I did not expect the tax rate to fall so dramatically. I considered it to be a red flag and a signal for further disappointments. Finally, the investment community was becoming critical of the company's chairman and CEO.

In sum, the business that I had purchased changed dramatically and had no catalysts. Simultaneously, the industry was undergoing a cyclical and structural change. The cyclical nature stemmed from the weakening economy, while the structural changes were due to the massive repositioning that was taking place among the distributors—new players were entering, while well-established participants were leaving the industry.

The following is a timeline of notable events that took place.

- August 12, 1999: A new CEO is named at Maytag.

- September 19, 1999: The company announces that second-quarter earnings will be flat; Wall Street lowers the company's earnings expectations; Maytag's stock falls 36 percent that day.

- September/October, 1999: With the stock down dramatically, I began to search for value in the company.

- February 14, 2000: Maytag announces, ahead of schedule, that it will not meet the previously expected earnings estimates; Wall Street analysts reduce their earnings expectation for the company; Maytag's shares drop another 27 percent.

- March/April, 2000: Having conducted due diligence for approximately five months, I buy shares based on my margin of safety assessment; at $29 per share, my downside was limited.

- March, 2000: Maytag confirms that it expects to earn $3.80 to $4.00 per share fiscal year 2000.

- May 11, 2000: At Maytag's annual meeting, shareholders win supermajority, which was nonbinding, but lost a proposal to declassify board members by a slim margin.

Exhibit 5.2   Stock Price of Maytag 1999 to 2002.

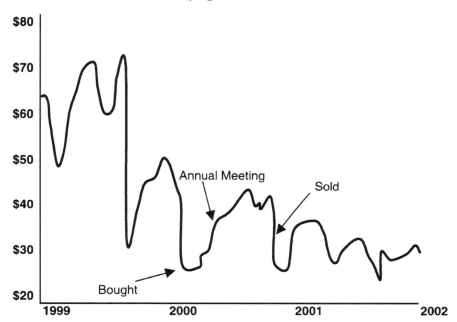

- July 25, 2000: Circuit City, one of the company's major distributors announces that it will exit the appliance business.

- August 16, 2000: Heilig-Meyers, another key distributor, announces plans to close 302 stores and exit the appliance business.

- August 2000: Maytag is still confident that it can meet the $3.80 earnings it had set for itself.

- August 2000: Retail giant Wal-Mart announces that it will enter the appliance business selling GE-branded products.

- August 24, 2000: Maytag's stock trades up to $41 per share on news that Maytag's management was in negotiations to sell the company. We sold a few shares to lock in some profits.

- August 28, 2000: Major competitor Whirlpool announces that it will not meet the earnings that Wall Street was expecting, citing Circuit City's exit from the distribution business as a key problem. Both Whirlpool and Maytag's stock prices drop.

- September 14, 2000: Maytag announces that it too will miss its earnings estimates.

- September/October, 2000: I reassessed my margin of safety level and recommended that we sell our stake in the company in the low $30s and avoid any possible of capital. I relied heavily on my margin of safety assessment to support the share price.

- November 9, 2000: The Chairman and CEO of Maytag resigns.

ASSESSING THE INVESTMENT OPPORTUNITY

"The difficulty never lies in identifying what a good business is today. The true difficulty is finding what will be a good business five or 10 years down the road."[1]

Jean-Marie Eveillard

AGOOD WAY TO EXPLAIN how an individual investor should approach a potential investment is to use an analogy. Warren Buffett often uses the game of baseball to explain how investors should think about new investment opportunities. He says that we should take our time and "wait for the right pitch" before investing. This is sound advice. The analogy used in this and in other parts of the book is the game of golf.

VALUE INVESTING AND THE GAME OF GOLF

Value investing is very similar to the game of golf. Just like the golfer, the value investor must be well schooled in patience and humility. As discussed in

[1]Sincere, M., *101 Investment Lessons from the Wizards of Wall Street* (Franklin Lakes: Career Press, 1999, p. 99).

Chapter 1, emotional discipline is critical to the success of both the investor and the golfer. In identifying an investment opportunity, one has to exercise a level of care in order to allow key understandings to surface.

Deciding on the type of investments to make is synonymous with managing one's course. Course management in golf refers to the way a player walks up to the ball, reflects upon it, and determines whether or not there are factors, such as the wind, the thickness of the grass, or the location of the ball, that can affect the shot. Similarly, in value investing there are several variables that one must consider before addressing the particular investment.

These variables may include the general economic environment, market sentiment, or earnings season. In addition, the value seeker makes a decision as to the type of opportunity that is presented, and then determines the right set of tools to explore the opportunity. Likewise, golfers make decisions as to what type of club to use, only after properly assessing the location of the ball, distance to the pin, and the environment.

Any golfer will tell you that a very important part of having good course management is having a solid game plan—knowing in advance how you plan to play each hole. The value investor has a specific approach for each investment opportunity, whether it is a cyclical company, a break-up opportunity, or a fast grower. Like in golf, investors have all the clubs they need in their bag of tools. Even though each tool or club is not needed to score, what is important is having all the necessary tools and knowing how to use each of them to generate specific results. Golfers can imitate Tiger Woods, and investors may pattern themselves after Warren Buffett. However, they cannot achieve their own level of success on the golf course or through investing, until they actually go out and practice using the tools that are available to them.

IDENTIFYING THE OPPORTUNITY

Investing is a game that uses different tools, employs different styles, and takes advantage of different opportunities. Some investors choose high-growth companies in new industries, while others invest only in industries they know well. Yet some value investors may choose any company so long as it has certain valuation characteristics—a low price to earnings ratio, for example.

Properly identifying the *type* of opportunity that is presented is critical to successful investing because the type of opportunity determines one's approach and the analytical tools to consider. Identifying an opportunity essentially entails answering the question: What circumstances have afforded me this opportunity?

The following are short examples of investment opportunities and how each is approached, and the appropriate tools used to evaluate the situation. This section uses filings from the SEC to provide the best description of each company. While professional investors have many resources at their disposal to gain information quickly about a company or a given situation, individual investors are often limited to the SEC filings online and other information on financial Web sites.

There are seven types of opportunities discussed here. The opportunities are categorized in the following manner: modest/slow growth, high growth, event driven, cyclical, temporarily depressed, hybrids, and value traps. Modest or slow-growth opportunities are those companies whose historical revenue growth is in line with the economy—somewhere in the neighborhood of 1 percent to 9 percent. High-growth companies typically post revenue growth numbers above 10 percent per year.

Event-driven opportunities are potential investments, which include high-quality, undervalued companies undergoing (or likely to undergo) complicated spin-offs, financial restructurings, breakups, and/or reorganizations to realize their true values. Opportunities in this area are plentiful. Event-driven opportunities are very common during bull markets. During this time, companies look at various options to unlock shareholder value. The management is typically more eager given the overall performance of the market. They also are beholding to shareholders who demand more from the management team.

Cyclical companies typically pattern the general economic cycles. Companies in cyclical industries are driven by capacity. The revenues of cyclical companies are very high when at or near the top of the cycle and low at or near through levels. Opportunities in this area are typically uncovered through in-depth studies of industries undergoing fundamental and secular changes, where there will be winners decided over time.

Temporarily depressed opportunities are similar to cyclical companies because both opportunities are based on depressed profits. These are typically undervalued companies that have been depressed for the "wrong" reasons. What separates them from cyclical companies is that they are often misunderstood or overlooked by the general market because of their complex structure or the presence of a temporarily negative catalyst, rather than due to the economy. For example, a company whose profits are temporarily depressed due to a prolonged employee strike or product recall may present good investment opportunities.

There are always companies that are "out of favor." However, potential investment candidates include companies that would make an attractive acquisition target for a financial or strategic buyer. Usually, these are well-positioned companies selling at low private-market, sum-of-the-parts, and/or asset valuations, with strong margin of safety levels.

Hybrid opportunities are those companies that possess a combination of circumstances. A cyclical company breaking itself up at the low level of its cycle can be an example.

Finally, value traps are attractively priced companies that do not possess catalysts or possess ineffective ones. Needless to say, these are not true investment "opportunities" to be gotten; rather, they are to be avoided.

APPLYING THE FIVE KEYS OF VALUE TO FIT THE OPPORTUNITY

MODEST AND SLOW-GROWTH BUSINESS: RH DONNELLEY CORPORATION IN 1998—THE APPROACH AND ANALYSIS

I approached the company using vertical analysis, whereby I examined the company's income statement from the revenues down to the earnings it had generated. I could have examined the business using ROE decomposition, but I wanted to get a better understanding of the dynamics of the industry and how the economics of the business worked. Vertical analysis provided a clear way for me to achieve this.

The yellow pages advertising industry grew about 5 percent per year, even in a downturn in the economy over the prior 10 years. Price increases contributed to about half of that growth. RH Donnelley was the largest independent marketer of yellow pages advertising in the United States. At the time, the company sold over $1 billion of advertising in 1997 and was the leader in all of its major markets. RH Donnelley was also a leading provider of prepress publishing services for yellow pages directories (including a majority of the directories for which it sells advertising). RH Donnelley provided services for over 300 directories when it separated from Dun & Bradstreet. This also included providing advertising sales for over 270 directories in 13 states, which collectively had a total circulation of approximately 30 million in 1997.

The company had a diversified customer base of approximately 500,000 businesses, many of which relied on yellow pages directories as their principal or sole form of advertising. In the prior 3 years, the company achieved an average advertising sales renewal rate ranging from 90 percent to 100 percent in its major markets. One of the more attractive aspects of

RH Donnelley's revenues was the fact that the company was strategically aligned, on a long-term basis, with the established and leading telephone service provider in each of its major markets. The company provided yellow page advertising, marketing, and sales in these markets through long-term contractual agreements with subsidiaries of the incumbent telephone companies, which included Ameritech Corporation, Bell Atlantic Corporation, and Sprint Corporation. RH Donnelley also had a lifetime partnership with a subsidiary of Ameritech and long-term contracts with subsidiaries of Sprint and Bell Atlantic, which extended through 2004 and 2005, respectively.

RH Donnelley's advertising sales and profitability were derived primarily from yellow pages advertising sales pursuant to long-term contractual relationships with subsidiaries of several of the country's largest local telephone service providers. Furthermore, a high level of recurring advertising sales, the leading market share position, and a diverse geographic and industry base of advertisers typified the company's business. RH Donnelley also had a very strong management team at both the corporate and operating levels.

However, the industry Management's Discussion and Analysis section in the company's 1998 Form S-4 under "Results of Operations" gave me more insight into the situation and revealed that such decline was temporary.

RH Donnelley has a strong competitive advantage in each of its markets primarily due to size, renewal rates, and expertise. Regarding size, the prior year the company sold over $1 billion of yellow page advertising, which accounted for approximately 9% of the $11.4 billion of yellow page advertising sold in the United States. All other independent marketers of yellow page advertising accounted for less than 10 percent of total U.S. yellow pages advertising sales, combined. Renewal rates had been a focus for the company. As a result, the company achieved high and stable advertising sales renewal rates, with three-year averages of approximately 91 percent overall. Consequently, there was a strong attraction to the company by value investors, due to the company's underlying business fundamentals.

The operating margins were exceptionally strong, as the company generated strong and predictable free cash flow with limited capital expenditures. Moreover, working capital needs were very modest given the nature of the business. As for valuation, I used the enterprise value to operating cash flow (earnings before interest, taxes, depreciation, and amortization) tool, given that the company had substantial debt and little capital expenditure requirements. At $16 per share, the company was trading at 5.5 times my 2000 operating cash flow projections, which was based on stable margins and 5-percent revenue growth. On an earnings per share basis, my analysis concluded that the company would be able to make at least $1.90

Excerpt from RH Donnelley's July 1998 Form S-4:

Gross advertising sales is the billing value of advertisements sold by the Company. Gross advertising sales in 1997 decreased 4.3%, from $1,115.6 million in 1996 to $1,067.2 million in 1997. In December 1997, Donnelley sold its East Coast proprietary yellow pages business (P-East) and in May 1996, Donnelley sold its West Coast proprietary yellow pages business ("P-West"). The decline in gross advertising sales in 1997 was primarily due to the sale of P-East, which accounted for gross advertising sales of $87.8 million in 1996 and $73.8 million in 1997, and the expiration of Donnelley's contract with Cincinnati Bell during August 1997, which led to a reduction in the related gross advertising sales from that contract from $65.0 million in 1996 to $50.1 million in 1997. Gross advertising sales in the Company's other markets, after adjusting for P-West's gross advertising sales of $2.1 million in 1996, decreased by 1.8%, from $960.6 million in 1996 to $943.4 million in 1997 due to lower sales for Bell Atlantic directories because of the rescheduling of certain directories in those markets, which created a shift in sales from 1997 to 1998. This decline was partially offset by gross advertising sales growth in Donnelley's Sprint markets (primarily Las Vegas), which was well above industry average levels. DonTech's gross advertising sales also increased by 1.3%, from $403.5 million in 1996 to $408.6 million in 1997.

Revenues are derived from commissions related to advertising sales and do not include revenues generated by sales of advertising by the DonTech partnership. Revenues decreased from $270.0 million in 1996 to $239.9 million in 1997, primarily reflecting the sale of P-East and the expiration of Donnelley's contract with Cincinnati Bell. Adjusted for P-East revenues of $95.1 million in 1996 and $78.0 million in 1997, P-West revenues of $2.2 million in 1996 and Cincinnati Bell revenues of $17.1 million in 1996 and $13.1 million in 1997, the Company's revenues declined 4.4% from $155.6 million in 1996 to $148.8 million in 1997. Revenues were adversely affected by scheduling shifts in the publication schedules for certain Bell Atlantic directories, which resulted in a 9.9% decrease in revenues for Donnelley in its Bell Atlantic markets, from $95.9 million in 1996 to $86.4 million in 1997. This decrease was partially offset by a 7.7% increase in revenues in Donnelley's Sprint markets, from $37.0 million in 1996 to $39.9 million in 1997; revenue growth was especially strong in Las

Vegas, where directories are published semiannually due to the strong economic growth in the Las Vegas market and resulting above-average growth in yellow pages advertising.

Partnership income and related fees decreased in 1997 by 2.1%, from $132.9 million in 1996 to $130.2 million in 1997. Donnelley receives partnership income primarily from two sources, the CenDon partnership and the DonTech partnership. Donnelley receives 50% of the profits generated by the CenDon partnership. Donnelley receives a percentage share of the profits generated by the DonTech partnership (which percentage share is 50% under the restructured DonTech partnership arrangement) and, beginning in the third quarter of 1997, also receives direct fees (Revenue Participation) from an affiliate of Ameritech which are tied to advertising sales generated by the DonTech partnership. These items are included in income from partnerships and related fees. Donnelley's income related to DonTech declined 4.3% in 1997, from $121.4 million in 1996 to $116.2 million in 1997, primarily due to a contractual reduction in Donnelley's share of DonTech's profits. In 1990, Donnelley accepted such contractual reductions in its share of DonTech's profits in return for amending the DonTech partnership agreement so that it would have no termination date, and these contractual reductions ended in 1997. A portion of the decline was also due to sales and production inefficiencies that arose from an unbalanced production schedule in which the majority of the directories with which DonTech is affiliated were published in the fourth quarter. In 1997, a two-year program was instituted that is intended to correct the imbalance and increase the effectiveness of DonTech's sales force and support operations. Donnelley's partnership income from CenDon increased 25.8% in 1997 from $9.7 million in 1996 to $12.2 million in 1997 due to sales growth in CenDon's Las Vegas markets that was well above industry averages.[2]

in the next 2 years, which implied a 7 times P/E ratio. At 5 times enterprise value to operating cash flow and 7 times P/E, the price seemed right.

Then I had to find the value. I searched the private equity deal summaries and came up empty. There was no perfect twin company that was publicly traded in the United States. I did find some luck looking abroad for

[2]RH Donnelley, Form S-4, July 17, 1998, pp. 31, 32.

publicly traded companies with similar assets. In fact, there were international companies that were being valued in the marketplace, at that time around 12 to 16 times enterprise value to operating cash flow. There was also a large public deal that had taken place at that time. That particular transaction included the acquisition of Yellow Books by a British company, for 13 times enterprise value to operating cash flow.

I took a closer look at Yellow Books and the motive of the British company to assess the rationale of the deal. Based on this deal and what I thought the market would pay for the business with RH Donnelley's characteristics, I reasoned that I would be able to sell my shares to the market at some point in the future. I believed that the market would pay 8 or 9 times enterprise value to operating cash flow, based on what other similar assets were sold for in the public markets. This would imply a stock price in the range of $28 to $32 per share.

I was very comfortable with the business; I liked the price of $16 and was convinced the company was worth at least $28 per share. Next, I looked for the fourth value lever: the catalyst. Given the nature of the business, I realized that there must be an internal catalyst to drive share price appreciation. I relied on management to continue to buy back shares and create shareholder value through restructuring opportunities. As long as the company was buying back their stock, my desire to have the stock reach fair value would soon be realized.

Finally, I assessed the company's margin of safety. Given the stability and predictability of RH Donnelley's revenues, cash flows, and market presence, the analysis led me to a safety level of $13 per share. This was all based on the assumption that if the company's stock traded below $13 for any length of time, it would make financial sense for the company to be taken private or sold. In addition, the asset values of the company yielded a price of close to $13. On this opportunity, my rationale was that my upside potential was 75 percent and my downside was 19 percent. The risk/reward was on my side.

HIGH GROWTH: NETWORK ASSOCIATES IN THE SUMMER OF 1999— THE APPROACH AND ANALYSIS

My investment in Networks Associates, Inc. was a challenge because nearly one-third of my margin of safety value was based on the market's exuberance and the overvaluation of certain assets. Network Associates was formed in December of 1997 as a result of a merger. The company is the leading developer and provider of software products, which addresses two of the most important concerns of information technology or IT professionals:

network security and network management. In the network security arena, the majority of the company's revenue had historically derived from its McAfee antivirus product line. Network Associates owned 42 percent of the consumer antivirus market in 1998—twice as much as its largest competitor. The company's share in the corporate market was nearly 43 percent. In the network management arena, the majority of the company's revenue came from its Sniffer product line. These two business divisions contributed to about 80 percent of Network Associates' revenues.

Excerpt from Network Associates' 1998 Form 10-K

Net revenue increased 45% to $612.2 million in 1997 from $421.8 million in 1996, and 51% from $278.9 million in 1995. The increases in net revenue are due to the increases in product revenue and services and support revenues described below.

Product revenue increased 49% to $510.8 million from $343.9 million in 1996, and 36% from $252.2 million in 1995. The increase in the growth rate in product revenues was primarily due to increases in the licensing of antivirus software products to new customers, renewing expiring antivirus licenses, continued acceptance of the Company's Sniffer products and continued acceptance of the Company's consulting and support services. The increase is also attributable to a lesser extent to the licensing of products (other than antivirus and Sniffer products) to new and existing customers as well as expansion into indirect product distribution channels and international markets. Finally, changes in 1995 in the Company's antivirus revenue recognition described below contributed to the increase in product revenue in both 1996 and 1995...[3]

Services and support revenues include revenues from software support, maintenance contracts, education, and consulting services, as well as those revenues from warranty, customer support, and maintenance contracts which are deferred and recognized over the related service period. Service revenues increased 30% to $101.4 million in 1997 from $77.9 million in 1996 and 192% from $26.7 million in 1995. The increase in services and support revenues resulted from growth in all categories of service revenues, principally due to the growth of the

---

[3]Network Associates, Form 10-K, December 1997, p. 29.

installed customer base and the resulting renewal of maintenance contracts. The high growth from 1995 to 1996 was due primarily to the Company initiating consulting and support services relating to the antivirus and network security software products.

International revenue accounted for approximately 28%, 24%, and 25% of net revenue for 1997, 1996, and 1995, respectively. The increase in international net revenue as a percentage of net revenue from 1996 to 1997 was due primarily to increased acceptance of the Company's products in international markets and the continued investment in international operations....[4]

At the time of my research, the antivirus business was expected to grow at 30 percent per year. There was a projected demand at twice as much as the growth rate of personal computers, simply because of the need for customers to protect themselves against viruses distributed by e-mail and Internet file downloads. The network management business was growing at 15 percent annually. Network Associates had the dominant share in the market, especially in North America. The company also had smaller businesses that were growing as well. Approximately 50 percent of its total revenue emanated from subscriptions. Overall, the combined revenue growth was expected to be in the 17 percent to 23 percent range.

However, there were several issues with this growth company. First, with concerns about the company's use of aggressive accounting looming, the management team had to prove to shareholders that they could indeed meet the growth objectives. Secondly, the Y2K scare was in full strength at the time, and there was uncertainty as to how much antivirus software would be sold in that environment. Thirdly, Network Associates was reorganizing its sales force, and there was concern that productivity was at risk. In fact, because of this information, some investors deemed Network Associates as a pure turnaround situation. Finally, there was skepticism among investors, particularly those of value orientation, as to whether or not the growth rate would turn into cash flow growth. This skepticism was due to accounting concerns and the fact that a good part of the growth came from an Internet division call McAfee.com, an Internet destination dedicated to updating, upgrading, and managing PCs over the Web.

[4]Network Associates, Form 10-K, December 1997, p. 30.

I liked the antivirus and network security business. It was the only area of technology in which I would participate. Unlike other technology-related companies for which change occurred regularly, the antivirus business, I reasoned, would be the same that day as it would be in 10 to 20 years. Down the road, the company would still be producing good programs to eliminate viruses. Computer viruses will always be a threat to communications, and it is not possible to write a software program that will forever destroy them.

Network Associates' price was decent, but not great. At $15, the company was trading at about 7 times enterprise value to operating cash flow, 17 times price to earnings, and around 1 times the enterprise value to normalized sales. The company was worth between $27 and $33 per share, based on the fact that among other assessments its closest competitor was trading at over 3 times sales.

As far as catalysts were concerned, I had identified six. First, operational improvements, specifically regarding the sales force and inventory management, I believed to be the most potent catalyst. Network Associates made some improvements at that time and recently reported that inventory was down to 12 weeks from 22 weeks. Secondly, the potential equity carve out of McAfee.com might have proven to be a potent catalyst for the stock because at the time, McAfee.com was among the top 40 most visited Web sites in the country. Risky as it may seem, I reasoned that the company's market value could range from $300 million to $700 million in the current market environment. Although I was paying nothing for McAfee.com, I was well aware of the outrageous valuations being given to dot-com companies at the time. At the low point of the valuation range, the carve out would be worth $3.50 per share in Network Associates' share value—an extra $3.50 per share value, which the market was ignoring.[5] Thirdly, the company was buying back $100 million worth of stock, which should spur stock price appreciation. Four, I reasoned that if the stock were to linger too long, it would be a prime take-out candidate given the company's market position, brand strength, and financial flexibility. Fifth, I also reasoned that the end of the Y2K "lockout" should help the company's revenue growth, as Network Associates' customers resumed spending on security. Finally, the upcoming release of Windows 2000 would help to achieve the revenue growth, as well as give the expected demand for new PCs to power Microsoft's new software.

[5]McAfee.com went public in December of 1999. NETA sold just 15% of McAfee, or over 6 million shares at $12, which more than quadrupled to $55 per share in three days, reaching a market cap of over $500 million. NETA's remaining pretax stake was worth over $400 million for its shareholders.

After considering the first four Keys of Value, I thought about my margin of safety levels. At $15 per share, I concluded that my safety level for the stock was somewhere near $12.50. This calculation was based on the $3.50 per share value of McAfee.com stock, which I expected to support Network Associates' stock. According to the most recently filed Form 10-Q, the company also had excess cash—the cash balance after subtracting all of the company's debt—of about $2.50 per share, and noncash asset values of just over $1 billion, which equated to nearly $7 per share in replacement value. In sum, my upside on the stock was a 100-percent return, and my downside was 17 percent. This investment that generated over a 90 percent return was one of the shortest and riskiest investments I had made.

THE APPROACH AND ANALYSIS OF AN EVENT-DRIVEN OPPORTUNITY: SYBRON INTERNATIONAL

In April of 2000, the following press release flashed on my computer screen:

Sybron International's April 2000, Form 8-K

SYBRON INTERNATIONAL ANNOUNCES RECORD EARNINGS AND SPINOFF OF DENTAL GROUP

MILWAUKEE (April 24, 2000). Sybron International Corporation (NYSE:SYB) announced today its financial results for the second quarter of fiscal 2000, the quarter ended March 31, 2000.

SECOND QUARTER AND FIRST HALF FINANCIAL RESULTS: Sybron had net income of $39.0 million for the second quarter of 2000, up 19.9 percent from net income from continuing operations in the like period a year ago. Net income for the first half of 2000 was $69.4 million, an increase of 24.3 percent from net income from continuing operations last year.

Diluted earnings per share for the second quarter were $0.37, an increase of 19.4 percent from the $0.31 diluted earnings per share from continuing operations in the second quarter of 1999. Diluted earnings per share for the first half of the year were $0.65, an increase of 22.6 percent from last year.

Net sales for the second quarter totaled $326.4 million, compared to $272.0 million for the second quarter of 1999, an increase of 20.0 percent. Sales increases were negatively impacted by the strengthening of the U.S. dollar by approximately $3.4 million. Without foreign currency effects, sales increased by 21.2 percent over our corresponding second quarter of 1999. Year-to-date, net sales at $624.6 million were up 20.0 percent from last year.

Cash flow continues to be strong as earnings before interest, taxes, depreciation, and amortization (EBITDA) for the quarter were $102.3 million as compared with $84.3 million for the same quarter of 1999, an increase of 21.3 percent. EBITDA for the first six months of the year was $191.5 million, an increase of 23.0 percent from the same period a year ago.

Internal sales growth this quarter was a robust 8.9 percent, made up of 11.0 percent in the dental segments and 7.7 percent in the laboratory segments.

Kenneth F. Yontz, Chairman, President and Chief Executive Officer, said, "I am extremely pleased with the Company's very positive and well-balanced performance this quarter and, in particular, the excellent rate of internal growth achieved by both the dental and laboratory segments. Again, the combination of solid operating performance throughout the Company, together with the addition of good profitable businesses through our acquisition program, has produced a healthy rate of sales and earnings growth."

SPINOFF OF DENTAL GROUP

Sybron International also announced today that its board of directors has decided to proceed with a spinoff of its dental group by way of a pro rata dividend of Sybron Dental Specialties, Inc. (SDS) stock to Sybron International shareholders. The spinoff is subject to a number of conditions, including the receipt of a ruling from the Internal Revenue Service that the transaction will be tax-free, and the effectiveness of a Registration Statement registering the SDS stock under applicable securities laws. The spinoff process is expected to take six to eight months.

When the spinoff is completed, Frank Jellinek, Jr., currently president of Sybron Laboratory Products Corporation (SLP), will become President and Chief Operating Officer of Sybron International, which will be renamed Apogent Technologies, upon approval by shareholders. He will also join the board of directors of Apogent.

Mr. Yontz, currently Chairman, President and CEO of Sybron International, will remain Chairman and CEO of Apogent Technologies and will become Chairman of SDS. Floyd W. Pickrell, Jr., currently President of SDS, will become President and CEO of the newly spun-off dental unit. Dennis Brown, Vice President and Chief Financial Officer of Sybron International, will also join the Board of Directors of SDS.

In commenting on the spinoff, Mr. Yontz stated that, "The time has come, given the quite different dynamics of the two businesses, to recognize that their abilities to grow and prosper, and to have independent access to capital markets, will be substantially enhanced if they are independent companies. Both of these businesses are market leaders in their fields, and this separation will ensure that their market leadership is not only maintained but strengthened."[6]

Sybron International announced plans to break up the company. In June of that same year, Sybron International's shares dropped significantly—as much as 41 percent—in the third quarter. The decrease in stock price related to the company's inventory problems with a major customer, resulting in a slower than expected growth in sales. I believed then that the customer and distributor-related problems that plagued the company's lab business were temporary negative catalysts and were well on the way to being corrected.

The analysis I had performed on Sybron International revealed that the sum of the company's parts was worth more than the whole. Sybron International has two divisions: Apogent Technologies, and Dental Products. Apogent manufactured consumable and labor-saving tools for a variety of research and clinical functions worldwide. These products included bottles, beakers, flasks, microscope slides, diagnostic rapid tests, etc. Apogent has significant market share in the markets in which they compete, which include biotech, pharmaceutical R&D, general research institutions, hospitals, and laboratories. Apogent's customers were primarily large original equipment manufactures and distributors. I reasoned that what would drive growth in this division would be genomics—the exploration of the human gene for a possible cure for disease. As a basic supplier of consumable research products, Apogent was well positioned to capitalize on the genomics revolution. Apogent generated a significant cash flow and had a history of steady and predictable earnings. Internal growth had been in the neighborhood of 5 to 6 percent, and over 20 percent including acquisitions. One of the top

[6]Sybron International, Corp., Form 8-K, April 24, 2000, p. 2.

executives of the company, who was a hard-charging manager with a proven record of generating shareholder value, ran this division.

The Dental Products division manufactures professional dental products, such as filling materials, bonding agents, dental burs, and impression materials, in addition to orthodontic materials such as brackets, bands, etc. They also make infection control products, such as sterilizers and disinfectants. Approximately 90 percent of revenues were derived from single-use consumable products. The company had very strong brands. The Dental Products division had leading market share in orthodontics—31 percent. The company's next biggest competitor had 18 percent market share. In dentistry, however, Sybron International had the #2 product.

At $25 per share, Sybron International was trading at less than 7 times firm value to operating cash flow, and 17 times price-to-earnings for 2001. Reasonable comparable companies for the genomic tools business were trading at 15 to 17 times firm value to operating cash flow and 25 times price-to-earnings; for the dental business, 9 times firm value to operating cash flow and 19 times price-to-earnings. On a sum-of-the-parts basis, Sybron International was worth at least $37 to $43 per share, generating a 60-percent upside potential based on the company's current price. There were two primary catalysts. The company will be doing a tax-free spin-off of the dental business and potential asset sales—selling some of the company's slow-growing businesses. My downside analysis generated a price of $22 per share based on take-out multiples that I had applied to the company on a sum-of-the-parts basis—implying a downside of 12 percent. What also reaffirmed my decision was the fact that several members of the board of directors had strong financial incentives to create value for outside owners, such as myself. Members of the board included Thomas Hicks of the leverage buyout firm Hicks, Muse, Tate & Furst, and well-known investor Robert Hass. In addition to being board members, both individuals were significant shareholders of the company, according to the latest proxy statement.

CYCLICAL COMPANIES

By definition, cyclical companies have temporary, industry-related issues, which cause the up and down nature of their stock prices.

LONG-TERM CYCLICAL: NEWHALL LAND & FARMING IN 1994
In 1994, there were substantial assets within Newhall Land & Farming Co. that were not being considered by the overall stock market. Newhall Land

was one of the first value investments at Fidelity. I believed that by selling off certain assets and with a change in the conditions of the local economy, Newhall's share price could double based on the value of its businesses. The company owned real estate properties, shopping malls, a utility company, farming land, and homebuilding operations, mainly in southern California. I began recommending the purchase of the company below $15 a share, based on the valuations that I had placed on the company's many business assets. I also took into consideration the company's own assessment appraised value of its assets, which was included in the company's Form 10-K. What follows is an excerpt from the 10-K.

Excerpt from Newhall Land & Farming's 1993 Form 10-K

The Company's primary business is developing master-planned communities. Since 1965, the Company has been concentrating its resources on developing the new town of Valencia on 10,000 acres of the 37,500-acre Newhall Ranch in accordance with a master plan designed to enhance the value of developed and undeveloped land. Preliminary planning is underway for another master-planned community on the 12,000 acres of the Newhall Ranch remaining in Los Angeles County. In 1993, the Company exercised an option on approximately 700 acres and purchased 160 acres in Scottsdale, Arizona, for a third master-planned community, with options remaining on an additional 1,400 acres. The master plan and zoning for the new planned community, McDowell Mountain Ranch, was approved by the Scottsdale City Council for development of over 4,000 homes and 70 acres of commercial property on a 3,200-acre site. Approximately 900 acres have been dedicated to the City of Scottsdale for open space.

Valencia, one of the nation's most valuable landholdings, is located in the Santa Clarita Valley, approximately 30 miles north of downtown Los Angeles and within 10 miles of the San Fernando Valley which has a population of over 1.3 million people. The Company's Newhall Ranch landholdings are bisected by Interstate 5, California's principal north-south freeway, and four major freeways intersect Interstate 5 within ten minutes of Valencia.

During the 1960s and 1970s, residential development dominated the activity in Valencia. In the 1980s, industrial development expanded eight-fold and the Santa Clarita Valley was the fastest growing area of unincorporated Los Angeles County. In the 1990s, Valencia is emerging from a residential and industrial suburb of Los Angeles to become the regional center for North Los Angeles County. Regional centers generate long-term increases in land values with the more intensive development of industrial and commercial business parks and shopping centers, along with a broader range of single-family and multifamily residential projects.[7]

APPRAISAL OF REAL PROPERTY ASSETS

Annually, the Company obtains appraisals of substantially all of its real property assets. The independent firm of Buss-Shelger Associates, MAI real estate appraisers, appraised the market value of the Company's real property assets to be $897,100,000 at December 31, 1993. The appraised assets had an aggregate net book value of $242,571,000 at December 31, 1993 and did not include oil and gas assets, water supply systems, cash and cash equivalents and certain other assets...[8]

The appraised values of the Company's land and income-producing properties in the Valencia master-planned community have increased from $222 million in 1984, the first year independent property appraisals were obtained, to $745 million in 1993, despite declines in recent years. On a per unit basis, the Company's net appraised value has increased from $11.74 to $21.04 over the same period...[9]

My focus was to buy the company at the "right" price, as it would be unclear as to when the positive catalyst, which would help Newhall reach its true value, would occur. The eventual turn of the southern California economy was unknown at this time. I was convinced of only three facts: 1) I was purchasing the company at a substantial discount to its tangible and adjusted book value, 2) the southern California economy would turn around *some* day, and 3) I was willing to wait for these catalysts to occur.

[7]Newhall Land & Farming Co., Form 10-K, December 31, 1993, p. 1.
[8]Newhall Land & Farming Co., Form 10-K, December 31, 1993, p. 3.
[9]Newhall Land & Farming Co., Form 10-K, December 31, 1993, p. 4.

Buying Newhall below the adjusted book value was the downside protection (i.e., my margin of safety). Over a two-year period, we purchased a position in the company. Three years later, after the local economy eventually rebounded, our initial investment in Newhall Land & Farming had doubled. While this may not seem to be an extraordinary return to some, I believe this investment was particularly prudent given its limited downside risk.

LONG-TERM CYCLICAL WITH A NEAR-TERM CATALYST: EATON CORPORATION IN 2000

Eaton Corp. was a global manufacturer of highly engineered products that serve industrial, vehicle, construction, commercial, aerospace, and semiconductor markets. The company had five divisions. By the end of that year, the truck components business was expected to contribute to 15 percent of sales, while automotive delivered 20 percent of sales. Fluid power accounted for 30 percent of sales. Industrial/commercial controls amounted to 25 percent, and semiconductor equipment contributed 25 percent of sales. The principal products included hydraulic products and fluid connectors, electrical power distribution and control equipment, truck drive train systems, engine components, ion implanters, and a wide variety of controls. Over 70 percent of sales was from North America, and worldwide sales were expected to reach $8.4 billion.

On February 24, 2000, prior to my interest in purchasing shares in the company, Eaton announced that it would engage Goldman, Sachs & Co. to study the feasibility of doing an equity-carve via an initial public offering of the semiconductor equipment segment. In July of that same year, Eaton completed an IPO of 16 million shares of the semiconductor unit, now called Axcelis. The shares were priced at $22, and traded as low as $9 when I became interested in the company.

Soon thereafter, Eaton announced that it would spin off its remaining 82-percent stake in Axcelis. The company held leading market shares in each of its niche markets. Eaton had the advantage by manufacturing highly engineered and proprietary products for a diverse group of customers. The company was also extremely profitable, generating consistent and strong free cash flows. The company had recently made a large acquisition, and was expected to capture significant cost savings. What follows is an excerpt from the company's most recent quarterly report at that time.

Eaton's stock was trading at 6.8 times P/E and 4 times enterprise value to operating cash flow, and 1.8 times adjusted book value. Historically, this was

Excerpt from Eaton Corp.'s March 2000 Form 10-Q

RESULTS OF OPERATIONS

Sales for the first quarter of 2000 were $2.33 billion, an increase of 40% above the comparable period in 1999. All business segments reported record sales in the first quarter of 2000...

Operating earnings per share during the first quarter of 2000, excluding restructuring charges and net gain on the sale of corporate assets, were $1.75, 50% above one year earlier...[10]

AUTOMOTIVE COMPONENTS

Automotive Components continued its consistent pattern of record performance and achieved all-time record sales in the first quarter of 2000 of $497 million, 4% above last year's record...[11]

FLUID POWER & OTHER COMPONENTS

Fluid Power and Other Components achieved all-time record sales in the first quarter of 2000 reaching $665 million, nearly 320% above year earlier results...[12]

INDUSTRIAL & COMMERCIAL CONTROLS

Industrial and Commercial Controls sales in the first quarter of 2000 reached a record $579 million, 13% ahead of last year...[13]

SEMICONDUCTOR EQUIPMENT

Semiconductor Equipment sales in the first quarter of 2000 were a record $141 million, 147% above last year's comparable results. Current industry forecasts are now calling for a worldwide rise in semiconductor capital equipment purchases this year of over 40%, as part of what is expected to be a multi-year industry rebound. The Company is fully participating in this trend. Operating profits were $27 million in the first quarter of 2000 compared to an operating loss of $12 million in last year's first quarter. These results reflect the benefits of the fundamental restructuring this business undertook during 1998 and early 1999...[14]

[10]Eaton Corp., Form 10-Q, March 31, 2000, p. 13.
[11]Eaton Corp., Form 10-Q, March 31, 2000, p. 13.
[12]Eaton Corp., Form 10-Q, March 31, 2000, p. 13.
[13]Eaton Corp., Form 10-Q, March 31, 2000, p. 14.
[14]Eaton Corp., Form 10-Q, March 31, 2000, p. 14.

the cheapest the company had ever been. If I applied an average multiple on P/E or enterprise value to operating cash flow, I would get to a fair value in the range of $73 to $77. On a discounted cash flow basis, using a 9-percent discount rate, I got $76 per share. This indicated an upside of 43 percent from my buy price of $53—not that great of a return until I assessed the downside scenario. My downside assessment was comprised of three components.

First, I was getting the Axcelis stake for free. Let me explain. I valued each of the divisions—excluding Axcelis—to get to a "stub" value—the part expected to be left over after the spin-off. I used operating cash flow multiples because the inputs for each division were readily available. I assigned a 7-times multiple on the industrial/commercial business, based on the valuation of a few of the division's competitors, and got $35 per share value. For the auto and truck components, I assigned a 4-times multiple to each of them to get $20 and $12 respectively, using the same valuation procedures.

The fluid power business carried a 5-times multiple and yielded a $30 per share value. Based on these numbers, the total firm value was $97 per share. I then subtracted debt obligations of $45 to get an equity value of $52. This seems to be no big surprise, given that Eaton's stock was trading at $53 at this time. But it was. This calculation did not include the 82% stake Eaton had in Axcelis, which meant I was getting the entire stake of Axcelis for $1 or virtually nothing. At the time, Axcelis was trading at around $10 per share.

Using the conversion rate of 1.1, for every share of Eaton I owned, I was guaranteed 1.1 shares of Axcelis. This gave me an $11 value in Axcelis, which was not accounted for in the stock price. This analysis implied that Eaton's stock should have been trading at $52 + $11, or $63 per share, not $53. Therefore, the first component of my margin of safety relied on the fact that I was only paying $1 for a stake in a company that was worth $11. I could afford the stock to go much lower. My second source of safety was in Eaton's replacement values and all assets, including Axcelis. Based on this reasoning, I came to $49 per share.

Finally, I reasoned that the take-out value of the enterprise was in the range of $50 per share, based on past deal valuation multiples in my sum-of-the-parts analysis. At $50, my downside on the stock would be a mere 6 percent with a 43-percent upside potential. The risk/reward was definitely in my favor. The most potent and perhaps the only real catalyst to help the stock reach my fair value was a turnaround in the cyclical nature of the business. At the time, diversified industrial companies were suffering from lower earnings guidance. That was okay. I was not concerned with the outlook for then, as I was confident that it would turn around in 18 to 24 months.

TEMPORARILY DEPRESSED VALUE; PACTIV CORPORATION IN 2000

Pactiv sold consumer products, such as plastic storage bags for food and household items, under the brand names "Hefty" and "Baggies." These products were sold through a variety of retailers, including supermarkets, mass merchandisers, and other stores where consumers purchase household goods. In addition to consumer products, the company manufactured plastic zipper closures for a variety of other packaging applications.

Many of the company's products have strong market positions. In foodservice packaging, Pactiv had, at the time, the number-one market share position in the United States and Canada in four of five main product categories based on unit volume. In addition, the company estimated that products representing 80 percent of sales of the protective packaging business held the #1 or #2 market share position in North America. In the United States, the company also had the leading market share position in disposable tableware.

Pactiv's breadth of product lines, its ability to offer "one-stop shopping" to customers, and its long-term relationship with key distributors contributed to its leadership position. The company also owned a 45-percent stake in Packaging Corporation of America, which was the sixth largest container-board and corrugated packaging products producer in the United States.

Pactiv was in a good business run by smart people. Historically, the company had grown through acquisitions. Excluding acquisitions, Pactiv's revenues grew about four percent to six percent per year. The company generated strong free cash flows and had one of the best management teams in the industry. Management's interest was aligned with shareholders, as evidenced by the fact that the management team required itself to own three to five times their base salary in Pactiv's stock.

However, the company's share price was hurting, primarily due to resin prices. A little more than 80 percent of Pactiv's sales came from products made out of plastic. Polyethylene and polystyrene comprised the bulk of Pactiv's resin purchases, making up about 75 percent of raw materials consumed by the company. Plastic resin prices had been rising since the prior year and were not expected to reverse course in the near term. Pactiv's profit margins suffered due to the sharp increase in resin prices.

At the current price of $9 per share, I reasoned that this was a good price to pay for the company. I looked at Pactiv on a "normalized" basis, by analyzing the company in an environment that excluded the peaks and troughs of resin prices. I concluded that the company could make at least $1.00 per share, as the prior year the company made $0.55 per share. With $600 million in normalized operating cash flow, I was purchasing the

Excerpt from Pactiv Corp.'s 1999 Form 10-K

OPERATING INCOME (INCOME (LOSS) BEFORE INTEREST EXPENSE, INCOME TAXES, AND MINORITY INTEREST)

The $13 million operating loss in 1999 included restructuring and other charges of $183 million and spin-off transaction expenses of $136 million. Operating income in 1998 was $283 million, which included restructuring charges of $32 million...[15]

Excluding the impact of unusual items, operating income was $306 million in 1999, a decline of 2.9% from the prior year. The favorable impact of 7% unit volume growth and restructuring savings in 1999 was more than offset by the decline in the spread between selling prices and material costs (principally polyethylene resin) which lowered gross margin as a percent of sales to 26.6% from 28.1% in 1998. In addition, operating income in 1999 was negatively impacted by higher operating costs for the corporate data center.

Consumer and foodservice/food packaging operating income declined 6.9% in 1999, as the favorable impact of 7% unit volume growth was more than offset by a decline in margins because of the rapid escalation of raw material costs.

Protective and flexible packaging operating income increased 8.7% in 1999, principally because of a 10% growth in unit volume and the positive effect of cost-reduction initiatives. Excluding the negative impact of foreign-currency exchange, operating income improved 13% in 1999.

The operating loss in the other segment was reduced to $27 million in 1999 from $31 million in 1998, as a result of reductions in corporate overhead costs and higher pension income, partially offset by an increase in expenses associated with operating the corporate data center...[16]

INCOME (LOSS) FROM CONTINUING OPERATIONS

The company recorded a net loss from continuing operations of $112 million ($0.67 per share) in 1999, compared with net income of $82 million ($0.49 per share) the previous year. Excluding the restructuring and other charges and spin-off transaction costs, net income for 1999 was $93 million ($0.55 per share), while 1998's net income was $102 million ($0.61 per share).[17]

[15]Pactiv Corp., Form 10-K, December 31, 1999, p. 12.
[16]Pactiv Corp., Form 10-K, December 31, 1999, p. 13.
[17]Pactiv Corp., Form 10-K, December 31, 1999, p. 13.

company at a valuation of 9 times P/E and 5 times enterprise value to operating cash flow. I reasoned that these were favorable prices to own Pactiv.

To calculate the company's fair value, I triangulated a valuation. I
employed sum-of-the-parts, discounted cash flows, and take-out valuations to come to a fair price of $17.83 or $18 per share. With the sum-of
the parts, I valued the food packaging, protective packaging, and the
company's stake in PCA differently. I used different twin companies for
each business and calculated the sum values on an operating cash flow
basis, and then subtracted the company's debt to arrive at the company's
equity value.

For discounted cash flows, I used a 10-percent discount rate and a 3-
percent terminal growth rate, given the nature of the business. My take-out
or deal valuation was based on prior deals in the packaging industry, which
I thought were appropriate to consider. I reasoned that I would be able to sell
my stake of the company at 8 to 10 times operating cash flow, assuming
only a modest operating cash flow growth rate. In aggregate, I arrived with
three different valuations from these methods, averaging out to be $17.83.

If I bought at $9, in the future, I would be able to sell my stake at $18.
The question then became: How will the stock go to $18 per share? The
most potent and obvious catalyst was the reduction of resin prices. Every
penny of resin price decline would equate to approximately $0.05 per share
in earnings for Pactiv. This was powerful economics. Given the quality of
the company and its management team, Pactiv's stock price was clearly
temporarily depressed.

Another catalyst, albeit less potent, was management's ongoing cost
cutting. In 1999 and early 2000, the company achieved substantial cost savings from plant closing to selling, general, and administrative (SG&A)
reductions. An ongoing debt reduction program and divestitures were also
catalysts. Earlier that year, Pactiv sold 85 percent of its stake of Packaging
Corporation of America, or 35 million shares, in an IPO at $12 per share.
The management team planned to use the after-tax proceeds to reduce debt.
Pactiv still held 6 million shares of Packaging Corporation of America,
which it planned to use for further debt reductions. The company also sold
several assets that were noncore to Pactiv's operations. Noncore divestitures resulted in over $100 million in cash and tax benefits.

My margin of safety was based on a calculation of the company's asset
values, which took into account the company's free cash flow generation
possibilities, brand value, market position, and product variety. The margin of
safety, which I thought it would take to make the company a prime candidate
to be taken private or sold, weighed on the share price. These exercises led

me to a share price of $7.50. With a limited downside and substantial upside, my investment in Pactiv Corp turned out to be a very worthwhile investment.

HYBRID OPPORTUNITIES

The restructuring on Thermo Electron Corporation in Chapter 4 is an example of a hybrid opportunity, where the situation was rich with catalysts of various types—new management, asset sales, divestitures, new strategy, spin-offs, share repurchases, etc. In such situations, value investors use a variety of tools specific to each case. They segment the opportunity and value each in isolation.

AVOIDING VALUE TRAPS

Value traps are inexpensively priced companies that do not possess positive catalysts or that may operate in declining industries. Here are some of the more common examples of potential value traps.

- Buying cheaply on valuation despite the fact that it may be a bad business

- Buying a cyclical company with low valuation at the top of its cycle

- Buying a stock solely because it has a low dollar value of say, $3 per share

- Buying simply the cheapest company in an industry without understanding the economics of the business

C H A P T E R

BUYING RIGHT AND BEING AN OWNER

> "…I could be the phoenix that would help a business rise from the ashes."[1]
>
> *Richard Rainwater*

WHEN INVESTORS "BUY RIGHT," they must identify excellent businesses, and they must also purchase them at good prices. It is pretty straightforward. Chapter 2 discusses how to identify good businesses and the tools needed for a thorough analysis. Chapter 3 discusses price and how to determine its attractiveness. In addition to what is discussed in Chapters 2 and 3, there is a third element in purchasing companies that is more of an art than a science. It entails the inclusion of the current environment in one's investment thinking.

There are three elements one should consider when purchasing shares of companies, and taking the current economic environment into consideration. First, follow Benjamin Graham's advice and think about the stock market as an owner/partner. Second, think about the economic environment without predicting the future. Third, think cyclically. Businesses and the economy operate in cycles, and not linearly. Avoid thinking that the strong trends will stay strong forever, and that companies undergoing hardship are always doomed.

---

[1]Train, J., *Money Masters of Our Time* (New York: HarperBusiness, 2000, p. 79).

THINK ABOUT THE STOCK MARKET AS AN OWNER/PARTNER

Mr. Market is perhaps the most well-known character among value investors. Benjamin Graham invented this fictional character as a way to help investors understand the overall stock market. Warren Buffett, one of Graham's disciples, says that Mr. Market is your partner in the stock market—but he is a very special kind of partner with special characteristics. Specifically, Mr. Market is very emotional and never gets discouraged if he is ignored.

There are a few critical understandings of Benjamin Graham's Mr. Market:[2] First, as your partner, Mr. Market can be very excited about the prospects of the stock market, and can offer you an extremely attractive price for your share of the business. During these times, Mr. Market will pay a high price for almost any publicly traded enterprise. In this environment, value investors typically reevaluate their current holdings with an eye towards selling shares of companies that are near their fair values or have assets that are impaired. Some value investors might sell despite the fact that fair value may have been reached a bit early. For example, if a value investor buys a company at $10 per share and expects to sell at $20 per share within a year, but the market irrationally values the stock at $20 only six months later, the value investor may indeed sell. In this case, the selling was prompted not by fundamental changes, but because the fair market value had already been reached. This is just one example of how the joyful Mr. Market works, at times, in favor of value investors.

Emotional discipline is key. Value investors do not sell shares of good companies for a quick profit, nor simply do they buy stocks because they are going up in the next hour. Buy high, sell higher is not a virtue for a disciplined buyer of businesses. In fact, Buffett has said, "the dumbest reason in the world to buy a stock is because it's going up."[3] Likewise, the value investor does not sell simply because the stock market is selling off.

Not surprisingly, Mr. Market often offers to sell you shares of businesses he owns at very low prices. At times, the prices may appear to be irrational. Recognizing when Mr. Market is in this mood is important. However, being able to separate the good companies from the not so good is critical. Employing the Five Keys of Value framework appropriately is paramount during the times when Mr. Market behaves irrationally. These are "buy" days for value investors.

[2]Cunningham, L. *The Essays of Warren Buffett* (New York: Cardozo Law Review, 2001, p. 64).
[3]Lowe, J. *Warren Buffett Speaks* (New York: McGraw-Hill, 1996, p. 97).

When Mr. Market feels discouraged, he typically sells the good companies along with the bad companies. It is in this environment that value investors feel the most comfortable in buying companies. Days like these are very easy to spot. Everything is down, say 5 percent to 10 percent, for reasons that are often short-lived. This market action does not always happen in the general market, but more often among specific sectors. For example, over the period of just one day, there could be a 20-percent drop in the share price of companies in the homebuilding industry, if certain adverse news makes its way to the general market. Or, a financial services company that is undergoing company-specific accounting issues may affect the value of other industry participants, merely through a business association. Again, these are the best opportunities for value investors. The sellers are irrational, or are selling on fear.

The next critical understanding of Mr. Market is whether to buy when he is depressed, or sell when he is joyful. The value investor knows that Mr. Market is not a thinker, and therefore should not be expected to help investors make decisions. Once again, he is not discouraged when he is ignored. He will come back day after day with new attempts to buy and sell businesses. Mr. Market does not get discouraged, simply because he has no return expectations, risk limitations, or investment style.

Understanding Mr. Market's mood gives value investors confidence in their decisions. There is little second-guessing once a decision is made. For example, if investors buy a stock at $20 per share, and it trades down to $15, value investors are more confident about their decision if the decrease in price is not based on the company's fundamentals. Stocks go up and down. This is what they do. Short-term performance of a stock is not relevant. Understanding this simple fact lifts an enormous burden from the shoulders of value investors, and raises their level of confidence.

This understanding also leads to the fourth key trait of Mr. Market; he exists to serve investors, not to advise them on their decisions. If Mr. Market is selling a business at a very high or low price, it should not be a signal for investors to take action. It is very important, as is discussed further in Chapter 8, for value investors to know what they plan to do prior to Mr. Market's offer, in order to eliminate the potential tendency to buy or sell businesses based on a reaction to the market. Many speculators and equity traders "invest" according to the swings of the market. Those who buy businesses do so proactively, making decisions backed by sound research that prepares them to take advantage of such price swings. Needless to say, this approach takes a high degree of discipline to employ.

Finally, given the fact that Mr. Market is not a thinker, Buffett states that if investors are not able to understand and value their own business better than Mr. Market, they should not be in the game of investing. Investors must be able to recognize an opportunity regardless of how Mr. Market is behaving. The true value investor must buy the best businesses at ridiculously low prices, and know when to sell shares of overvalued companies.

MR. MARKET AS A DISCIPLINARY TOOL

Approaching the stock market with Mr. Market in mind is very useful to value investors because it strengthens their emotional discipline. This is accomplished in several ways. First, understanding that Mr. Market is emotional in his decision making gives the value investor comfort during market fluctuations. As pointed out in earlier chapters, these fluctuations are actually welcomed by value investors who are looking to buy good businesses at superb prices.

Second, because value investors expect the market to act foolishly at times, they can be a bit more patient in understanding and valuing potential investment opportunities. Missing price targets is seldom a problem. If value investors "miss" a favorable price offered by the market in a given day, they are confident that Mr. Market will be foolish in its valuation of the same company again in the future.

THINK ABOUT THE ECONOMIC ENVIRONMENT WITHOUT TRYING TO PREDICT IT

Most investors focus on the leading economic indicators to get a better grasp of the market. The Conference Board publishes the economic indicators at the beginning of each month. There are three types of indicators produced by the Conference Board: lagging, coincident, and leading.[4] By definition, the data for the lagging indicator, based on events that have occurred in the general economy, include items such as unemployment data, and the consumer price index for services and commercial and industrial loans. The coincident indicator occurs at the same time as the general economy. The leading indicators are useful to investors because they can signal that the general market has peaked or that the overall economy is bottoming. The leading indicators include:[5]

1. Average weekly hours in manufacturing
2. Average weekly initial claims for unemployment insurance

[4]The indicators, variables, and general usefulness are drawn from the Web site of the Conference Board at *www.conference-board.org.*

[5]Leading indicators are drawn from the Web site of the Conference Board at *www.conference-board.org.*

3. Manufacturers' new orders on consumer goods and materials
4. Vendor performance (slower deliveries diffusion index)
5. Manufacturers' new orders of nondefense capital goods
6. Building permits for new private housing units
7. Stock prices (500 common stocks)
8. Money supply (M2)
9. Interest rate spread (10-year Treasury bonds less federal funds)
10. Index of consumer expectations

Value investors typically do not attempt to predict the direction of the economy or the general market. As a group, they rarely comment publicly on the general stock market, let alone economic variables that affect them. Buffett has often said that he focuses almost entirely on individual companies, rather than the overall market. Indeed, value investors use a specific approach to get the information needed in order to make informed decisions on when to buy and sell. The fact that value investors do not spend time predicting the direction of the market does not mean that they as a group do not pay attention to the general environment of the stock market.

In fact, there is a mental framework that one should employ when addressing the market. The intellectual framework is as follows: Be aware of the direction of interest rates and corporate profits, and be mindful of inflation. Interest rates are one of the most critical factors that affect a firm's valuation. In a 1999 *Fortune* article, Warren Buffet sums up the impact of interest rates to the general market best. "[Interest rates] act on financial valuations the way gravity acts on matter: The higher the rate, the greater the downward pull."[6]

There are several types of interest rates that are quoted by the market: the prime rate, the discount rate, T-bills, the Federal funds rate, etc. While all of these types of interest rates typically move in the same direction almost simultaneously, the most important rate is the Federal funds rate. The Federal funds rate is the interest rate that banks must pay other banks for reserves. A higher rate means that banks will have fewer reserves and will lend less money. The lower the rate, the more reserve banks can have, which makes them able to lend more money for the economy to grow. Of course, this has an effect on the yield curve, which is a graph that shows the interest rate in relation to short-term and long-term bonds. The graph typically slopes upward to show that short-term rates are often lower than long-term

---

[6]*Fortune*, "Mr. Buffett on the Stock Market," November 22, 1999, p. 212.

rates, given the fact that lenders generally require higher rates for longer-term loans. This "curve" inverts when short-term rates are higher or near equal to long-term rates, after the Fed raises rates to slow down the economy.

All else being equal, knowing the direction of the Federal funds rate helps investors determine the direction of short-term rates, and ultimately the yield curve. This has a significant and direct impact on the overall health of the economy and corporate profits.

After-tax corporate profits are equally important. Value investors buy businesses as a form of investment, in order to recoup their investments plus additional sums of money in the future. Investors in companies can only get out of a business what the business earns over time.[7] The expected return on the initial investment, which is based on business fundamentals as well as economic-driven factors, is very critical. The business fundamentals are clear and are discussed in detail in Chapter 2. They include the quality of the business, management's ability, and the competitiveness of the industry. The economically driven factors include the direction of interest rates and inflation.

Inflation is monitored very closely by investors because of its powerful impact on real returns, and its ability to redistribute wealth between lenders and borrowers. For example, a lender today may receive fewer real dollars in the future than were hoped for if inflation rises too quickly. In such case, the wealth is redistributed from the lender to the borrower, who effectively borrowed cheaper funds than were believed. Inflation also affects savings and corporate profitability. There are three indexes that track inflation—the gross domestic product (GDP) deflator, the Producer Price Index (PPI), and the Consumer Price Index (CPI). The GDP deflator casts a very wide net by including virtually all final goods and services from the government, the foreign sector, and investment by businesses. Dividing the current GDP by the real GDP of a chosen year gives us the deflator. The data used in this calculation is available on a quarterly basis. The PPI and CPI data, on the other hand, are available monthly.

The PPI is often considered a leading indicator because it uses a basket of goods that are used in finished goods. The PPI index is reported the second week of each month. The CPI is perhaps the most widely used index to gauge inflation. It uses a sample basket of goods and services, and prices those goods on a monthly basis. The CPI is very reliable and is used to indicate the cost of living for the general population. Investors use one or all of these indexes to gauge inflation. In addition to the three indexes, other

---

[7]*Fortune,* "Mr. Buffett on the Stock Market," November 22, 1999, p. 216.

factors, such as capacity-utilization, the National Association of Purchasing Manager's Index, and the unemployment rate, may be used as well.

Value investors' awareness of interest rates, corporate profits, and inflation help them buy right by getting a better understanding of the mood of Mr. Market. However, this approach in understanding the market is useless without the proper mental discipline in place.

THINK CYCLICALLY

Value investors use an analytical approach to the market. They think cyclically. Products have cycles, and so do industries, the economy, and the broader stock market. The problem with most investors is that they think in a linear fashion, assuming that the good times will always stay good and the bad times will never recover. Warren Buffett makes the case that investors often miss great opportunities in the market or get coerced into buying at market peaks because of their "unshakable habit: looking into the rear-view mirror instead of through the windshield."[8] This is part of the herd mentality. Buffett goes on to explain. "Once a bull market gets under way, and once you reach the point where everybody has made money no matter what system he or she followed, a crowd is attracted into the game that is responding not to interest rates and profits but simply to the fact that it seems a mistake to be out of stocks. In effect, these people superimpose an I-can't-miss-the-party factor on top of the fundamental factors that drive the market...Through this daily reinforcement, they become convinced that there is a God and that He wants them to get rich."[9]

Investors benefit greatly when they think and invest in cycles. It is important to sell the high performers, since the good times are not going to last forever. It is just as critical to buy selectively the excellent businesses undergoing difficult times, because some hard times do not last forever. The key is in identifying the proper catalysts.

STEPPING BACK TO REEVALUATE

How can understanding the environment help the investor buy right? Putting the proper emphasis on certain levers during a particular market environment helps the value investor buy right. In buying right, the investors carefully select the tools at their disposal, given the situation and the economic factors at work. Identifying catalysts is a critical factor in a bull market, while having an ample margin of safety is paramount in a down market. For

[8]*Fortune,* "Mr. Buffett on the Stock Market," November 22, 1999, p. 214.
[9]*Fortune,* "Mr. Buffett on the Stock Market," November 22, 1999, p. 216.

example, if one buys a company in a bull market, and that same company is growing 20 percent every quarter, it is critical that the investor is confident in the sustainability of the ongoing catalysts that allow such performance to occur. With such high expectations, a slowdown in growth to say 15 percent can be catastrophic for several reasons. In this situation, this fast-growing stock was probably not cheap when considered on an absolute or a relative basis, and may have limited safety levels built into the stock price as well. Therefore, any slight disappointment is more likely to have a greater impact on stock price, as there was little holding up the stock price all along.

Another reason why high-flying growth stocks may get decimated when growth is slowing is because of opportunity costs. In bull markets, high performers are plenty; investors have more options and often "dump" companies that have a different outlook or have questionable growth characteristics. When buying solid companies in bear markets, these businesses often lack catalysts. Therefore, the lever that should be most secure is that of margin of safety. To buy right is to purchase a piece of a good business at a great price, while staying cognizant of the economic and market environment in which the company operates.

DOLLAR COST AVERAGING

Timing can be an important element for successful investing, despite the fact that no one will ever be able to "time" the market to generate above-average returns. While some may claim to be market timers, the reality is that we all fall short of being able to interpret the future. Dollar cost averaging is a method investors use to improve their ability to time the mood swings of Mr. Market.

Investors have choices as to how they wish to invest their money. One may choose to invest all funds in a particular opportunity in one transaction, or use the dollar cost averaging method. Buying large shares of a company all at once involves an incredible ability to time the market accurately. When employing the dollar cost averaging method, one invests a portion of one's funds and buys more as the stock falls to attractive price levels. Not surprisingly, the key here is discipline—allowing oneself not to pay a nickel more than what would be purchased in a single transaction. By purchasing shares incrementally, investors increase their average price, while gaining more conviction in the investment. By investing little by little, dollar cost averaging allows the investor to understand the business better.

Most investors commit a certain amount of money to buy shares in a particular company. For example, let's assume you have $5000 to invest in one company, and have identified a great business. After applying the Five

Keys of Value framework, you have determined that a reasonable price to pay for the business is $15 per share. You can purchase all of the shares at once, or you can buy in small to large portions. If the stock trades at $15, you may decide to purchase 50 shares at this price, while buying 100 or more shares if the stock reaches $13 per share. As long as investors remain disciplined (i.e., not paying more than their reasonable price) they are guaranteed, due to the law of averaging, to own the company at a more favorable price level than what they were willing to pay.

Dollar cost averaging is a very good method to ensure that one "buys right," as most investors have the tendency to buy when stock prices are going up rather than down. Dollar cost averaging, with a price level not exceeded by the investor, helps investors control the urge to buy a stock on its way up. Buying on the upside all too often results in paying a premium for companies. Dollar cost averaging works best in volatile markets, where unknowns about the economy, for example, are plentiful and Mr. Market is jittery.

Dollar cost averaging, however, does not work well in bull markets, where stocks tend to appreciate. This gives investors little opportunity to "average down" their cost basis. In such situations, investors using dollar cost averaging often find themselves not investing all allocated funds for a particular company, due to an unexpected increase in stock price.

Unfortunately, depending on the amount to be invested, dollar cost averaging can be expensive. Buying shares of a company in several different transactions can lead to significant commission fees, and, in turn, can decrease returns. Therefore, while institutional investors may find dollar cost averaging a helpful tool, it may not be cost-effective for the individual investor with limited funds.

In order for dollar cost averaging to be financially worthwhile, one must assess the amount of funds available to invest, and then decide if it makes economic sense to handle the investment in this manner. While the commission fees charged for each transaction may differ, the investor must be keenly aware of the dollar amount required to make each transaction cost-effective before using this method. With the onslaught of on-line brokers competing for customers, the discounts on commission fees should continue. Soon, dollar cost averaging will be economical for most of us.

OWNERSHIP IS A VERB WHEN MONITORING YOUR INVESTMENTS

Value investors are proud owners as they buy and sell businesses, not trade stocks. They take great care and patience in identifying, analyzing, and ultimately, making the decision to own a piece of a great business. Owning a business has its challenges, rewards, and responsibilities. The challenges and rewards are obvious.

The responsibilities for each individual investor are twofold. First, as an outsider, the investor must know as much about the company as possible. Second, an investor must hold management accountable for creating value for all stakeholders, including its customers, employees, and ultimately, shareholders. Owning companies takes time and effort, as it should. It includes reading and analyzing annual and quarterly reports, keeping up with industry journals, listening to news clips, and monitoring one or more twin companies in the same industry. For the professional investor, this list also includes company visits, and meeting with industry experts, management teams, and competitors. Attending annual meetings is also important.

OWNERS' RIGHTS

When you own a share of a company, you own a piece of a business. The reason why companies issue shares is because the company believes that it can take capital from investors and generate attractive returns. The capital is often used to expand the business or invest for the future.

For stockholders, there are several benefits to owning shares in a company. One benefit is the right to participate in the profits of the company and have influence over major decisions regarding the company, such as corporate governance. Shareholders only have one risk as the owners of a company—the risk of losing their capital investment.

The board of directors of any company works for shareholders; they represent shareholders in making executive-level decisions that will have a material impact on the company's stock price. There are several different types of shares that one might own. The most common types of shares in a public company include common, series, and preferred.

Common shares typically give the holder voting rights and equal access in all profits of the company. Given these rights, common shareholders are invited to special meetings with the company. Series shares (e.g., Series A, Series B, etc.) typically do not come along with voting rights. It is a mechanism for a company to raise money without losing control of the organization. Depending on how each series is structured, it may have its own special privileges.

Preferred shareholders possess special rights and privileges over common shareholders. For example, if a company were to be liquidated, the preferred shareholders would be paid before common shareholders. Preferred shareholders also enjoy a dividend, but do not benefit if the company improves in profitability. However, these shareholders have no voting rights, unless their dividends have been withheld for a certain number of years. Preferred stockholders do have the opportunity to convert their shares to common shares at some point in the future.

Common equity holders have very special rights with the organization. Shareholders immediately have rights once they purchase shares, and these rights are relinquished once those shares are sold. There are also shareholder rights plans. The management team of the company typically chooses those plans, and the shareholders vote on them.

Shareholders also have the right to receive an annual report on a regular basis, as well as other essential financial statements, including quarterly reports and earnings announcements that inform shareholders on the current conditions of the company. Shareholders are invited every year to the company's annual meeting where they are able to ask questions of the CEO and other officers about the management aspects of the business.

In June of 2001, the U.S. Securities and Exchange Commission's chief accountant offered 16 rights of investors during a recent speech.[10]

1. All investors have the right to equal and fair treatment.
2. Investors have the right to officers and directors who treat the stockholders' money with fiscal responsibility and due care as if it were their own.
3. Investors have a right to management—from the board of directors on down—that fosters a corporate culture of integrity, honesty and adherence to the spirit as well as the letter of the law.
4. Investors have the right to officers and management who shoot straight—who tell the owners of the company the complete story, without omission, without hype, without spin, and without delay.
5. Investors have a right to officers and directors who foster a corporate culture in which people don't cut corners just so they can report favorably on the achievement of individual or corporate goals.
6. Investors have a right to management that understands their job is to manage the business, not the earnings.
7. They have the right to a management team that clearly understands it is the steward of the stockholders' company, that it serves the stockholders, that it is not the stockholders' master.
8. Investors have a right to timely and consistently transparent disclosures that reflect the true economics of the business, including complete and

---

[10]Lynn, T., U.S. Securities and Exchange Commission, "Speech by SEC Staff: The Investor's Bill of Rights: A Commitment for the Ages," June 18, 2001.

unbiased financial disclosures of all matters management or the auditors would want to know if they were investing in the company themselves.

9. Investors have the right to independent auditors that act on behalf of investors as challenging skeptics who must be convinced, rather than vendors who must make sales.

10. Investors have the right to an independent, inquisitive, financially literate and actively engaged audit committee that views its mandate broadly and that acts as the representative of shareholders.

11. Investors have the right to an active board of independent, knowledgeable and diligent directors who understand they are elected by and for all of the shareholders, not the CEO.

12. Investors are entitled to a corporate governance system that will ensure the company and management will seek the approval of investors on important matters affecting shareholder interests such as new or expanding stock option plans.

13. Investors have a right to real analysis performed by real analysts, who place the investors' best interests before their relationship with management and a mission to bring in the next deal.

14. Investors have the right to fair securities markets, where trades are executed at the best possible price.

15. Investors have the right to timely and transparent disclosures of actual fund performance by all funds that take their money, and

16. Investors have the right to regulators and standard setters who put the investor first, and that encourage rather than impede investor protection and efficient markets.

ASSESSING QUARTERLY EARNINGS ANNOUNCEMENTS AS A TOOL

Companies provide earnings announcements every three months. Quarterly announcements are designed to inform shareowners as to the goings-on of their company. Investors are able to get on a company's mailing list through the company's Web site or by calling the investor relations department. In addition, there are several Web sites that have earnings calendars to inform investors of upcoming corporate financial announcements.

From company to company, earnings announcements have a very similar reporting structure. The headline typically summarizes the progress of the past quarter. Written in bold-faced letters, the caption provides a summary of the quarter using metrics considered most important to investors. For example, cell phone companies may highlight subscriber growth numbers, while a homebuilding company may focus on backlog orders. The caption varies from industry to industry and company to company.

The first paragraph of most announcements provides investors with the earnings figures for the quarter. They are presented in total, as well as on a per-share basis. A comparison between the current and previous quarter earnings, as well as the quarter a year prior, is also provided. Members in the investment community refer to such assessments as year-over-year and sequential comparisons. Companies also provide earnings that exclude what are called "one-time" items. These one-time items can either increase or decrease earnings, and can include a sale of a business or a restructuring charge. An explanation is typically given as to why earnings may be abnormally high or low for a given quarter, due to this specific and fleeting event.

The next pieces of data provided are the sales for the quarter, or what analysts refer to as the "top line" numbers. The investment community pays very close attention to the sales number, as it is often the most important part of the announcement, particularly for companies with negative earnings. As with earnings, the sales figure is also given on a year-over-year and on a sequential basis comparison, with reasons for abnormal results.

After the bottom line and top line numbers are discussed, the quarterly announcement also provides other items found in the income statement that investors deem important. This may include the operating income for the quarter, gross margins, new orders, etc. This area is important in explaining the strength and weakness of the top and bottom line numbers.

The next part of the earnings announcement is the management's explanation of the quarter, including information on what has transpired in the given period, and the future outlook of the business. The tone of this portion is very important. Because the stock market is often forward-looking, the outlook projected by management often goes a long way in determining investor sentiment. Here, the management team may decide to discuss the various business lines of the organization and its performance. Management often concludes by giving investors guidance as to what it thinks the company will earn in the next few quarters. Investors take this guidance very seriously, as these numbers will be used as a base to determine their own projections. Investors may choose to add to the earnings number suggested if they think that the management team is too conservative. On the other hand, there may be a need for a reduction in the numbers, if management is believed to be aggressive or unrealistic in its outlook.

After a paragraph or two on legal issues that allow the company to make "forward-looking" statements without being held liable, the text of the announcement typically concludes with a brief paragraph describing the company. The financial statement and analysis follow, including an income statement, the most current balance sheet, and a management's analysis of the financial data presented.

The income statement is presented in two time periods: the current quarter, representing three months of performance, and year-to-date, which represents the performance of the company since the beginning of the fiscal year.

A THREE-STEP PROCESS TO ANALYZING EARNINGS ANNOUNCEMENTS

The most important aspect in analyzing earnings announcements is to understand what the numbers mean, not what they are. What they are today is history, what they imply for the future is not. The value of a business is based on what is to come.

Step 1: Look at the trends in the numbers. For example, take a critical eye to the top line and margins, and how they relate to management's outlook for the company. Calculate the percentage changes on a sequential basis, as well as for year-over-year. You may also want to do a similar analysis for prior earnings announcements, especially if the company in question is a new investment. Percentage change calculations for the income statement and balance sheet can be a tedious task, particularly over multiple quarters. However, this information can be extremely useful as potential red flags jump right out of the page.

If the trend in sales, for example, is heading south while management has been very upbeat over the past quarters, one might be suspicious about management's capability to project future activity. Significant changes from one quarter to the next, without proper explanation in the announcement, might be a signal that further investigation is needed.

Step 2: Get behind the numbers by taking a closer look at each key line item in the income statement and balance sheet, in order to assess what may be implied for the next few quarters. The financial statements included in earnings announcements are typically not audited. Therefore, it is up to the investors to take a closer look into the quality of not only the message, but also the data being provided by management.

Revenues are based on sales made in the current period, even if it has not been collected and/or does not include cash from a prior period. Value investors look carefully to assess whether or not the company has overstated revenues for the current quarter, as companies try to account for as much revenues as possible before the end of the quarter. Generally speaking, operating expenses typically generate revenues in the same quarter. This would include all materials used in the products, labor, R&D, and administrative expenses. An abnormally high or low operating expense number should be examined to determine the source. Low operating expenses in a quarter yield higher operating margins, and the reverse is true for high operating expenses.

What is often included in the operating expense segment are the one-time events or restructuring charges. Management considers these items to be unusual gains or losses. Unfortunately, however, the "one-time" events recur quarter after quarter for many companies. It is often up to the investor to decipher whether a "one-time" item is truly one-time. Value investors consider recurring one-time events in companies' reports red flags, as it may signify unstable business models. The problem with restructuring charges is that management can use them to improve future earnings. This involves taking charges to reduce depreciation today, in order to improve the earnings for tomorrow.

Value investors rely heavily on the footnotes of the announcements to help guide them in deciding what to do with such charges. The footnotes often provide ample information as to whether or not an item is truly one-time in nature or a recurring event. After taking into account the content of the footnotes, the investor should make the necessary adjustments accordingly. In addition to restructuring charges, gains or losses associated with "accounting changes," "discontinued operations," and "extraordinary items" should be checked for accuracy.

Having assessed the revenue numbers and the operating expense, the investor gets a decent grasp as to what the operating income or earnings before interests and taxes implies about the future. One might choose to obtain a company's earnings before interests, taxes, depreciation, and amortization from a particular quarter by adding back the depreciation and amortization.

To assess the company's earnings, the investor continues to analyze carefully the income statement. The next area of focus should be the net interest expense line item. The vast majority of interest expense is from loans the company has from banks (bank debt) and funds borrowed from the public (bonds). The interest expense is often reported as a net number and includes income from investments, marketable securities, and cash in the bank. Net interest expense can be abnormally low in a given quarter if interest income was high for the same period. Investors must make sure that a reduction in net interest expense is sustainable on a forward-looking basis. A quick assessment of the company's debt level also helps in this effort.

Next, changes in tax rates are assessed to get net income. The goal here is to determine whether the company's current tax rate is sustainable, and whether or not they have been consistent with prior reported time periods.

Abnormally low tax rates in a given quarter, compared to previous quarters, should be investigated before arriving at net income or net earnings. To get earnings per share, the investor uses the fully diluted share count number to account for claims to earnings from all equity holders.

For the balance sheet, depending on the industry and the circumstance, the focus is typically on the current assets and the company's total debt. Current assets include items such as inventory, accounts receivable, marketable securities, and cash. Management has a great deal of room to adjust these numbers on a quarterly basis. For example, management might change the way it accounts for inventory, in order to take advantage of inflation. This could be done by switching from the first-in-first-out (FIFO) accounting method to the last-in-first-out (LIFO) way. Accounts receivable are reviewed to determine if there has been an abnormally high increase or a significant decrease in reserves for bad debts.

Regarding the company's debt, one typically assesses the company's long-term and short-term debt and notes payable to see if there are any unexplained significant changes.

Step 3: Think about your reasons for purchasing the company and ask yourself whether or not anything has changed. Some value investors make a habit of writing down the key reasons why they own a particular company. During market fluctuations these reasons are reviewed. If the stock trades at favorable levels with no significant changes, more shares are purchased.

Writing down the key reasons for stock ownership is also useful in assessing quarterly earnings announcements. Again, quarterly announcements are required by management to give investors an update on the state of the investor's company. Value investors use this update to reevaluate why they own the company. Active business owners continually reevaluate their reasoning; it is as if they are running the company themselves. It is the best way investors can be assured to catch adverse changes in strategy or operations, which may permanently impair the assets of the firm.

ASSESSING PACTIV CORPORATION'S EARNINGS PRESS RELEASE

After calculating the percentage changes of last year's current quarter to this year's quarter, two numbers in the income statement caught my attention. First, selling, general, and administrative expenses decreased 35 percent on a year-over-year basis. This was good news because it was an indication that management was executing the cost reduction plan that had been outlined. The second number that changed drastically was short-term debt, which decreased 96 percent since the beginning of the fiscal year. The company was deleveraging its balance sheet by reducing the amount of

---

Case Study: Pactiv Corp Third-Quarter Earnings Announcement

Below is the earnings announcement:

*PACTIV ANNOUNCES SHARP INCREASE IN
THIRD-QUARTER NET INCOME OPERATING
MARGINS UP SIGNIFICANTLY, CASH FLOW STRONG*

LAKE FOREST, Ill.—(BUSINESS WIRE)—Oct. 26, 2000—Pactiv Corporation (NYSE: PTV) today reported third-quarter 2000 net income from continuing operations of $38 million, or $0.24 per share, up sharply from $4 million, or $0.01 per share, last year. Net income in 1999 was comprised of $4 million, or $0.01 per share, from continuing operations, and $8 million, or $0.05 per share, from discontinued paperboard operations. Third-quarter 1999 net income was adversely impacted by an abnormally high tax rate of 87 percent related to the repatriation of overseas earnings in connection with Pactiv's November 4, 1999, spin-off from Tenneco, Inc. Last year's third-quarter earnings per share would have been $0.10 if calculated using the current tax rate of 42 percent.

Sales in the third quarter were up 4.5 percent after adjusting for the impact of unfavorable foreign currency exchange, divestitures, and discontinued product lines. The increase was driven primarily by core product growth in the Consumer and Foodservice/Food Packaging segment. Reported sales of $730 million were 3.2 percent lower than last year.

Operating income in the third quarter of $100 million rose 45 percent from $69 million in the third quarter of 1999. Despite significantly higher raw material costs, third-quarter operating margin of 13.8 percent exceeded 1999's level of 9.1 percent as a result of pricing actions and the impact of cost improvements implemented since the company's spin-off. Gross margin continued to improve, increasing 0.7 percentage points to 30.0 percent compared with the second quarter of 2000. SG&A expense at 10.1 percent of sales was almost five percentage points below the comparable 1999 level.

"Our primary objective in 2000 has been to increase margins and reshape Pactiv to reflect its true earnings potential," said Richard L. Wambold, Pactiv's chairman and chief executive officer. "We are very pleased with the strong sequential improvement in gross margin which increased 2.4 percentage points since the first quarter. In the third quarter we again saw positive results from our continuing efforts to recover raw material cost increases and reduce other costs," Wambold continued.

As a result of strong cash flow in the quarter, total debt declined to $1.7 billion, down $89 million from second-quarter levels and $395 million from year-end 1999. In addition, the company has completed its $100 million stock repurchase program in which it repurchased 11.7 million shares at an average cost of $8.50 per share.

BUSINESS SEGMENT RESULTS

CONSUMER AND FOODSERVICE/FOOD PACKAGING

Third-quarter sales for the Consumer and Foodservice/Food Packaging unit rose 5.4 percent when adjusted to reflect divestitures and discontinued product lines. Sales were strong in Hefty(R) consumer products and foodservice disposables. Third-quarter operating income for the segment of $72 million increased 33 percent compared with $54 million last year. Operating margin in the third quarter advanced to 13.5 percent from 10.2 percent in the third quarter of 1999 and 13.2 percent in the second quarter of 2000 as a result of pricing actions taken to offset higher resin costs and the continued pruning of low-margin business.

Hefty(R) waste bags continued to post very strong sales and retained the number one market-share position in the grocery, mass merchant, and drug store category. In Foodservice/Food Packaging, execution of the company's "one-stop shopping" strategy continued in the third quarter with the opening of a new regional distribution center in Covington, Georgia. Distributors in 55 percent of the country can now place a single order for multiple products and receive a consolidated shipment from a single regional distribution center, resulting in improved customer-service levels and lower company inventories. This improved service capability will be expanded to 80 percent of the country in the fourth quarter with the opening of a Midwest distribution center. Full nationwide coverage will be provided in 2001.

PROTECTIVE AND FLEXIBLE PACKAGING

Third-quarter sales increased 2.2 percent excluding the unfavorable effect of foreign currency exchange and businesses divested in late 1999. Operating income was $12 million in the quarter compared with $19 million last year but, as expected, showed improvement over the $10 million earned in the second quarter of 2000. Third-quarter operating margin was 6 percent, up from the second-quarter level of 4.9 percent, as pricing actions began to offset prior-period raw material cost increases.

"Our actions to address performance in this segment began in North America in the second quarter, and we are beginning to see the related benefits. As we discussed last quarter, our focus is on regaining margin lost to resin cost increases. Additional actions to enhance operating efficiencies in both North America and Europe will be initiated later this year," Wambold explained.

YEAR-TO-DATE RESULTS

For the nine-month period, Pactiv's net income from continuing operations increased significantly to $106 million, or $0.65 per share, from $56 million, or $0.33 per share, in 1999. Adjusting for the impact of unfavorable foreign currency exchange, divestitures, and discontinued product lines, year-to-date sales rose 7.9 percent.

Nine-month reported net income was $240 million, or $1.47 per share, which was comprised of $106 million, or $0.65 per share, from continuing operations and $134 million, or $0.82 per share, from discontinued operations. For the same period in 1999, the company incurred a net loss of $138 million, or $0.83 per share, which represented the net of income from continuing operations of $56 million, or $0.33 per share, loss from discontinued operations of $155 million, or $0.93 per share, an extraordinary loss of $7 million, or $0.04 per share, and loss from a change in accounting principle of $32 million, or $0.19 per share. Reported sales for the first nine months of 2000 increased slightly, to $2.2 billion, versus 1999.

OUTLOOK

With respect to fourth-quarter earnings, the company remains comfortable with its previous guidance of about $0.26 per share. Looking toward 2001, the company reaffirms its previously stated goal of increasing earnings per share in the 12- to 15-percent range...[11]

---

[11]Pactiv Corporation Earnings Announcement, October 26, 2000.

debt it had on its balance sheet. Debt to capitalization had dropped to 52 percent, down from as high as 60 percent at the beginning of the year. I also calculated the accounts payable turnover, inventory turnover, and accounts receivable turnover, to see how effective the management was at making the most of these three components of working capital.

Step 2: I reviewed the percentage changes that I had calculated and was satisfied with their implications. Sales were down 3 percent in the current quarter because the company sold some assets and discontinued a few product lines. Also, the top line was affected by lower currency exchange rates. I expected the next few quarters to be a bit stronger because these items, while unpredictable, were one-time events.

I calculated the operating margins for this quarter by dividing operating income by sales. Operating margins for the third quarter increased from 9 percent to 14 percent, due to the company's ability to raise prices to offset higher materials costs. This was very good news, as it suggested to me that the company had pricing power over its customers. The company evidenced this ability by being able to pass the increased material costs on to its customers. I also noticed a $4 million decline in net interest expense. After a brief look at the balance sheet, I reasoned that it was due to a decline in the company's debt. My thought was that the company must be using its free cash flow to pay down its debt. This was a signal that Pactiv was becoming financially stronger as a company, despite the high production costs the business encountered.

The drastic decline in the company's tax rate also caught my attention. I calculated the effective tax rate by taking the operating income and subtracting the net interest income to get a pretax earnings number. For the third quarter of 2000, Pactiv's pretaxed earnings were $66 million, and $31 million in 1999. Next I took the income tax expense figure and divided it by the pretaxed earnings number. The analysis revealed that Pactiv had an effective tax rate of 87 percent in 1999 and 42 percent in 2000. This vast reduction in the tax rate, or the abnormally high rate in 1999, was an anomaly. I deemed the current low tax rate to be sustainable because 1999 was an extraordinary year for the company, as Pactiv was spun off from its parent company, Tenneco, Inc. Experience indicated that spin-off years are typically filled with unusual items.

Next, I looked at the company's discontinued operations number. While the amount was only $8 million, I wanted to gain a level of confidence that it was indeed a one-time, nonrecurring event. As it turned out, the $8 million gain was the result of a sale the company made of one particular division. I was satisfied after reviewing the year-to-date numbers. I did, however, take a closer look at the discontinued operations and extraordinary charges to obtain a greater comfort level with the two.

Step 3: There were five reasons I listed as to why I owned Pactiv Corp. After analyzing the earnings report, my assessment of the company a few months back had not changed:

1. **The company generates strong free cash flow, driven by excellent brands with great market shares.** Nothing had changed. In fact, the cash flows were likely to get stronger from my vantage point, given that the company was able to raise prices and operating margins and reduce interest expense.

2. **The management team is very strong and has the proper financial incentives in place.** Nothing had changed.

3. **Cost cutting and asset sale opportunities are significant and real.** Nothing had changed. The company was underway with the cost-cutting program and divestitures, as evidenced by the one-time gains from the asset sales and the increase in margins.

4. **Raw materials costs, such as resin, are unsustainably high. A reduction in cost will go straight to the bottom line.** Raw materials costs, particularly resin prices, were still on the rise. I still believed this high price, due in part to high oil prices, was a temporary negative catalyst that had to be "waited" out.

5. **The company was cheap on a private-market basis. It was likely to be a take-out candidate if the stock continued to languish, based on the stability of its free cash flows.** Nothing had changed except that with the increase in the company's debt capacity, it was becoming a more attractive candidate.

GETTING THE MOST OUT OF THE CONFERENCE CALL

Participation in conference calls is typically reserved for professional money managers and analysts. For an individual, listening to a replay or a Webcast can be just as important. In fact, the most sophisticated investors never ask questions during conference calls. They simply listen to the questions being asked by others and the responses of management.

But if the desire to participate in the call is overwhelming, investors should focus their questions on such things as the risks to cash flow and matters specifically relating to the company's financial health. For example, on a Pactiv conference call I might ask for further detail on the cost-cutting efforts, new products, or management's priority list for the use of the company's free cash flow, et cetera.

VOTING RIGHTS

Shareholders have the right to vote on major issues affecting the company. These issues can vary from merger proposals to electing new board members. As common shareholders, the more stock you own, the greater influence you can have on the company. But every vote counts, and the management teams of publicly traded companies take votes very seriously. Longer-term shareholders may submit proposals themselves.

Generally, each share equals one vote. However, some companies issue different classes of stocks with different voting powers. These types of shares are often controlled by a small number of entities that control the company.

Shareowners receive a proxy statement before the annual meeting. This legal document contains information on which shareholders must vote for approval of the management team's upcoming plans. The proxy statement also shows items such as the compensation of top executives and the company's stock chart compared to its peer group.

Voting is done at the company's annual meeting. However, you can vote by absentee ballot via email, or some companies will allow you to vote over the telephone or on-line at *www.proxyvote.com*.

BUY AND HOLD, BUT NOT FOREVER

Buying shares of a company and holding them for a long time, say 5 to 10 years, has its advantages and disadvantages. For individuals who are not investing on a full-time basis, the buy-and-hold strategy can be appealing. Once the shares are bought, investors need not watch the daily price fluctuations of the stock to decide whether or not to sell. More time can be spent on obtaining a better understanding of the business that they own. In addition, the buy-and-hold strategy helps with tax planning. Long-term investors benefit from lower capital gains tax rates.

Using the Five Keys of Value appropriately leads to a sound investment strategy. This philosophy of investing shows that long-term investing works best, because investors would be very confident on the business, the price paid, the events that need to occur to spur continued share price appreciation, and the downside if nothing happens. The key is having the appropriate patience and discipline to weather the down markets, while staying calm during times when the market is overheated.

One negative attribute of the buy-and-hold strategy is that your investment may be too early to benefit from any catalytic results. The longer you wait, the smaller your returns will be due to inflation. In addition, holding a company for a long time frame certainly implies that the company purchased 10 years ago is most likely a different company today. As a result, many investors consider 3 to 5 years ample time to allow companies to generate adequate returns, without a significant change in business models.

In general, I believe the buy-and-hold strategy is a good one; it is the duration that matters. Too short of a duration is more like trading, rather than investing. Holding for too long reduces real returns, and most likely changes the reasons for ownership. Business buyers in the private equity and leverage buyout game typically consider a 3- to 5-year time horizon when making an investment. The actual length of time for holding any company might be "forever," if the fundamentals continue to improve year after year. However, it is important to establish a finite exit point, in order to calculate the value of a company and assess management's expectations. Therefore, one might conclude that 5 to 10 years may be too long in the modern era, and that 3 to 5 years is perhaps a more appropriate time frame for owning a stock.

WHEN TO SELL

While remaining disciplined, value investors often wait patiently for Mr. Market to determine when companies are bought and sold. Some companies are undervalued for a brief period of time, even if for just a few days. I purchase companies when the market "allows" me to gain shares at a significant discount. Therefore, some positions may be smaller than others, not because the opportunity is less compelling, but because the market allows me to take only a small position at that time. Once I have identified outstanding companies that fit my investment discipline, and I have gained an ownership position, subsequent selling occurs when the following arises.

1. My ongoing research reveals deterioration of the business fundamentals or permanent impairment to the assets of the firm.
2. The company reaches its fair value.
3. The catalyst that I identified prior to making the investment is unlikely to materialize, or is proven ineffective.

C H A P T E R 8

GENERATING VALUE IDEAS AND BUILDING AN INDEPENDENT PORTFOLIO

GENERATING VALUE INVESTMENT IDEAS: TURNING OVER EVERY STONE

Value investors primarily use three resources to find the best possible investment opportunities for their portfolios. These resources include the use of financial publications and other media, computer-generated screens, and your "network." Combing through the financial publications for signals of value, manipulating computerized databases, and making the most of a network of like-minded value investors are the first steps in a long and often tedious process of identifying the best companies for fundamental analysis. Many investors use these techniques. However, it is the way in which one group uses these methods that defines them as value investors. Ultimately, good ideas are hard to find, and great ideas may only come around once a year.

Unique approaches generate unique investment prospects. While both are well-known and accomplished value investors, Warren Buffett and Benjamin Graham's screens may have emphasized different characteristics.

Benjamin Graham's screen criteria may have looked like this:

- Price-to-earnings ratio less than 15 times

- Price for the enterprise less than 1.2 times net tangible assets

- Assets-to-liabilities ratio must be greater than 2 to 1

- Long-term debt not greater than 1.1 times net current assets
- Market capitalization greater than average company in peer group

Warren Buffett's screen may look like this:[1]

- Simple and predictable business
- Evidence of management of superior quality and integrity
- Intrinsic value of the company growing faster than inflation
- After-tax earnings greater than $10 million
- Above average return on equity with little leverage
- Earnings growth greater than inflation over the past 10 years

The distinction one can make between the two is that Graham concentrated on price, while Buffett searches for value and later determines an appropriate price.

USING THE FINANCIAL MEDIA: SEARCH FOR VALUE, THEN WAIT FOR THE RIGHT PRICE

There are several financial media venues that help investors identify good companies, including TV, radio, the Internet, and print publications. Channels and programs such as CNBC, Bloomberg Television, CBS Market Watch, CNNfn, Louis Rukeyser's Wall Street, etc., have one or more Web sites, and some produce radio programs and magazines. They are all excellent. The most useful mechanism, however, for many patient business buyers, is the old-fashion print media. Printed information allows investors to take their time understanding what is being presented. After digesting the important tidbits, investors can make marks on the page, taking a quick calculation of various metrics of interest.

There are several paths that investors take when searching for value ideas in financial publications. Some take a straightforward approach by skimming through each story. Other investors jump around, targeting specific areas of the publication in their own customized ways. While seemingly different, there is a common thread among these approaches: value investors know what to look for and where to search. There are three items the value investor hopes to find when reading financial publications: 1) company/industry-specific knowledge, 2) potential catalysts, and 3) insight into valuation. Company and industry-specific knowledge relates to in-depth analysis on

---

[1]Berkshire Hathaway, Inc., 1994 Annual Report, page 21.

targeted companies or an entire industry that corporate publications may offer. Catalyst identification can come from a variety of items, from stories high-lighting a change in management to articles on new product breakthroughs.

Stories of announced business transactions often give value investors insight into the valuation of certain business enterprises. Attempting to gain insight into the valuation of companies from the perspective of knowl-edgeable, and some not-so-knowledgeable industry players essentially entails searching for proposed business combinations and transactions. Information about entire companies or divisions of companies that are being bought and sold can be found in a variety of financial publications. In the process, specifically looking for commonly used valuation multiples, such as price to book, revenue per customer, units per home, usage per day, etc., helps the investor value companies using these types of reported trans-action multiples as reference points.

There are dozens of publications that investors can choose from to help them search for value. These publications, both on-line and in print, vary in reporting style, level of focus, and subscription costs. Some publications err more on the side of "reporting" the events of the day, while others focus on analyzing the news and anticipating future outcomes.

Professional value investors use a variety of publications and subscription services, combing through as much financial news as possible. The individual value investor has fewer options, as the subscription costs can be prohibi-tive, and access to such services can be limited. Some of the best publications that are financially accessible to both the professional and the individual investor are the newspapers *The Wall Street Journal, Barron's,* and *Investor's Business Daily,* and the magazines *BusinessWeek, Fortune,* and *Forbes.* Every investor is different, and there is no "right" way of reading any financial publication.

***Searching for value in* The Wall Street Journal.**   There are three business-related sections to *The Wall Street Journal:* the First section, Marketplace, and Money & Investing. The First section includes all of the day's top stories, covering such categories as business and politics. This section is written in a way that allows the reader to glance quickly at the key stories of the day and the in-depth stories that are often exclusives. The Marketplace section has an emphasis on the development of new markets. The final business section, Money & Investing, provides analysis and explanations on a variety of topics that relate to investing. This section also includes the vast number of invest-ment metrics on stocks, mutual funds, currencies, bonds, etc.

A typical journey through the daily *Wall Street Journal* might resemble the following: First, the individual glances at the "What's News" column on the first page of the paper. The value investor looks for catalysts or valuation insights here. If a story is of some interest based on value characteristics, the investor may wish to read the entire article.

Next, value investors can turn to the "Index to Businesses" column if they have a particular company of interest and would like to read any updates that may be included in the current issue. Glancing at this column early in the search for ideas serves another purpose. Often, investors put certain ideas on the shelf if there is no clear reason to purchase the company in its current state. This index list may ignite a new found interest in some of the companies that may have not been value candidates in the past.

After skimming through the index, the investor might go to one of the most often overlooked catalyst hideouts, the "Who's News" column. This segment features changes in top management of companies. The value investor is well aware of the fact that changes in leadership within the executive suite often signal forthcoming changes to the valuation of businesses. Perhaps the best prospects are those companies with low profit margins operating in high-profit-margin industries.

The investor then turns to the "Stock Market Data Bank." Here, the investor glances through the stock price highs and lows from the previous day, looking for companies with significant declines in price of say, 25 percent or more, or companies in the same industry. For example, when significant declines occur in one sector, they often present the best opportunities to find value. Sector declines are often due to external and temporary reasons, such as an increase in interest rates by the Federal Reserve, or poor earnings results from an industry leader. The market often overreacts and provides an opportunity for the long-tem investor, who is able to identify the best companies with the cheapest valuations in the industry. The challenge is to avoid value traps as discussed in Chapter 7. Investors can also look at specific industry performances to assess where opportunities can be found. For example, if an industry is down say 20 percent, it may represent an attractive area to search for value opportunities. The value investor can glance over to the previous column, "Abreast of the Market/Small Stock Focus," to get a sense of the market's activity, or on some days, look at smaller companies in this column.

The investor is able to do deeper research in the "Industry/Corporate Focus" segment. It is here that *The Wall Street Journal* takes a detailed look at an industry or a company to uncover its most pressing issues and future prospects. For the individual investor, this is often an excellent place to begin building company-specific or industry knowledge. While professional value investors have the luxury of visiting with company management for a consult, individual value investors can obtain expert-quality research from this section of the paper. Investors can also look to "Marketing & Media" for similar insight, paying closer attention to the breaking stories. Saving articles of interest from these two columns, and filing them in industry or company-specific folders, is a habit for many professional value investors. Individuals should do the same.

Finally, with the information provided in the paper, the investor can get a perspective on the economy. This can be particularly useful in getting an early look at potential external catalysts that may have an impact on industries, companies, or both.

***Finding value in* Barron's.**   *Barron's* is perhaps the most cherished publication in the value investment community. Every Saturday, the community comes together to get an update on the latest news and analysis in the market. It is very clear that *Barron's* financial pages are full of interesting ideas, fresh perspectives, and analysis that often uncover hidden values and highlight overlooked opportunities. The key for investors, of course, is having the ability to sift through the vast amount of information.

Navigating through the pages of *Barron's* on Saturday mornings is a very special time for many investors. Needless to say, every investor approaches this weekly publication differently. Some read page by page, while others target specific sections. The following are a few sections that value investors use in the search for opportunities. The first place where many value investors begin their search is "Up & Down Wall Street." This column often contains interesting perspectives on the general market and one or two investment ideas.

The Mutual Funds section of the paper is often read to get the profile of the week. *Barron's* typically profiles one notable investor in this section. Here, the value investor reads about interesting ideas, while assessing the rationale of the investor being profiled. This section is particularly helpful if it profiles a manager that the reader thinks highly of, and fortunately, this is often the case. Keeping a list of ideas in this section for your independent review is a good way to guarantee a decent list of ideas annually.

The next area that is of interest is the 13D Filings. Here, *Barron's* publishes a list of companies for which 13Ds have been filed. This filing reports an investor's intention to unlock shareholder value in a particular company or simply increase or decrease his or her holdings. This section often signals potential catalysts in the form of management changes or future restructurings. The "Research Reports" section can also highlight potential opportunities. While value investors rarely take Wall Street analysts' recommendations at face value, it is worthwhile to read an analyst's reasoning for recommending a "buy" or "not buy" for a particular company's stock. Often found on the same page is the "Insider Transaction" section that shows recent filings by officers or directors of companies who are interested in buying or selling shares of their own companies. Significant transactions are often worth taking a closer look into, as they may signal changes in management's outlook on the company.

Next, the value investor might turn to the "Winner & Losers," "Charting the Market," and "Market Laboratory" sections of the paper. These three sections together give the investor a solid grasp of where the potential values may be, by noting industries that seem to be oversold and gaining insight as to why such activities have occurred. Finally, *Barron's* has a list of companies in the publication's Index that the value investor may find worthwhile to explore.

***Identifying potential targets:* Investor's Business Daily.**   The *Investor's Business Daily* has become more widely used over the years as a tool for new ideas. In addition to the news of the day, it provides its own proprietary charts and ratings on companies considered best performers by the editors. The list is derived from over 10,000 companies. Due to this unique feature, this publication is not only a newspaper—value investors consider it a tool.

Like other financial publications, there are various ways in which one can make the best use of *Investor's Business Daily.* Many investors, after skimming the top stories on the front page, go directly to the "Where The Big Money's Flowing" table that shows the companies with a plummeting share price and high trading volumes. This is often a place to find great bargains for value seekers. Other areas in the newspaper such as "The Big Picture" and "Industry Groups" can help value investors understand the sectors that may be ignored by the general market. The daily illustration of "52-week Highs and Lows" may prove to be a great place to search for value as well. Many investors typically use these tables for further analysis, isolating certain industries or studying parts of the economy.

The "New America" section describes companies with the best outlooks for the future. While many of these new companies are expensive, learning more about them and their respective industries can give clues as to how the industries will evolve. Two forces in industry analysis discussed in Chapter 2 are the threat of new entrants and substitute products. In this section, a future threat to stable industries may be revealed, as well as industries that are growing very quickly. Similar observations can be made by looking at "Stocks in the News," "Internet & Technology," and "Follow the Leaders."

Identifying potential targets in **BusinessWeek, Fortune, Forbes,** *and* **Value Line.** *BusinessWeek* is read from the back to front by many investors. *Fortune* and *Forbes* are used in similar fashions. Starting form back to front, with *BusinessWeek* as an example, readers glance at the list of companies in the current issue found in the "Index of Companies." Next is *"BusinessWeek* Investor Figures of the Week," where the publication displays the key performance measures of the market for the week. There is also a series of articles that are specific to investors, called *BusinessWeek* Investor. These articles often analyze companies' and CEOs' performance. Many investors often find themselves regular readers of certain columns, written by well-known contributors and editors of these publications—Robert Barker and Gene Marcial at *BusinessWeek,* and Andy Serwer and Herb Greenberg at *Fortune.* Other well-regarded, useful, and just as effective financial publications include *The New York Times, The Financial Times,* and *Bloomberg Magazine.*

MASTERING COMPUTER SCREENS: HUNT FOR ATTRACTIVE PRICES, THEN SEARCH FOR VALUE

Reading through financial publications can be a very tiresome task. While it is advantageous to read every single publication when in search for value, it is nearly impossible to do so in an effective manner. The assumption is that individuals, as well as professional investors, have other things to do rather than keep up with every daily, weekly, and monthly publication that may reveal the next great investment opportunity.

Computer screens are basically the use of a database that stores stocks of interest and is updated regularly with data that can be easily manipulated to meet a certain set of statistical criteria. The objective is to sift through the database for shares of companies with a particular characteristic. For example, one may want a list of all health care companies trading at less than 15 times earnings, with a debt-to-capitalization ratio of less than 40 percent, and with enterprise value-to-operating cash flow of less than 6 times. A list of all companies with the desired parameters would be generated. There are several Web sites that provide screening services.

With the advances of technology and the average home computer, individual investors have about as many resources as professional money managers when it comes to getting information. Today any individual can obtain unlimited amounts of data effortlessly, uncovering information from just about any publicly traded company in the world. The amount of information available to individual investors is enormous. More importantly, screening processes that were once available to professional money managers are now just a click away for individual investors. There are numerous Web sites that offer screening programs for free.

Access to these sites is good, but it can be dangerous for those who are unable to manipulate the numbers for themselves and interpret their meaning. Hence, a screening program done by someone other than the user is of little value, and value investors realize this. Unfortunately, many others do not, and they may buy shares of companies based on the criteria of others. This move can prove to be a bad one, depending on the given environment. The screening criteria that might have worked well for Benjamin Graham may not work for you today. Even if one were given a fresh, modern, and proprietary list of investment candidates using the criteria of a well-respected investor, success may not be guaranteed for casual users. It is only when they fully understand the rationale behind the investor's screening parameters and how to rationalize the findings, further that true value can be found. It is important to know and understand the search criteria used for all screens, even from those of great investors. Needless to say, blind purchases of any sort without understanding the weaknesses of a screen can lead to financial disasters.

Investors use the framework and begin their screening process. Consistency is paramount. Graham and Buffett are consistent in that their criteria are similar to the ways they approach investments—one being more technically oriented than the other. It is important to be more open to ideas when using the screens than during the actual analytical process. Inflexibility can cause one to miss opportunities. It is better to cast a wider net, given the scarcity of good ideas.

There is a wide range of variables that one can choose from when screening stocks. The following is a list of the more commonly used criteria:

- Return on equity
- Operating margins
- Free cash flow growth
- Price to earnings

- Price to sales
- Price to book
- Dividend characteristics
- Earnings growth
- Share price performance
- Enterprise value to cash flow
- Market capitalization

Generating screens is an art, not a science. All investors have their own dimensions that they would like to see in a given screen. For example, some investors prefer companies with a specific ratio of interest coverage or price-to-earnings multiple. Absolute numbers, while they may be helpful at first, can be a very destructive element if not used properly and in the correct environment. Therefore, it is best not to use certain numbers as a "rule of thumb." In the blueprint below, only a few absolute numbers are given to avoid this rule of thumb stigma.

Screening for ideas: A blueprint

Good business: Search for companies with high ROEs, earnings quality and growth, free cash flow, sustainable competitive advantages, and outstanding management.

Cheap price: Depending on the industry, search for companies with price-to-earnings ratio less than 15, price to sales less than 1.5, at or near private market valuations, and at least 40-percent discount to fair value.

Obtainable value: Search for companies off 50 percent or more from 52-week highs in bull markets, and off 60 percent of highs in bear and sideway markets; cyclical companies; and industry leaders in commodity and low-tech industries.

Candidate for catalysts: Search for companies with extremely low margins in high-margin industries; companies trading at, near, or below net cash on their balance sheets; and companies trading below net asset value or private market values.

Margin of safety: Search for companies with pristine balance sheets, with no or very little debt compared to other industry players, tangible book values, and companies trading near take-out or liquidation values.

BUILDING YOUR PORTFOLIO

One of the most effective ways value investors exploit their investment prowess is to concentrate their efforts on a small number of companies in a portfolio. Many in the investment community refer to concentrated portfolios as "focus investing." The objective is to concentrate on a few well-researched companies that have the greatest opportunities to generate superior returns. This is primarily because concentrated portfolio returns do not correlate to the general market. These companies are typically the companies that value investors know best, and for which they have the greatest level of conviction.

The genesis of focused investing lies in the value investor's belief that good opportunities are hard to uncover. Therefore, the value investor believes that one should wait for the right company, at the right time, with the right price. Investors have to be patient and wait for the perfect investment.

One of the first elements needed for investors who wish to invest in a concentrated way is to prepare themselves emotionally for the volatility that such portfolios experience. Value investors employing a focused portfolio strategy must have firm convictions on their abilities to assess business values, because the often aggressive fluctuations in stock prices and portfolio performance can make confident investors second-guess their decisions. As a result, volatility is seen differently among investors.

While most investors shy away from volatility, disciplined value investors see volatility as opportunity. They buy when the price is right, sell when fair value is reached, and ignore the price fluctuations in between. Focus investing is a very good portfolio strategy, but many are not focused because they find it difficult to become comfortable with the expected level of volatility in the performance of the portfolio.

In a concentrated portfolio, volatility is higher because the stock movement of individual securities has more of an impact on the limited number of stocks in the portfolio. Many argue that this level of risk offsets possible rewards. Those who oppose focus investing fall short in their reasoning because volatility is not a risk. Volatility is merely the price you pay for making concentrated bets. Investors must be able to stomach large swings of value in their portfolios. What gives the value investor comfort in employing this portfolio strategy is the fact that focus investing rewards those who buy businesses over those that simply "pick" stocks. Stocks go up and down to various degrees. That is what they do. The challenge for investors is knowing when, during the ups and downs, they should buy or sell. The answer lies not in the sentiment of the general market, but in the economics of each individual business.

There is no difference in buying an entire company. In fact, this is exactly how value investors perceive stock ownership—as purchasing companies in the form of securities. It is with this perspective that the value investor knows what to monitor and how to react during the daily gyrations of stock price. Buffett said it best: "The art of investing in public companies successfully is little different from the art of successfully acquiring subsidiaries [of companies]. In each case, you simply want to acquire, at a reasonable price, a business with excellent economics and able, honest management. Thereafter, you need only monitor whether these qualities are being preserved."[2]

The success of a focused portfolio depends heavily on the investor's ability to identify and assess the value of businesses. Fortunately, having a concentrated portfolio places a premium on the very thing that value investors do best—identifying good businesses and buying them at great prices. Good businesses at attractive prices are rare and hard to find.

Many focused investing practitioners characterize their strategy with a different number of companies. It is common for individual value investors to have 5 to 10 companies in their portfolios while their investment clubs or professional value investors can own 15 or more.

There are several reasons why concentrating on a few companies makes sense. The first reason pertains to the quality of research. With fewer companies on hand, the investor is able to reach the level of company-specific knowledge that value investors require for each investment. While many believe vigorously in portfolio diversification, some academics have found that having a limited number of stocks yields similar results.

A study done at the University of Chicago Business School set out to prove that the average equity portfolio in the United States, holding 130 stocks, is far too many. To test this theory, the researchers "drew from a pool of all listed companies to construct portfolios ranging in size from 1 to 500. They discovered that adding securities decreased portfolio risk, but that most of this advantage dissipates rapidly once the number of holdings exceeds 16" stocks in the portfolio.[3] Another study indicated that one can achieve 85 percent of the diversification that is required by most investors in a portfolio with 15 companies, and that diversification only increases to 95 percent with 30 companies in the portfolio.[4]

---

[2]Cunningham, L. *The Essays of Warren Buffett: Lessons for Corporate America* (New York: Cardozo Law Review, 2001, p. 91).

[3]*Bloomberg Personal Finance,* "Do More With Less," March 1998. Professors Lawrence Fisher and James Lorie conducted the study.

[4]Hagstrom, R., *The Warren Buffett Portfolio* (New York: John Wiley & Sons, 1994, p. 191).

Considering the mental limitations in mastering a large number of companies and the academic research supporting a focused portfolio, a final supporting reason for focused portfolios is actual evidence of success. For this, we need look no further than the Oracle of Omaha. Warren Buffett believes that diversification only makes sense for those investors who lack knowledge and understanding.[5]

A diversified portfolio helps to hedge against ignorance. Buffett suggests that investors should focus on 5 to 10 investments in their portfolios.[6] At the end of the day, it is a personal decision investors make as to the number of companies they have in their portfolios. More importantly, investors have to consider their investment objective, time horizon, and tolerance level for financial pain given the expected volatility.

The positives and negatives of focus investing are well known and researched in the investment community. Yet there is still one misperception of focused investing: If you have a concentrated portfolio, you are not diversified. Investing in several different industries, investment types, or both, can diversify focused portfolios. For example, a value investor can have 10 companies in 7 different industries ranging from packaging to medical devices. Investors can also have a company undergoing a restructuring, a few companies in cyclical industries, and a few high-growth companies. The right mix of investment types and industries is key to increasing an investor's chance of generating adequate performance. Buffet's concentrated portfolio has ranged from life insurance to newspapers to soft drinks. In 1999, when Buffett auctioned off his wallet with a stock tip hidden inside, he recommended a real estate company.

Those who oppose focused investing believe that diversification limits volatility and helps to give investors security, arguing that if one company performs miserably other companies in a well-diversified portfolio will help mitigate the impact. This kind of reasoning is why the vast majority of professional money managers underperform the market index. Such thinking brings mediocrity, and emphasis is placed not on identifying and buying great companies but on spreading bets. The rationale is that if one buys 100 stocks in a portfolio, he or she is sure to get a few winners.

Receiving mediocre or market returns should never be the objective of an actively managed portfolio, nor should it be for the individual investor. There are less expensive ways to get these returns such as those gained using low-cost index funds. Investors who overdiversify risk have their personal

---

[5]Hagstrom, R., *The Warren Buffett Portfolio* (New York: John Wiley & Sons, 1994, p. 191).
[6]Hagstrom, R., *The Warren Buffett Portfolio* (New York: John Wiley & Sons, 1994, p. 9).

portfolios resemble that of an index fund. A focused portfolio is geared towards creating wealth, while a diversified portfolio is geared towards capital preservation.

The specific approach that nonprofessional investors should take in building their own portfolios is the following:

1. Prepare mentally and emotionally for the volatility in performance.
2. Use the Five Keys of Value framework in a highly disciplined manner.
3. Own between 10 and 20 but preferably 15 good businesses at excellent prices.
4. Allocate wisely—invest more in the companies you like best.

APPENDIX A

BUSINESS ASSESSMENT TOOLS

In general, ratios are most useful when they are used in a historical context as well as relative to the particular company's peer group.

Tool	Formula	What It Tells You
Accounts receivable turnover -	Sales ÷ Accounts receivable	The number of times accounts receivable have been turned into cash. It also shows the relationship between revenues and receivables for a particular business.
Acid test ratio	(Cash + Cash equivalents + Accounts receivable) ÷ Current liabilities	Used the same way as the working capital ratio, without dependence on inventory. This test is more stringent.
Asset coverage	Total assets ÷ Long-term debt	This ratio indicates how secure the debt is, based on the amount of assets in the firm. All else equal, the level of security increases as this ratio increases.
Asset turnover	Sales ÷ Total assets	Assesses how well the company has managed its assets. Efficiently run companies typically have a high asset turnover ratio.
Average interest rate	(Interest expense − Accounts payable) ÷ Liabilities	This is a rough assessment of how much the company is being charged for its borrowed funds.

Tool	Formula	What It Tells You
Average sale period	365 days ÷ Inventory turnover	The amount of time it takes, in days, to sell inventory.
Book value per share	Shareholders' equity ÷ Shares outstanding	Comparing book value across firms can help identify undervalued opportunities. It also helps to assess what shareholders would receive if the assets of the firm were to be sold. Debt holders would be paid first, and equity holders would receive the remaining. It is best used for companies with low levels of goodwill as a percentage of their book values.
Cash flow-to-assets	Cash flow from operations ÷ Total assets	This is a monitoring tool. Historical trends of this ration signal whether a company is likely to run into financial difficulty.
Cash turnover	Sales ÷ Cash	Helps determine how effective management is at turning cash into revenues. A relatively high ratio indicates that management has been effective.
Collection ratio	Accounts receivable /(Sales ÷ 365)	This is used to assess the amount of days it would take for a company to collect on its invoices that are still outstanding.
Current ratio	Current Assets ÷ Current liabilities	The short-term debt-paying ability of the firm to retire immediate liabilities.
Day's sales receivables	Accounts receivable /(Annual sales ÷ 360)	Measures the amount of days of uncollected sales in the company's receivables. This number can be computed on a quarterly basis as well using 90 days in the denominator and a quarterly sales figure.
Debt-to-asset ratio	Total debt ÷ Total assets	This indicates how the company's assets are financed. A ratio above one implies that the majority of the assets of the firm are financed by debt.
Debt-to-capitalization ratio	(Short-term debt + Long-term debt) ÷ (Shareholders' equity + Short-term debt + Long-term debt)	This shows how dependent a company is on its use of debt. The higher the ratio, usually the more risky the investment.

Tool	Formula	What It Tells You
Debt-to-equity ratio	(Short-term debt + Long-term debt) ÷ Shareholders' equity	The amount of assets provided by debt holders, for each dollar of assets provided by equity holders.
Dividend payout ratio	Dividends per share ÷ Earnings per share	Measures how strong and secure the company's dividends are. The lower the ratio the more secure.
Dividend yield	Dividends per share ÷ Market price per share	This is the return based on the cash dividends being provided by a stock. It can be used to assess margin of safety levels if the cash dividends are secure. An abnormally high yield can signal that a company is being undervalued or that management might reduce the dividend.
Earnings per share (EPS)	Net income ÷ Shares outstanding	Perhaps the most widely used assessment tool, EPS measures accounting profits and not cash. It can best be used to compare firms among various industries.
Gross margins	Gross profit ÷ Sales	Determines how much the selling price is above costs.
Interest coverage	Operating income ÷ Interest expense	This reveals how much of the interest payments is covered by the company's operations. Ratios should be well above one, for healthy companies.
Inventory turnover	Cost of goods sold ÷ Average inventory during period	The number of times a company's inventory has been sold during the year. A low turnover is usually not a good sign because it means that the product has been sitting in a warehouse.
Net margins	Net income ÷ Sales	The percentage of sales captured in net income.
Operating cash flow ratio	Cash flow from operations ÷ Current liabilities	The ability of the firm to retire immediate liabilities using the cash flow from operations.
Operating margins	Operating income ÷ Sales	A good ratio to monitor the operational efficiencies of a company from one period to the next. It is also indicates whether or not a company will be able

to make a profit.

Tool	Formula	What It Tells You
Return on assets (ROA)	Net income ÷ Total assets	Indicates how effective management has been at employing the assets of the firm. ROA is often called ROI, return on investment.
Return on equity (ROE)	Net income ÷ Shareholders' equity	Often used as a measure of profitability, operational effectiveness, and a firm's financial leverage.
Sales-to-fixed assets	Sales ÷ Fixed assets	This ratio can gauge whether or not a company has too much or too little capacity, given the revenues being generated.
Times interest earned	Earnings before interest expense and income taxes ÷ Interest expense	The level of strength the company has in making due on its interest expense payments.
Working capital	Current assets − Current liabilities	This is a test of a company's liquidity. It is a company's ability to pay off current liabilities by using current assets only. The greater the working capital, the more liquid the company.
Working capital-to-sales ratio	Working capital ÷ Sales	This is a forecasting tool. It allows investors to determine how much working capital is needed, given the projected sales.

APPENDIX B

ANALYZING WALL STREET ANALYSTS' RECOMMENDATIONS[1]

ESEARCH ANALYSTS STUDY publicly traded companies and make buy and sell recommendations on the securities of those companies. Most specialize in a particular industry or sector of the economy. They exert considerable influence in today's marketplace. Analysts' recommendations or reports can influence the price of a company's stock—especially when the recommendations are widely disseminated through television appearances or through other electronic and print media. The mere mention of a company by a popular analyst can temporarily cause its stock to rise or fall—even when nothing about the company's prospects or fundamentals recently has changed.

Analysts often use a variety of terms—buy, strong buy, near-term or long-term accumulate, near-term or long-term overperform or underperform, neutral, hold—to describe their recommendations. But they rarely urge investors directly to sell the stocks they cover. One study showed that, in the year 2000, less than one percent of brokerage house analysts' recommendations were "sell" or "strong sell" recommendations. As a result, many industry professionals interpret a "hold" recommendation to mean "sell."

[1]U.S. Securities and Exchange Commission: : "Analyzing Analyst Recommendations," *http://www.sec.gov/investor/pubs/analysts.htm.*

While analysts provide an important source of information in today's markets, investors should understand the potential conflicts of interest that analysts might face. For example, some analysts work for firms that under-write or own the securities of the companies the analysts cover. Analysts themselves sometimes own stocks in the companies they cover—either directly or indirectly, such as through employee stock-purchase pools in which they and their colleagues participate.

As a general matter, investors should not rely solely on an analyst's recommendation when deciding whether to buy, hold, or sell a stock. Instead, they should also do their own research—such as reading the prospectus for new companies or for public companies, the quarterly and annual reports filed with the SEC—to confirm whether a particular invest-ment is appropriate for them in light of their individual financial circum-stances. This alert discusses the potential conflicts of interest that analysts face and provides tips for researching investments.

WHO ANALYSTS ARE & WHO THEY WORK FOR

Analysts historically have served an important role, promoting the efficiency of our markets by ferreting out facts and offering valuable insights on com-panies and industry trends. They generally fall into one of three categories:

SELL-SIDE
These analysts typically work for full-service broker-dealers and make rec-ommendations on the securities that they cover. Many of the more popular sell-side analysts work for prominent brokerage firms that also provide investment banking services for corporate clients—including companies whose securities the analysts cover.

BUY-SIDE
These analysts typically work for institutional money managers—such as mutual funds, hedge funds, or investment advisers—that purchase securi-ties for their own accounts. They counsel their employers on which securities to buy, hold, or sell, and stand to make money when they make good calls.

INDEPENDENT
These analysts typically aren't associated with the firms that underwrite the securities they cover. They often sell their research reports on a subscription or other basis. Some firms that have discontinued their investment banking operations now market themselves as more independent than multiservice firms, emphasizing their lack of conflicts of interest.

POTENTIAL CONFLICTS OF INTEREST

Many analysts work in a world with built-in conflicts of interest and competing pressures. On the one hand, sell-side firms want their individual investor clients to be successful over time because satisfied long-term investors are a key to a firm's long-term reputation and success. A well-respected investment research team is an important service to customers. At the same time, however, several factors can create pressure on an analyst's independence and objectivity. The existence of these factors does not necessarily mean that the research analyst is biased. But investors should take them into account before making an investment decision. Some of these factors include the following.

INVESTMENT BANKING RELATIONSHIPS

When companies issue new securities, they hire investment bankers for advice on structuring the deal and for help with the actual offering. Underwriting a company's securities offerings and providing other investment banking services can bring in more money for firms than revenues from brokerage operations or research reports. Here's what an investment banking relationship may mean:

*   **The analyst's firm may be underwriting the offering**—If so, the firm has a substantial interest—both financial and with respect to its reputation—in assuring that the offering is successful. Analysts are often an integral part of the investment banking team for initial public offerings—assisting with "due diligence" research into the company, participating in investor road shows, and helping to shape the deal. Upbeat research reports and positive recommendations published after the offering is completed may "support" new stock issued by a firm's investment banking clients.

    1. **Client companies prefer favorable research reports**—Unfavorable analyst reports may hurt the firm's efforts to nurture a lucrative, long-term investment banking relationship. An unfavorable report might alienate the firm's client or a potential client and could cause a company to look elsewhere for future investment banking services.

    2. **Positive reports attract new clients**—Firms must compete with one another for investment banking business. Favorable analyst coverage of a company may induce that company to hire the firm to underwrite a securities offering. A company might

be unlikely to hire an underwriter to sell its stock if the firm's analyst has a negative view of the stock.

- **Brokerage Commissions**—Brokerage firms usually don't charge for their research reports. But a positive-sounding analyst report can help firms make money indirectly by generating more purchases and sales of covered securities—which, in turn, result in additional brokerage commissions.

- **Analyst Compensation**—Brokerage firms' compensation arrangements can put pressure on analysts to issue positive research reports and recommendations. For example, some firms link compensation and bonuses—directly or indirectly—to the number of investment banking deals the analyst lands or to the profitability of the firm's investment banking division. Other firms tie compensation or bonuses to the amount of business the firm does with a particular issuer. These practices may give the analyst an incentive to help ensure that the company continues its investment banking relationship with the brokerage firm.

- **Ownership Interests in the Company**—An analyst, other employees, and the firm itself may own significant positions in the companies that an analyst covers. Analysts may also participate in employee stock-purchase pools that invest in companies that they cover. And in a growing trend called "venture investing," firms and analysts may acquire a stake in a start-up by obtaining discounted, pre-IPO shares. These practices allow analysts to profit, directly or indirectly, from owning securities in companies that they cover. Some say that owning the stocks that analysts cover "puts their money where their mouths are." Others say that someone who owns a stock ordinarily wishes to see it appreciate in price. In addition, firms or analysts— through the employee buying pools they participate in, or otherwise— may act against their own recommendations, selling stock in a company even as the analyst reiterates a "buy" or other favorable rating and issues a positive report about the company's prospects.

DISCLOSURE

The rules of the National Association of Securities Dealers, Inc. (NASD) and the New York Stock Exchange require analysts in some circumstances to disclose certain conflicts of interest when recommending the purchase or sale of a specific security. For example, analysts generally must divulge the fact that they or the brokerage firm they work for own certain types of financial positions in a recommended security. Analysts must also disclose it when their firms make a market in the security or had an investment banking relationship with the company during the past three years. Since analysts rarely make such disclosures during interviews with the news media, you should understand that the absence of disclosure doesn't always mean that there are no conflicts. Conflict of interest disclosures commonly appear in the footnotes of written research reports or in small print on the back cover. If you find one of these disclosures, it is important to understand what it may mean.

A disclaimer that says..."The firm and/or affiliates and employees have or may have a long or short position or holding in the securities, options on securities, or other related investments of issuers mentioned herein."
...may mean "While I'm recommending that you buy ABC, Inc."...

a.   I own stock in ABC, Inc.

b.   My colleagues at the firm own stock in ABC, Inc.

c.   An employee stock purchase pool I belong to owns stock in ABC, Inc.

d.   The firm I work for owns stock in ABC, Inc.

e.   Entities related to the firm I work for own stock in ABC, Inc.

f.   I, my colleagues, or my firm have short positions in the stock of ABC, Inc.

g.   Any combination of the above.

h.   All of the above.

A disclaimer that says..."The firm may have, within the last three years, served as manager or comanager of a public offering of or makes markets in the securities of any or all of the companies mentioned."
...doesn't tell you whether or not the analyst's employer...

a.   Is currently acting as an underwriter of public offerings of the recommended securities.

b.   Has served within the past three years as the lead or managing underwriter of public offerings for the stock of the recommended companies.

c.   Has an ongoing investment banking relationship with the companies issuing the recommended securities.

d.   Stands to make money when investors buy or sell stock in the recommended companies because the analyst's firm is a market maker in those stocks.

e. Any combination of the above.

f. All of the above.

The fact that an analyst—or the analyst's firm—may have a conflict of interest does not mean that the recommendation given is flawed or unwise. But it's a fact you should know and consider in assessing whether the recommendation is wise for you.

It's up to you to educate yourself to make sure that any investments that you choose match your goals and tolerance for risk. Remember that analysts generally do not function as your financial advisors when they make recommendations—they're not providing individually tailored investment advice, and they're not taking your personal circumstances into consideration.

UNCOVERING CONFLICTS

It is difficult for individual investors to know for sure whether and to what extent any conflicts exist. But there are steps that you can take to identify some.

IDENTIFY THE UNDERWRITER
Before you buy, confirm whether the analyst's firm underwrote a recommended company's stock by looking at the prospectus, which is part of the registration statement for the offering. You'll find a list of the lead or managing underwriters on the front cover of both the preliminary and final copies of the prospectus. By convention, the name of the lead underwriter—the firm that stands to make the most money on the deal—will appear first, and any comanagers will generally be listed second in alphabetical order. Other firms participating in the deal will be listed only in the "Underwriting" or "Plan of Distribution" sections of the final supplement to the prospectus. You can search for registration statements using the SEC's EDGAR database at *www.sec.gov/edgar.shtml*. The final supplement to the prospectus will appear in EDGAR as a "424" filing.

RESEARCH OWNERSHIP INTERESTS
A company's registration statement and its annual report on the Form 10-K will tell you who the beneficial owners of more than five percent of a class of equity securities are. The registration statement will also tell you about private sales of the company's securities during the past three years. But when neither a recent registration statement nor an annual report is available, it's much harder to confirm independently whether an analyst, the firm, or

other employees at the firm own a company's stock. That's because the federal securities laws do not generally require investors to report their ownership in any given company—unless the investor is an officer, director, or beneficial owner of more than five percent. In those cases, you may be able to ascertain ownership by checking the following SEC forms:

- **Schedules 13D and 13G**—Any person who acquires a beneficial ownership of more than five percent must file a Schedule 13D. Schedule 13G is a much abbreviated version of Schedule 13D that is only available for use by a limited category of "persons," such as banks, broker-dealers, or insurance companies.

- **Forms 3, 4, and 5**—Officers, directors, and beneficial owners of more than 10 percent must report their holdings—and any changes in their holdings—to the SEC on Forms 3, 4, and 5.

- **Form 144**—If an analyst or a firm holds "restricted" securities from the company—meaning those acquired in an unregistered, private sale from the issuer or its affiliates—then investors can find out whether the analyst or the firm recently sold the stock by researching their Form 144 filings.

Except with respect to the securities of foreign private issuers, filers must send Schedules 13D and 13G electronically using the SEC's EDGAR system. While the SEC does not require that Forms 3, 4, 5, or 144 be sent electronically, some filers choose to do so. If you can't find a form on EDGAR, please contact the SEC's Office of Public Reference by telephone at (202) 942-8090, or by email at publicinfo@sec.gov. You can also check the "Quotes" section of the Nasdaq Stock Market's Web site at *http://www.sec.gov/cgi-bin/goodbye.cgi?quotes.nasdaq.com.*

UNLOCK THE MYSTERY OF "LOCK-UPS"

If the analyst or the firm acquired ownership interests through venture investing, the shares generally will be subject to a "lock-up" agreement during and after the issuer's initial public offering. Lock-up agreements prohibit company insiders—including employees, their friends and family, and venture capitalists—from selling their shares for a set period of time without the underwriter's permission. While the underwriter can choose to end a lock-up period early—whether because of market conditions, the performance of the offering, or other factors—lock-ups generally last for 180 days after the offering's registration statement becomes effective.

After the lock-up period ends, the firm or the analyst may be able to sell the stock. If you're considering investing in a company that has recently conducted an initial public offering, you'll want to check whether a lock-up agreement is in effect and when it expires, or if the underwriter waived any lock-up restrictions. This is important information because a company's stock price may be affected by the prospect of lock-up shares being sold into the market when the lock-up ends. It is also a data point you can consider when assessing research reports issued just before a lock-up period expires—which are sometimes known as "booster shot" reports.

To find out whether a company has a lock-up agreement, check the "Underwriting" or "Plan of Distribution" sections of the prospectus. That's where companies must disclose that information. You can contact the company's shareholder relations department to ask for its prospectus, or use the SEC's EDGAR database if the company has filed its prospectus electronically. For companies that do not file on EDGAR, you can contact the SEC's Office of Public Reference by telephone at (202) 942-8090, or by email at publicinfo@sec.gov. There are also commercial Web sites that you can use for free that track when companies' lock-up agreements expire. The SEC does not endorse these Web sites and makes no representation about any of the information or services contained on these Web sites.

HOW YOU CAN PROTECT YOURSELF

Investors are advised to do their homework before investing. If you purchase a security solely because analysts said that the company was one of their "top picks," you may be doing yourself a disservice. Especially if the company is one you've never heard of, take time to investigate.

- Research the company's financial reports using the SEC's EDGAR database at *http://www.sec.gov/edgar.shtml*, or call the company for copies. If you can't analyze them on your own, ask a trusted professional for help.

- Find out if a lock-up period is about to expire, or whether the underwriter waived it. While that may not necessarily affect your decision to buy, it may put an analyst's recommendation in perspective.

- Confirm whether or not the analyst's firm underwrote one of the company's recent stock offerings—especially its IPO.

- Learn as much as you can about the company by reading independent news reports, commercial databases, and reference books. Your local library may have these and other resources.

- Talk to your broker or financial advisor and ask questions about the company and its prospects. But bear in mind that if your broker's firm issued a positive report on a company, your broker will be hard-pressed to contradict it. Be sure to ask your broker whether a particular investment is suitable for you in light of your financial circumstances.

Above all, always remember that even the soundest recommendation from the most trustworthy analyst may not be a good choice for you. That's one reason why we caution investors never to rely solely on an analyst's recommendation when buying or selling a stock. Before you act, ask yourself whether the decision fits with your goals, your time horizon, and your tolerance for risk. Know what you're buying—or selling—and why.

A P P E N D I X **C**

THE CRITICAL FAILINGS OF EBITDA

This appendix is an excerpt of the June 2000 report by Moody's titled "Putting EBITDA In Perspective."[1] *All of the following material is copyrighted by Moody's Investors Services, and it is printed here with permission of Moody's.*

EBITDA ignores changes in working capital and overstates cash flow in periods of working capital growth.

Following the Money—Working Capital Affects Cash Flow: EBITDA is insensitive to the actual collection of cash because it ignores fundamental changes in working capital that are otherwise calculated when deriving net cash from operating activities. A company may complete its earnings cycle (book revenues and recognize operating income) but not collect cash until a later period.

Earnings are not cash, but merely reflect the difference between revenues and expenses, which are accounting constructs. Thus, it is important to scrutinize revenue recognition policies, especially for capital intensive start-ups.

Moreover, a material increase in the average age of a company's accounts receivable, together with a sharp growth in sales, could produce an unfavorably wide gap between cash and earnings. Likewise, an acceleration

---

[1]Stumpp, P., Marshella, T., Rowan, M., McCreary, R., Coppola, M. "Putting EBITDA In Perspective: Ten Critical Failings of EBITDA as the Principal Determinant of Cash Flow," (New York: Moody's Investor Service, June 2000).

in cash payments to trade creditors as payment terms tighten would also produce an unfavorably wide spread between a company's reported expenses and the cash it actually has available in a given accounting period.

EBITDA can be a misleading measure of liquidity.
The analysis of liquidity is dynamic. An analysis of an issuer's financial flexibility should consider many factors in addition to total cash inflows and outflows. EBITDA, however, provides limited insight into evaluating liquidity. EBITDA and other cash flow measurements, such as cash sources from operations, provide only a simple construct over a defined period of time. They provide no qualitative information about a company's sources and uses of cash, its access to liquidity, or the strength of its liquidity facilities.

In assessing liquidity, Moody's considers the potential near-term claims on the issuer and compares these to all likely near-term sources of cash. The analysis begins with a critical evaluation of an issuer's sources (internal and external) and uses of cash. We then analyze a series of reasonable stress scenarios, and assess the company's ability to meet both its operating needs and its debt obligations under these scenarios.

This is followed by a close examination of the company's contingency funding plans for a period of stress caused by either company-specific concerns or by a general market disruption. EBITDA fails to consider the following elements that are critical to assessing an issuer's liquidity:

- Potential near-term claims on cash, including direct obligations as well as contingent obligations

- The issuer's confidence sensitivity

- The strength and stability of cash flow

- The level of necessary or committed capital spending

- Funding needs to support working capital

- Vulnerability to reduced access to capital markets

- The liquidity of the issuer's assets

- The strength of a company's liquidity facilities

Liquidity is access to cash. EBITDA doesn't capture a company's ability to cover debt service from earnings. A company could have a strong reported consolidated EBITDA but not the cash to pay interest. Cash could be in an unrestricted subsidiary and thus reinvested, or cash could be in a foreign subsidiary and might be subject to restrictions on the repatriation of cash and/or the withholding of taxes on dividends. These factors, in turn, could delay the timing and decrease the amount of cash received.

Analysis of a company's ability to cover debt service from earnings must also consider the significance of seasonality or other timing factors. A high interest coverage ratio is of limited value if, for example, the interest is due in June and the earnings are not realized until December. Thus, the analysis of sources and uses is critical. It is also important to pay attention to the adequacy of a company's liquidity to provide for such timing differences.

EBITDA does not always coincide with the receipt of cash. Take the case of a wireless service company that recently sold a block of communication towers to an independent service company at a gain over the net book value of the towers. The wireless company entered into a lease with the buyer of the towers to enable it to continue to maintain the equipment on the towers. Postsale, one would expect the company's EBITDA to be reduced by the amount of the lease payment.

However, the wireless service provider, who received cash for the towers at the time of sale and used the proceeds to repay debt, followed sale-leaseback accounting, which defers and amortizes the gain on the sale over the term of the lease. The transaction was expected to have no effect on EBITDA because the amortization of the gain would offset the cost of the lease. Nonetheless, in this example, cash came into the company at the time of sale, and EBITDA in periods following the sale overstates cash flow by the amount of the deferred gain recognized.

EBITDA does not consider the amount of required reinvestment—especially for companies with long-lived assets.

EBITDA is a better measurement for companies whose assets have longer lives—it is not a good tool for companies whose assets have shorter lives or for companies in industries undergoing a lot of technological change. The use of EBITDA as an indicator of debt coverage implies that funds generated by noncash charges for depreciation are not needed for reinvestment for ordinary capital expenditures. Although it is acknowledging the fungibility of cash, this assumption would be conceptually valid only if a company's future capital investments are to be funded from excess cash balances or from the proceeds of new financing or asset sales.

If a company relies on funds from operations to finance new capital investments, however, depreciation may not be available for debt service. In such instances, capital expenditures should be deducted from EBITDA. The term "maintenance CAPEX" is often used as an indicator of the level of required reinvestment, but this term is not consistently applied and could imply a smaller amount of reinvestment than that which is actually required in the longer term.

Moreover, due to inflation, the investment needed to maintain the physical plant will generally be greater in current dollars than depreciation of prior capital expenditures. Some industries afford management more flexibility with respect to the timing and amount of capital spending. Deferring or reducing capital expenditures, however, could lower a business's productive capacity and efficiency, both of which are very important, particularly in highly leveraged companies.

Furthermore, there are instances in which book depreciation may not equal economic depreciation. In these cases, companies must reinvest more than depreciation expense to maintain the plant. This is particularly relevant in capital intensive industries, where assets are bought at an extremely high price and subsequently written down. In these cases, companies will continue to have to reinvest the old ("prewritedown") level of depreciation.

EBITDA says nothing about the quality of earnings. Sometimes EBITDA should be limited to just EBIT.

EBITDA is probably best assessed by breaking down its components into EBIT, Depreciation, and Amortization. Generally speaking, the greater the percentage of EBIT in EBITDA, the stronger the underlying cash flow. To the extent that EBITDA contains a high amount of depreciation and amortization, it is important to evaluate whether funds provided by such noncash charges are truly available for debt service. To the extent that a company relies on cash from operations to finance new capital investments, then depreciation or amortization may not be entirely available for debt service.

EBITDA is an inadequate stand-alone measure for comparing acquisition multiples.

EBITDA is commonly used as a gauge to compare acquisition prices paid by companies and/or financial sponsors and is thought to represent a multiple of the current or expected cash flow of an acquired company. Although this measurement can be used as a rough rule of thumb, it is important to remember that EBITDA does not always correspond to cash flow. Moreover, users of this approach should be aware that EBITDA multiples create an illusion of making acquisition prices appear smaller.

For example, a 6.5-times EBITDA multiple for a company whose EBITDA consists of 50 percent of EBITA and 50 percent of depreciation, equates to a materially higher 13-times multiple of operating earnings plus amortization. Industries each have their own cash flow dynamics, making it difficult to assess EBITDA multiples without taking such sector differences into account. Nonetheless, even within a single industry, the value of using EBITDA multiples is limited by the fact that they convey only partial information about the acquired company.

Even though EBITDA acquisition multiples may reflect qualitative differences between two companies in the same industry, the actual multiples convey little about the underlying businesses. (For example, two companies may be in the same industry, but one may have a subsidiary that is in a different line of business with different profitability and investment requirements.) Moreover, differing EBITDA multiples may convey little vital information such as an upgrade to the plant and the accompanying ability to roll out new services.

In general, EBITDA acquisition multiples convey no specific information about the following.

- Quality of an acquired company's EBITDA, including its mix of EBIT, depreciation, and amortization

- Extent and nature of an acquired company's contingent obligations, liquidity, and debt maturity profile

- State of the acquired company's working capital that could pose an immediate cash drain on the consolidated entity

- Quality of an acquired company's asset base, its management, the markets that it serves, or its growth prospects

- Extent of "earn-outs," which could materially increase the acquisition multiple

- History or stability of an acquired company's earnings

- Effects of differing accounting policies

- Extent of manipulation based on short-term adjustments to earnings, including temporary cutbacks in marketing or administrative expenses

EBITDA ignores distinctions in the quality of cash flow resulting from differing accounting policies—not all revenues are cash.
Different accounting policies can have a profound effect on EBITDA, making that measurement a poor basis for the comparison of financial results across firms. Accounting policies can affect the quality of earnings, and therefore EBITDA. The most profound impact on EBITDA, however, relates to the manner in which revenues are recognized. In particular,

accounting policies that accelerate revenues—or the recognition of revenues without near-term realization of cash—makes EBITDA a poor basis for the comparison of cash flow among companies.

Revenue recognition policies that don't correlate with the receipt of cash include "barter" transactions commonly used by Internet companies, "pre-need" services revenues of deathcare companies—for which cash is placed in a trust, and revenues of timeshare companies that correspond to mortgage notes receivable. Revenues that are reported under percentage-of-completion (POC) accounting can similarly result in a significant gap between EBITDA and cash.

EBITDA is not a common denominator for cross-border accounting conventions.

EBITDA can vary for the same company depending on whether it was calculated based on U.S. GAAP or on GAAP used in a foreign country. Foreign country accounting standards and practices often differ from U.S. GAAP in terms of revenue recognition, methodologies that capitalize rather than expense costs, goodwill recognition, and fixed asset depreciation. Even modest differences can be very meaningful when debt service is thin.

EBITDA offers limited protection when used in indenture covenants.

EBITDA is commonly used as a component in indenture covenants that restrict the permissible levels of debt incurrence. While there are many variations to these tests, debt incurrence tests based on EBITDA are typically structured in one of three ways.

1. Consolidated Cash Flow to Fixed Charges—with *consolidated cash flow* defined as net income, plus provision for taxes, plus consolidated interest expense including the interest component of all payments associated with capital lease obligations, plus depreciation and amortization, plus certain one-time issuance expenses—and with fixed charges generally defined as consolidated interest expense whether paid or accrued, capitalized interest and interest expense on indebtedness that is guaranteed, and all dividend payments on preferred stock.

2. Consolidated Coverage Ratio—defined as the aggregate amount of consolidated EBITDA of the company and its restricted subsidiaries for the most recent four consecutive fiscal quarters ending prior to the date of such determination, for which consolidated financial statements of the company are available, to consolidated interest expense for such four fiscal quarters, in each case for each fiscal

quarter of the four fiscal quarters ending prior to the issue date on a pro-forma basis, to give effect to acquisitions as if they had occurred at the beginning of such four-quarter period.

3.   Maximum Leverage Ratio—defined as pro-forma debt of the company and its restricted subsidiaries on a consolidated basis, divided by annualized pro-forma EBITDA of the company and its restricted subsidiaries.

EBITDA can drift from the realm of reality.

As evidenced throughout this special comment, EBITDA can easily be manipulated through aggressive accounting policies relating to revenue and expense recognition, asset writedowns and concomitant adjustments to depreciation schedules, excessive adjustments in deriving "adjusted pro-forma EBITDA," and by the timing of certain "ordinary course" asset sales, to influence quarterly results. In addition, users of EBITDA should be alert to the following.

- Be aware of situations in which management decisions have been taken to make cash flow appear more robust. Revenue loading or expense cutbacks made to enhance the sale prospects or price of a company can often bolster EBITDA, albeit on an unsustainable basis. Underfunding marketing expenses may make short-run EBITDA vibrant at the expense of long-run growth. Moody's recently rated the bank debt of a single product manufacturer in connection with that company's sale by its parent in early 2000. The company's sales were $366 million, and in rating the notes, we noticed that marketing costs were cut 35 percent from $126 million to $82 million. While the company reports a strong $121 million of EBITDA and no permanent sacrifice of volume or market share to date, credit statistics remain very vulnerable to a restoration of marketing spending to historic levels. Such a return may be needed in order to thwart competition and to maintain market share.

- Companies with excessive "noise" in their earnings should prompt serious questions as to whether unusual charges should be "added back" to show a normalized EBITDA. Such charges could be a symptom of fundamentally low returns or questionable viability.

- Cash flow that is heavily influenced by asset sales may not be recurring. It is important to distinguish between one-time asset sales, such as sales of fiber channel capacity, and recurring sales, such as refurbished pagers or used equipment sold by rental service companies.

EBITDA is not well suited for the analysis of many industries because it ignores their unique attributes.

EBITDA is a tool more relevant to basic industries dominated by capital-intensive, long-lived asset classes. Steel companies, for instance, can live off of the fat without need of new furnaces. But EBITDA has evolved from asset classes with long lives (20 or more years) to companies that have considerably shorter asset lives (3–5 years) and that need continual reinvestment to maintain their asset base. EBITDA also fails to consider the specific attributes of a number of industries, including the following.

*   **Cable TV Industry:** Cable companies need to reinvest amounts comparable to depreciation over time to upgrade technology that is constantly changing. Amortization is a continuing source of cash flow and can be looked at for debt service.

*   **Deathcare Industry:** Deathcare companies use EBITDA, but this is not an accurate representation of cash flow, and many of the companies have demonstrated an intensive need for working capital. Deathcare companies provide funeral and cemetery services on an "at-need basis" (at the time the death) or on a "preneed basis" (in advance of death). Accounting policies differ among companies and are also affected by state laws that require proceeds of certain preneed sales to be put into a trust. Revenues are recognized for preneed sales of cemetery interment rights (or plots), related services (funeral services or interment services), and merchandise sales (casket), together with the concurrent recognition of related costs when the customer contracts are signed. This raises a number of issues:

    1. The services provided are performed at a later date, and such costs are subject to inflation.
    2. Many states require that proceeds from preneed sales, merchandise, and services be paid into trust funds.
    3. Deathcare companies often provide credit for such services that can extend as long as 84 months.

    Thus, there is a gap created between EBITDA and cash. EBITDA is further misleading because some companies capitalize and subsequently amortize marketing and advertising expenses as opposed to recognizing them as a current period expense.

*   **Exploration and Production Industry:** The quality, durability, and proximity of EBITDA to discretionary cash flow varies greatly for petroleum exploration and production (E&P) companies. An issuer's

ability to maintain a given level of EBITDA is affected by its ability to sustain productive CAPEX outlays, commodity price fluctuations, production risk, and drilling risk. EBITDA also needs to be assessed in the context of reserve life on proven developed reserves and adjusted for CAPEX needed to sustain production.

1. A substantial and constant level of CAPEX is needed to replace the production that generated reported EBITDA in the first place.

2. The natural gas and oil price component of EBITDA can swing widely between reporting periods.

3. The production life of total proven reserves and proven developed reserves will differ widely among firms. One firm's reserve life may be only 5 years, while another's may be 10 or more. The cash burn rate, drilling, and liquidity risks of the short-lived firm is much higher than that of the long-lived firm.

4. EBITDA risk is closely linked to the proven developed reserve life. Only proven, developed, producing reserves generate cash flow, and the higher-risk proven, undeveloped reserves need time and CAPEX to bring to production.

5. The unit-finding and development costs associated with replacing reserves can vary widely among firms and should be assessed relative to the unit cash margins those reserves will produce over the price cycle.

6. A firm with an eight-year reserve life may have a large pocket of high-margin, but very short-lived, higher-risk production masking low-margin, higher-cost, but long-lived production.

7. In some cases, production from an individual new natural gas well may decline 50 percent, or more in the first year, before flattening out at low levels in the third year.

Accounting policies can also affect EBITDA. Some E&P companies use "successful efforts" accounting whereby exploration expense and dry hole costs are expensed, while other E&Ps use "full cost" accounting that capitalizes exploration and dry hole costs. For E&Ps that use successful efforts, exploration and dry hole expenses should be added back to EBITDA (yielding EBITDAX) to make it comparable to EBITDA (EBITDAX) for E&Ps using the "full cost" method. Both "successful efforts" and "full cost" accounting capitalize development costs—costs incurred in bringing proven but undeveloped reserves to production.

- **Fiber Channel Building Industry:** Fiber channel builders have a business plan that calls for them to sell limited amounts of fiber assets and to use their unsold fiber capacity to generate a recurring revenue stream. EBITDA for fiber channel builders is highly affected by the one-time sales of fiber capacity. Construction and development expenses are capitalized. Thus, EBITDA contains both the revenues related to the one-time sale plus amortization of capitalized construction and development costs attributed to the capacity sold. While EBITDA may reflect cash derived during the period, it is highly influenced by one-time sales since no more revenues can be gleaned from the fiber capacity sold.

- **Homebuilding Industry:** There are three basic issues with using EBITDA for homebuilders:

    1. EBITDA contains very little depreciation.
    2. Homebuilders can affect earnings by capitalizing marketing costs. It is important to look at the degree to which marketing expenses are capitalized and subsequently amortized.
    3. Homebuilders often buy land, and it takes time to get approvals for development and to actually build the infrastructure for communities even before a home is built.

    To look at a meaningful measure of interest coverage, certain adjustments have to be made. Homebuilders capitalize interest in connection with the development of land. When this interest is amortized it is in the cost of goods sold (instead of amortization). Thus, to arrive at a numerator to serve as a comparative measurement across companies, it is important to adjust EBITDA for the amount of interest that is amortized through cost of goods sold. The denominator is interest incurred rather than interest expense, to get to a better measure of economic debt service.

- **Paging Industry:** Providers of paging and other wireless messaging services derive the majority of revenues from fixed periodic fees. Operating results benefit from this recurring revenue stream with minimal requirement for incremental selling expenses or other fixed costs. Many paging companies often take back used paging equipment from subscribers that lease pagers, refurbish them, and sell them into the resale channel for used pagers. The refurbished pagers are sold at a margin over the net book value of the depreciated pager plus the costs of refurbishment. Paging companies have considerable latitude with respect to the timing of such resales. They can, for example, mask declining revenues from core services by selling a larger than normal volume of refurbished pagers into the resale market. EBITDA does not discriminate between earnings from core paging services and sales of refurbished pagers. Moreover, EBITDA does not detect unusual variations in the volume of product sales from one quarter to another. EBITDA can be influenced by the amount of depreciation ascribed to the units of pagers sold. The equipment margin, and consequently EBITDA, can be made larger, depending on the pool of refurbished pagers sold.

• **Restaurant Industry:** Depreciation should not be viewed as a continuing source because there is a need to reinvest in modernizing the restaurants and updating themes. Certain restaurant themes need to be refreshed about every seven years to address changing tastes and styles; otherwise there may be a steady erosion in cash flow.

• **Rental Services Industry:** Rental service companies can temporarily get away with not reinvesting depreciation if the fleet is young. But, this can not last indefinitely. Over time, depreciation will need to be reinvested to maintain the fleet. EBITDA for companies in the rental services industry can be affected by the volume and timing of used equipment sales.

• **Theater Exhibition Industry:** Movie theater exhibition companies have a large PP&E component on the balance sheet. They need to reinvest depreciation over a period of time to adapt to changing technology and industry innovation, and thus EBITDA should not be the basis for additional leveraging. In a very short period, theater exhibition has evolved from the "town theater" to "duplex" to "triplex" to "multiplex" (8–16 screens) to "megaplex" (18–24, 30, or more screens with stadium seating), and technology has changed to digital sound and is evolving to digital projection. Without reinvestment of depreciation, these entities lose their ability to compete. Because of the widespread use of leases in the theater exhibition industry, leverage covenants based simply on EBITDA may not comprehensively constrain leverage including the growing obligations under operating leases. Thus, debt, plus capitalized operating leases-to-EBITDA, plus rents, provides a more effective means of gauging financial leverage, and is also more effective for comparative analytical purposes due to divergent financing strategies for sector participants.

- **Timeshare Companies:** For companies in the timeshare industry, revenues from the sales of vacation intervals consist mostly of promissory notes. In general, 10 percent of timeshare sales are realized in cash, and the remaining 90 percent consists of mortgage receivables due over 7 years. However, once a timeshare sale is booked, the entire sale is accounted for as revenue. Thus, EBITDA does not reflect cash flow available to the company. Moreover, due to varying methods of reporting EBITDA within the timeshare industry, the computation of EBITDA may not be comparable to other companies in the timeshare industry that compute EBITDA in a different manner. Some timeshare operators sell their receivables through some form of securitization in order to finance operations. When this sale is made, companies often recognize an immediate gain attributable to the favorable spread on the mortgage notes receivable rate over the securitization rate. This is also a noncash item since no cash is realized until there are payments on the mortgage receivables.

- **Trucking Industry:** In general, EBITA is the better determinant of the financial health of a trucking company. Equipment replacement is critical since trucks are short-lived assets. If depreciation is not reinvested, the wheels literally fall off. In addition, and unlike ocean-going shipping, for example, depreciation is a close proxy in terms of what needs to be spent to maintain the fleet and is almost always very close to CAPEX on a normalized basis. Without fleet renewal, there can be a vicious downward spiral as maintenance costs quickly increase and utilization rates decrease.

D

MANAGEMENT'S PLAN TO RESTRUCTURE A COMPANY

THERMO ELECTRON ANNOUNCES MAJOR REORGANIZATION PLAN[1]

- Company to be Split into Three Independent Entities: Thermo Electron to Focus on Measurement and Detection Instruments; Thermo Fibertek and Medical Products Businesses to be Spun Off as Dividends to Thermo Electron Shareholder

- Businesses with Aggregate Revenues of $1.2 Billion to be Sold

WALTHAM, Mass., January 31, 2000—Thermo Electron Corporation (NYSE-TMO) announced today that its board of directors has authorized a major reorganization plan that will vastly simplify Thermo Electron by splitting the company into three independent public entities, two of which will be spun off as dividends to Thermo Electron shareholders. As part of the plan, which is expected to take about one year to complete, the company has designated for sale businesses with aggregate revenues of $1.2 billion. This is in addition to businesses with approximately $150 million in revenues sold since May 1999. Ultimately, Thermo Electron will become one integrated, publicly traded company.

The "new" Thermo Electron will focus on its core business—measurement and detection instruments. Thermo Electron also plans to spin off

[1]Thermo Electron Corp., January 31, 2000. Form 8-K.

as a dividend to Thermo Electron shareholders its Thermo Fibertek subsidiary and a newly created medical products company. As a stand-alone public entity, Thermo Fibertek will continue to broaden the use of its separation technologies for process industries and commercialize new fiber-based composite products. The new medical products company, which will be formed by combining several existing businesses, will provide medical equipment and systems to the healthcare industry. Once the process is complete, each of these three companies will have its own entirely separate and independent board of directors and management team.

Richard F. Syron, chairman, president, and chief executive officer of Thermo Electron, said, "This is a bold plan to deliver shareholder value by creating three independent, focused companies that have strong prospects for growth. Further, we believe this plan will allow the 'new' Thermo Electron to become the preeminent provider of measurement and detection instruments. Thermo Electron will be a highly integrated, tightly managed operating company. While still a broad-based instrument company addressing needs in virtually every industry, we plan to invest significant resources—through internal R&D, strategic partnerships, and complementary acquisitions—in growing our expanding product and technology portfolio serving customers in the life sciences and telecommunications industries.

"In addition, we believe we will create added value for Thermo Electron shareholders by spinning off two focused companies that also have substantial opportunities for growth. Shareholders who have struggled in the past with the company's complexity should benefit from the simplified structure and well-defined strategy. Each of the three entities that will emerge from this plan has the scale and business fundamentals to be a strong, stand-alone company," said Syron. "With a clear mission and approach, each management team will be able to concentrate on the specific issues and needs facing the customers it serves. As independent entities, these companies will have greater access to capital, which, in turn, will enable them to build on their leading market positions. We believe this will allow each company to become a superior competitor, thereby offering greater value to customers and shareholders." Syron concluded, "Thermo Electron was founded on the principle of identifying and nurturing new technologies and bringing them to the marketplace. With this new structure, we believe each company will be able to continue the Thermo Electron tradition of product innovation and excellence, while creating even greater opportunities for commercial success."

The three new companies that will be formed from Thermo Electron are:

THERMO ELECTRON—MEASUREMENT AND
DETECTION INSTRUMENTS:

Thermo Electron will focus solely on its measurement and detection instruments business. Thermo Electron is already a world leader in the instrument industry, with 1999 instrument revenues of approximately $2.3 billion. The "new" Thermo Electron will provide instruments for the life sciences, telecommunications, analytical, process control, laser, optical components, precision temperature-control, and environmental-monitoring markets. Currently these technologies are designed and distributed through a number of public and private companies, including Thermo Instrument Systems and its subsidiaries: Thermo Optek, ThermoQuest, Thermo BioAnalysis, ONIX Systems, ThermoSpectra, Metrika Systems, Thermo Vision, and Thermo Environmental Instruments, as well as through Thermedics Detection and Thermo Sentron. Under the plan, public subsidiaries would be "spun in" or merged into Thermo Electron, ultimately creating one integrated public company.

Spectra-Physics Lasers, acquired by Thermo Instrument in February 1999, will remain a public company while Thermo Electron continues to evaluate this business.

Richard Syron will remain chairman, president, and chief executive officer of Thermo Electron, and Earl R. Lewis will continue to serve as president of the instruments business.

THERMO FIBERTEK—SEPARATION TECHNOLOGIES AND
FIBER-BASED PRODUCTS:

Thermo Fibertek is a leading provider of separation technologies for the pulp and paper industries and is known for its service, product quality, and technological innovation. The company is a worldwide leader in recycling equipment and water-management systems, and the number one competitor worldwide for paper-machine accessories. As an independent company, Thermo Fibertek will be better positioned to raise capital for investment in additional technologies and businesses that would allow it to expand its core business. Thermo Fibergen, which will remain a subsidiary of Thermo Fibertek after the proposed spinoff, will aggressively fund the continued development and growth of its fiber-based composite business. In 1999, the companies had consolidated sales of approximately $225 million.

Thermo Fibertek's obligations relating to its outstanding convertible debentures will not be affected by the spinoff; the debentures will remain convertible into Thermo Fibertek common stock and will continue to be guaranteed by Thermo Electron.

William A. Rainville will remain president and chief executive officer of Thermo Fibertek. The company is expected to be renamed before the spinoff to shareholders, which is anticipated to occur by early 2001.

MEDICAL PRODUCTS:

Thermo Electron has had a growing presence in the medical products industry through a number of wholly owned businesses and public subsidiaries. Currently, Thermo Electron is the number one player in neurodiagnostic and monitoring equipment, and holds the number two position worldwide in respiratory and pulmonary care products. Several of Thermo Electron's healthcare businesses will become part of a new medical products company that will include its neurodiagnostic, patient-monitoring, auditory, respiratory and pulmonary care, enteral feeding systems, and medical polymers product lines. In 1999, these businesses had sales of approximately $335 million. As an independent, focused entity, the new medical products company will be better positioned to market its products and respond to customer demands in today's competitive healthcare arena. Thermo Cardiosystems and Trex Medical will not be part of the new medical products company. See "Divestitures" below.

Thermo Electron is currently conducting an extensive search for a president and chief executive officer of this new medical products company, considering both internal and external candidates. The company will fill the position before the spinoff to shareholders, which is expected to occur by early 2001.

DIVESTITURES:

Over the next 12 months, the company also plans to sell businesses with aggregate sales of approximately $1.2 billion. This is in addition to businesses with approximately $150 million in revenues sold since May 1999. Thermo Electron believes that these businesses would better prosper within other strategically aligned organizations that can provide greater focus, resources, and targeted marketing strength. The additional businesses that are expected to be sold include, among others, the following: Thermo Cardiosystems, Trex Medical, the Thermo TerraTech businesses, Thermo Coleman, Peek, NuTemp, Thermo Trilogy, and Peter Brotherhood. In the aggregate, the company does not currently expect to incur losses from the disposition of these businesses.

The proceeds from these divestitures will be retained by Thermo Electron for reinvestment in future acquisitions and product development efforts related to measurement and detection instruments.

SPIN-INS:

Thermo Electron has already announced the terms for, and is proceeding with, the spin-ins of ThermoTrex, ThermoLase, Thermo TerraTech, ThermoRetec, and The Randers Killam Group. Under the plan, Thermo Electron would also spin in Thermo Optek, ThermoQuest, Thermo Bio-Analysis, Metrika Systems, ONIX Systems, Thermo Instrument Systems, Thermedics, and as previously announced, Thermo Sentron, Thermedics Detection, and Thermo Ecotek—described in brief below.

THE THERMO INSTRUMENT GROUP:

Because Thermo Instrument Systems currently owns more than 90 percent of the outstanding shares of Thermo Optek and ThermoQuest common stock, each of these two companies is expected to be spun in for cash through a "short-form" merger, at $15.00 and $17.00 per share, respectively.

In addition, Thermo Instrument will make cash tender offers of $28.00 per share for Thermo BioAnalysis, $9.00 per share for Metrika Systems, and $9.00 per share for ONIX Systems, in order to bring its own equity ownership in each of these businesses to at least 90 percent. If successful, each of these companies would then be spun into Thermo Instrument through a short-form merger at the same cash prices as the tender offers.

Following these tender offers, Thermo Instrument, in turn, would be taken private. Thermo Electron plans to conduct an exchange offer, in which Thermo Electron common stock would be offered to Thermo Instrument minority shareholders in exchange for their Thermo Instrument common stock in order to bring Thermo Electron's equity ownership in Thermo Instrument to at least 90 percent. If successful, Thermo Instrument would then be spun into Thermo Electron through a short-form merger. Thermo Instrument minority shareholders would also receive shares of Thermo Electron common stock in exchange for their Thermo Instrument shares in the merger at the same exchange ratio that is being offered in the exchange offer. The company expects to announce the exchange ratio for this transaction shortly after conducting the tender offers for Thermo BioAnalysis, Metrika Systems, and ONIX Systems.

THE THERMEDICS GROUP:

Thermedics will make cash tender offers of $8.00 per share for Thermedics Detection and $15.50 per share for Thermo Sentron in order to bring its own equity ownership in each of these companies to at least 90 percent. If successful, each of these companies would then be spun into Thermedics through a short-form merger at the same cash prices as the tender offers.

Following these tender offers, Thermedics, in turn, would be taken private. Thermo Electron plans to conduct an exchange offer, in which Thermo Electron common stock would be offered to Thermedics minority shareholders in exchange for their Thermedics common stock, in order to bring Thermo Electron's equity ownership in Thermedics to at least 90 percent. If successful, Thermedics would then be spun into Thermo Electron through a short-form merger. Thermedics minority shareholders would also receive shares of Thermo Electron common stock in exchange for their Thermedics shares in the merger at the same exchange ratio that is being offered in the exchange offer. The company expects to announce the exchange ratio for this transaction shortly after conducting the tender offers for Thermedics Detection and Thermo Sentron.

THERMO ECOTEK:

Because Thermo Electron currently owns more than 90 percent of the outstanding shares of Thermo Ecotek common stock, Thermo Electron will spin in this company through a short-form merger. Thermo Ecotek minority shareholders will receive 0.431 shares of Thermo Electron common stock in exchange for each share of Thermo Ecotek stock held. Under Thermo Electron's new focused strategy, Thermo Ecotek is no longer a core business, and Thermo Electron is evaluating its strategic options for this company. In the meantime, Thermo Ecotek will proceed with its ongoing power projects using its own resources to fund development.

Upon completion of the respective spin-ins, outstanding obligations under the Thermo Instrument, Thermedics, and Thermo Ecotek convertible debentures will be assumed by Thermo Electron, and these debentures will become convertible into Thermo Electron common stock. Thermo Electron's guarantee obligations under other subsidiary debentures and its obligations under its own debentures will remain ongoing obligations of Thermo Electron.

TIMING:

Thermo Instrument and Thermedics expect to conduct their respective subsidiary tender offers during the second quarter of 2000. The Thermo Optek, ThermoQuest, and Thermo Ecotek short-form mergers are expected to be completed by the end of the second quarter of 2000. Thermo Electron expects to conduct the exchange offers for Thermo Instrument and Thermedics during the third quarter of 2000.

The spinoffs of Thermo Fibertek and the new medical products company, as well as the planned divestitures, are expected to take up to a year
to complete.

Thermo Electron's board has been advised by McKinsey & Company,
Inc.; J.P. Morgan & Co., Inc.; and The Beacon Group Capital Services,
LLC in its development of this plan.

CONDITIONS:

All of the transactions described here are subject to a number of conditions,
including the following.

The proposed spinoffs of Thermo Fibertek and the new medical products
company will require: a favorable ruling by the Internal Revenue Service
regarding the tax treatment of the spinoffs; Securities and Exchange Commission (SEC) clearance of necessary filings; final Thermo Electron board
action; and other customary conditions. In addition, the spinoff of the new
medical products company will be conditioned on the successful completion
of the proposed Thermo Instrument and Thermedics spin-ins.

The spin-ins of Thermo Optek, ThermoQuest, and Thermo Ecotek will
require SEC clearance of necessary filings. The tender offers for Thermo
BioAnalysis, Metrika Systems, ONIX Systems, Thermo Sentron, and Thermedics Detection, as well as the proposed exchange offers for Thermo
Instrument and Thermedics, will require: establishment of exchange ratios
for the proposed Thermo Instrument and Thermedics exchange offers; the
receipt of acceptances from enough minority shareholders so that Thermo
Instrument's, Thermedics', or Thermo Electron's (as applicable) equity ownership in each of the proposed spin-in companies reaches at least 90 percent;
and other customary conditions. In addition, depending on the exchange
ratio that is set, and the number of Thermo Electron shares outstanding at the
time of the transaction, the issuance of Thermo Electron common stock in
the Thermo Instrument spin-in may require the approval of Thermo Electron's
shareholders, per New York Stock Exchange rules...

APPENDIX E

DESCRIPTIONS OF SEC FORMS

OVERVIEW OF THE MOST COMMON CORPORATE FILINGS[1]

The following is a short description of the most common corporate filings made with the SEC. Many of these filings are now made through the SEC's EDGAR system and are available electronically.

Form ADV

This form is used to apply for registration as an investment adviser or to amend a registration. It consists of two parts. Part I contains general and personal information about the applicant. Part II contains information relating to the nature of the applicant's business, including basic operations, services offered, fees charged, types of clients advised, educational and business backgrounds of associates, and other business activities of the applicant.

Annual Report to Shareholders

The Annual Report to Shareholders is the principal document used by most public companies to disclose corporate information to shareholders. It is usually a state-of-the-company report including an opening letter from the Chief Executive Officer, financial data, results of continuing operations, market segment information, new product plans, subsidiary activities, and research and development activities, on future programs.

[1]U.S. Securities and Exchange Commission: "Descriptions of SEC Forms," *http://www.sec.gov.*

Form BD

This form is used to apply for registration as a broker or dealer of securities, or as a government securities broker or dealer, and to amend a registration. It provides background information on the applicant and the nature of the business. It includes lists of the executive officers and general partners of the company. It also contains information on any past securities violations.

Form D

Companies selling securities in reliance on a Regulation D exemption or a Section 4(6) exemption from the registration provisions of the 1933 Act must file a Form D as notice of such a sale. The form must be filed no later than 15 days after the first sale of securities.

For additional information on Regulation D and Section 4(6) offerings, ask for a copy of the Regulation and the pamphlet entitled: "Q & A: Small Business and the SEC" from the Commission's Publications Unit, or see the Small Business Section of the Commission's Web site.

Form 1-A

Regulation A provides the basis for an exemption for certain small offerings (generally up to $5 million in any 12-month period). Companies selling securities in reliance on a Regulation A exemption from the registration provisions of the 1933 Act must provide investors with an offering statement meeting the requirements of Form 1-A.

For additional information on Regulation A, ask for a copy of the Regulation and the pamphlet entitled "Q & A: Small Business and the SEC" from the Commission's Publications Unit, or see the Small Business section of the Commission's Web site.

Form MSD

This report is used by a bank or a separately identifiable department or division of a bank to apply for registration as a municipal securities dealer with the SEC, or to amend such registration.

Form N-SAR

This is a report to the Commission filed by registered investment companies on a semiannual and annual basis, at the end of the corresponding fiscal periods. Unit investment trusts, however, are required to file this form only once a year, at the end of the calendar year. The form contains information about the type of fund that is reporting sales charges, 12b-1 fees, sales of shares, identity of various entities providing services to the investment company, portfolio turnover rate, and selected financial information.

Prospectus

The prospectus constitutes Part I of a 1933 Act registration statement. It contains the basic business and financial information on an issuer with respect to a particular securities offering. Investors may use the prospectus to help appraise the merits of the offering and make educated investment decisions.

A prospectus in its preliminary form is frequently called a "red herring" prospectus and is subject to completion or amendment before the registration statement becomes effective, after which a final prospectus is issued and sales can be consummated.

Proxy Solicitation Materials (Regulation 14A/Schedule 14A)

State law governs the circumstances under which shareholders are entitled to vote. When a shareholder vote is required and any person solicits proxies with respect to securities registered under Section 12 of the 1934 Act, that person generally is required to furnish a proxy statement containing the information specified by Schedule 14A. The proxy statement is intended to provide security holders with the information necessary to enable them to vote in an informed manner on matters intended to be acted upon at security holders' meetings, whether the traditional annual meeting or a special meeting. Typically, a security holder is also provided with a "proxy card" to authorize designated persons to vote his or her securities on the security holder's behalf in the event that the holder does not vote in person at the meeting. Copies of definitive (final) proxy statements and proxy cards are filed with the Commission at the time they are sent to security holders. For further information about the applicability of the Commission's proxy rules, see Section 14(a) of the 1934 Act and Regulation 14A.

Certain preliminary proxy filings relating to mergers, consolidations, acquisitions, and similar matters are nonpublic upon filing; all other proxy filings are publicly available.

1933 Act Registration Statements

One of the major purposes of the federal securities laws is to require companies making a public offering of securities to disclose material business and financial information in order that investors may make informed investment decisions. The 1933 Act requires issuers to file registration statements with the Commission, setting forth such information, before offering their securities to the public. (See Section 6 of the Securities Act of 1933 for information concerning the "Registration of Securities and Signing of Registration Statement," and Section 8 of the Securities Act of 1933 for information on "Taking Effect of Registration Statements and Amendments Thereto.")

The registration statement is divided into two parts. Part I is the prospectus. It is distributed to interested investors and others. It contains data to assist in evaluating the securities and to make informed investment decisions.

Part II of the registration statement contains information not required to be in the prospectus. This includes information concerning the registrants' expenses of issuance and distribution, identification of directors and officers, and recent sales of unregistered securities as well as undertakings and copies of material contracts.

(Investment companies file 1933 Act registration statements that are, in many cases, also registration statements under the Investment Company Act of 1940. For descriptions of registration statements filed by these issuers, see the following section.)

The most widely used 1933 Act registration forms are as follows:

- **S-1:** This is the basic registration form. It can be used to register securities for which no other form is authorized or prescribed, except securities of foreign governments or political subdivisions thereof.

- **S-2:** This is a simplified optional registration form that may be used by companies that have been required to report under the 1934 Act for a minimum of 3 years and have timely filed all required reports during the 12 calendar months and any portion of the month immediately preceding the filing of the registration statement. Unlike Form S-1, it permits incorporation by reference from the company's annual report to stockholders (or annual report on Form 10-K) and periodic reports. Delivery of these incorporated documents as well as the prospectus to investors may be required.

- **S-3:** This is the most simplified registration form, and it may only be used by companies that have been required to report under the 1934 Act for a minimum of 12 months and have met the timely filing requirements set forth under Form S-2. Also, the offering and issuer must meet the eligibility tests prescribed by the form. The form maximizes incorporating by reference information from 1934 Act filings.

- **S-4:** This form is used to register securities in connection with business combinations and exchange offers.

- **S-8:** This form is used for the registration of securities to be offered to an issuer's employees pursuant to certain plans.

- **S-11:** This form is used to register securities of certain real estate companies, including real estate investment trusts.

- **SB-1:** This form may be used by certain "small business issuers" to register offerings of up to $10 million of securities, provided that the company has not registered more than $10 million in securities offerings during the preceding 12 months. This form requires less detailed information about the issuer's business than Form S-1. Generally, a "small business issuer" is a U.S. or Canadian company with revenues and public market float less than $25 million.

- **SB-2:** This form may be used by "small business issuers" to register securities to be sold for cash. This form requires less detailed information about the issuer's business than Form S-1.

- **S-20:** This form may be used to register standardized options where the issuer undertakes not to issue, clear, guarantee, or accept an option registered on Form S-20, unless there is a definitive options disclosure document meeting the requirements of Rule 9b-1 of the 1934 Act.

- **Sch B:** Schedule B is the registration statement used by foreign governments (or political subdivisions of foreign governments) to register securities. Generally, it contains a description of the country and its government, the terms of the offering, and the uses of proceeds.

- **F-1:** This is the basic registration form authorized for certain foreign private issuers. It is used to register the securities of those eligible foreign issuers for which no other more specialized form is authorized or prescribed.

- **F-2:** This is an optional registration form that may be used by certain foreign private issuers that have an equity float of at least $75 million worldwide, or are registering nonconvertible investment-grade securities, or have reported under the 1934 Act for a minimum of three years. The form is somewhat shorter than Form F-1 because it uses delivery of filings made by the issuer under the 1934 Act, particularly Form 20-F.

- **F-3:** This form may only be used by certain foreign private issuers that have reported under the 1934 Act for a minimum of 12 months and that have a worldwide public market float of more than $75 million. The form also may be used by eligible foreign private issuers to register offerings of nonconvertible investment-grade securities, securities to be sold by selling security holders, or securities to be issued to certain existing security holders. The form allows 1934 Act filings to be incorporated by reference.

- **F-4:** This form is used to register securities in connection with business combinations and exchange offers involving foreign private issuers.

- **F-6:** This form is used to register depository shares represented by American Depositary Receipts ("ADRs") issued by a depositary against the deposit of the securities of a foreign issuer.

- **F-7:** This form is used by certain eligible, publicly traded Canadian foreign private issuers to register rights offers extended to their U.S. shareholders. Form F-7 acts as a wraparound for the relevant Canadian offering documents. To be registered on Form F-7, the rights must be granted to U.S. shareholders on terms no less favorable than those extended to other shareholders.

- **F-8:** This form may be used by eligible, large publicly traded Canadian foreign private issuers to register securities offered in business combinations and exchange offers. Form F-8 acts as a wraparound for the relevant Canadian offering or disclosure documents. The securities must be offered to U.S. holders on terms no less favorable than those extended to other holders.

- **F-9:** This form may be used by eligible, large publicly traded Canadian foreign private issuers to register nonconvertible investment-grade securities. Form F-9 acts as a wraparound for the relevant Canadian offering documents.

- **F-10:** This form may be used by eligible, large publicly traded Canadian foreign private issuers to register any securities (except certain derivative securities). Form F-10 acts as a wraparound for the relevant Canadian offering documents. Unlike Forms F-7, F-8, F-9, and F-80, however, Form F-10 requires the Canadian issuer to reconcile its financial statements to U.S. Generally Accepted Accounting Principles ("GAAP").

- **F-80:** This form may be used by eligible, large publicly traded Canadian foreign private issuers to register securities offered in business combinations and exchange offers. Form F-80 acts as a wraparound for the relevant Canadian offering or disclosure documents. The securities must be offered to U.S. holders on terms no less favorable than those extended to other holders.

- **SR:** This form is used as a report by first-time registrants under the Act of sales of registered securities and use of proceeds therefrom. The form is required at specified periods of time throughout the offering period, and a final report is required after the termination of the offering.

Investment Company Registration Statements

Investment companies also register their securities under the 1933 Act. However, many of the forms used are also used as registration statements under the Investment Company Act of 1940.

Mutual funds, the most common type of registered investment company, make a continuous offering of their securities and register on Form N-1A, a simplified, three-part form. The prospectus, or Part A, provides a concise description of the fundamental characteristics of the initial fund in a way that will assist investors in making informed decisions about whether to purchase the securities of the fund. The statement of additional information, Part B, contains additional information about the fund that may be of interest to some investors but need not be included in the prospectus. Part C contains other required information and exhibits.

Closed-end funds, unit investment trusts, insurance company separate accounts, business development companies, and other registered investment companies register their securities and provide essential information about them on other registration forms, as listed below. All the forms listed are used for registration under both the 1933 Act and 1940 Act unless otherwise indicated.

- **N-1A:** This form is used to register open-end management investment companies ("mutual funds").

- **N-2:** This form is used to register closed-end management investment companies ("closed-end funds").

- **N-3:** This form is used to register insurance company separate accounts organized as management investment companies offering variable annuity contracts.

- **N-4:** This form is used to register insurance company separate accounts organized as unit investment trusts offering variable annuity contracts.

- **S-6:** This form is used to register securities issued by unit investment trusts (1933 Act only).

- **N-14:** This form is used to register securities issued by investment companies in connection with business combinations and mergers (1933 Act only).

Other Securities Act Form: Form 144

This form must be filed as notice of the proposed sale of restricted securities or securities held by an affiliate of the issuer in reliance on Rule 144 when the amount to be sold during any three-month period exceeds 500 shares or units or has an aggregate sales price in excess of $10,000.

1934 Act Registration Statements

All companies whose securities are registered on a national securities exchange, and, in general, other companies whose total assets exceed $10,000,000 ($10 million) with a class of equity securities held by 500 or more persons, must register such securities under the 1934 Act. (See Section 12 of the 1934 Act for further information.)

This registration establishes a public file containing material financial and business information on the company for use by investors and others, and also creates an obligation on the part of the company to keep such public information current by filing periodic reports on Forms 10-Q and 10-K, and on current-event Form 8-K, as applicable.

In addition, if registration under the 1934 Act is not required, any issuer who conducts a public offering of securities must file reports for the year in which it conducts the offering (and in subsequent years if the securities are held by more than 300 holders).

The most widely used 1934 Act registration forms are as follows:

- **10:** This is the general form for registration of securities pursuant to Section 12(b) or (g) of the 1934 Act of classes of securities of issuers for which no other form is prescribed. It requires certain business and financial information about the issuer.

- **10-SB:** This is the general form for registration of securities pursuant to Sections 12(b) or (g) of the 1934 Act for "small business issuers." This form requires slightly less detailed information about the company's business than Form 10 requires.

- **8-A:** This optional short form may be used by companies to register securities under the 1934 Act.

- **8-B:** This specialized registration form may be used by certain issuers with no securities registered under the 1934 Act that succeed to another issuer that had securities so registered at the time of succession.

- **20-F:** This is an integrated form used both as a registration statement for purposes of registering securities of qualified foreign private issuers under Section 12 or as an annual report under Section 13(a) or 15(d) of the 1934 Act.

- **40-F:** This is an integrated form used both as a registration statement to register securities of eligible publicly traded Canadian foreign private issuers or as an annual report for such issuers. It serves as a wrap-around for the company's Canadian public reports.

Interpretive Responsibility:

Division of Corporation Finance—Office of Chief Counsel (Except for Form 20-F, as to which the Office of International Corporate Finance should be consulted.)

OTHER EXCHANGE ACT FORMS

Form TA-1

This form is used to apply for registration as a transfer agent or to amend such registration. It provides information on the company's activities and operation.

Form X-17A-5

Every broker or dealer registered pursuant to Section 15 of the Exchange Act must file annually, on a calendar or fiscal-year basis, a report audited by an independent public accountant.

Forms 3, 4, and 5

Every director, officer, or owner of more than 10 percent of a class of equity securities registered under Section 12 of the 1934 Act must file with the Commission a statement of ownership regarding such security. The initial filing is on Form 3 and changes are reported on Form 4. The Annual Statement of beneficial ownership of securities is on Form 5. The forms contain information on the reporting person's relationship to the company and on purchases and sales of such equity securities.

Form 6-K

This report is used by certain foreign private issuers to furnish information: (i) required to be made public in the country of its domicile; (ii) filed with and made public by a foreign stock exchange on which its securities are traded; or (iii) distributed to security holders. The report must be furnished promptly after such material is made public. The form is not considered "filed" for Section 18 liability purposes. This is the only information furnished by foreign private issuers between annual reports, since such issuers are not required to file on Forms 10-Q or 8-K.

Form 8-K

This is the "current report" that is used to report the occurrence of any material events or corporate changes that are of importance to investors or security holders and previously have not been reported by the registrant. It provides more current information on certain specified events than would Forms 10-Q or 10-K.

Form 10-C
This form must be filed by an issuer whose securities are quoted on the Nasdaq interdealer quotation system. Reported on the form is any change that exceeds five percent in the number of shares of the class outstanding and any change in the name of the issuer. The report must be filed within 10 days of such change.

Form 10-K
This is the annual report that most reporting companies file with the Commission. It provides a comprehensive overview of the registrant's business. The report must be filed within 90 days after the end of the company's fiscal year.

Form 10-KSB
This is the annual report filed by reporting "small business issuers." It provides a comprehensive overview of the company's business, although its requirements call for slightly less detailed information than required by Form 10-K. The report must be filed within 90 days after the end of the company's fiscal year.

Form 10-Q
The Form 10-Q is a report filed quarterly by most reporting companies. It includes unaudited financial statements and provides a continuing view of the company's financial position during the year. The report must be filed for each of the first three fiscal quarters of the company's fiscal year and is due within 45 days of the close of the quarter.

Form 10-QSB
The Form 10-QSB is filed quarterly by reporting small business issuers. It includes unaudited financial statements and provides a continuing view of the company's financial position and results of operations throughout the year. The report must be filed for each of the first three fiscal quarters and is due within 45 days of the close of the quarter.

Form 11-K
This form is a special annual report for employee stock purchase, savings, and similar plans, interests in which constitute securities registered under

the 1933 Act. The Form 11-K annual report is required in addition to any other annual report of the issuer of the securities (e.g., a company's annual report to all shareholders, or Form 10-K).

Form 12B-25
This form is used as a notification of late filing by a reporting company that determines that is unable to file a required periodic report when first due without unreasonable effort or expense. If a company files a Form 12b-25, it is entitled to relief, but must file the required report within 5 calendar days (for a Form 10-Q or 10-QSB) or within 15 calendar days (for a Form 10-K, 10-KSB, 20-F, 11-K, or N-SAR).

Form 13F
This is a quarterly report of equity holdings by institutional investment managers having equity assets under management of $100 million or more. Included in this category are certain banks, insurance companies, investment advisors, investment companies, foundations, and pension funds.

Form 15
This form is filed by a company as notice of termination of registration under Section 12(g) of the 1934 Act, or suspension of the duty to file periodic reports under Sections 13 and 15(d) of the 1934 Act.

Form 18
This form is used for the registration on a national securities exchange of securities of foreign governments and political subdivisions thereof.

Form 18-K
This form is used for the annual reports of foreign governments or political subdivisions thereof.

Schedule 13D
This Schedule discloses beneficial ownership of certain registered equity securities. Any person or group of persons who acquire a beneficial ownership of more than 5 percent of a class of registered equity securities of certain issuers must file a Schedule 13D reporting such acquisition together with certain other information within 10 days after such acquisition. Moreover, any material changes in the facts set forth in the Schedule generally precipitates a duty to file promptly an amendment on Schedule 13D.

The Commission's rules define the term "beneficial owner" to be any person who directly or indirectly shares voting power or investment power (the power to sell the security).

Schedule 13G
Schedule 13G is a much abbreviated version of Schedule 13D that is only available for use by a limited category of "persons" (such as banks, broker/dealers, and insurance companies), and even then only when the securities were acquired in the ordinary course of business and not with the purpose or effect of changing or influencing the control of the issuer.

Schedule 13E-3
This schedule must be filed by certain persons engaging in "going private" transactions. The schedule must be filed by any company or an affiliate of a company who engages in a business combination, tender offer, or stock purchase that has the effect of causing a class of the company's equity securities registered under the 1934 Act (1) to be held by fewer than 300 persons, or (2) to be delisted from a securities exchange or interdealer quotation system. The filer must disclose detailed information about the transaction, including whether the filer believes the transaction to be fair.

Schedule 13E-4
This schedule (called an Issuer Tender Offer Statement) must be filed by certain reporting companies that make tender offers for their own securities. In addition, Rule 13e-4 under the 1934 Act imposes additional requirements than an issuer must comply with when making an issuer tender offer.

Schedule 13E-4F
This schedule may be used by a Canadian foreign private issuer that makes an issuer tender offer for its equity shares (provided that U.S. holders hold less than 40 percent of the class of shares subject to the offer). It serves as a wraparound for the relevant Canadian disclosure documents. The Canadian issuer must comply with relevant Canadian tender offer regulations.

Information Statement (Regulation 14C/Schedule 14C)
Schedule 14C sets forth the disclosure requirements for information statements. Generally, a company with securities registered under Section 12 of the 1934 Act must send an information statement to every holder of the registered security who is entitled to vote on any matter for which the company is not soliciting proxies. (If the company solicits proxies, Regulation 14C/Schedule 14A may be required.)

Schedule 14D-1

Any person, other than the issuer itself (see Schedule 13E-4), making a tender offer for certain equity securities registered pursuant to Section 12 of the 1934 Act, which offer, if accepted, would cause that person to own over five percent of that class of the securities, must at the time of the offer file a Schedule 14D-1. This schedule must be filed with the Commission and sent to certain other parties, such as the issuer and any competing bidders. In addition, Regulation 14D sets forth certain requirements that must be complied with in connection with a tender offer.

Schedule 14D-1F

Any person making a tender offer for securities of a Canadian foreign private issuer may use this schedule if U.S. holders hold less than 40 percent of the class of securities that is the subject of the offer and if the bidder extends the tender offer to U.S. holders on terms that are at least as favorable as those extended to any other holder. The schedule serves as a wraparound for the relevant Canadian disclosure documents. In addition, the tender offer must comply with relevant Canadian requirements.

Schedule 14D-9

This schedule must be filed with the Commission when an interested party, such as an issuer, a beneficial owner of securities, or a representative of either, makes a solicitation or recommendation to the shareholders with respect to a tender offer that is subject to Regulation 14D.

Schedule 14D-9F

Schedule 14D-9F may be used by a Canadian foreign private issuer or by any of its directors or officers when the issuer is the subject of a tender offer filed on Schedule 14D-1F. The schedule is used to respond to tender offers. The schedule serves as a wraparound for the relevant Canadian disclosure documents. In addition, the filer must comply with all relevant Canadian requirements.

TRUST INDENTURE ACT OF 1939—FORMS

- **T-1:** This form is a statement of eligibility and qualification of a corporation to act as a trustee under the Trust Indenture Act of 1939.

- **T-2:** This form is basically the same as Form T-1 except it is to be used for individual, rather than corporate trustees.

- **T-3:** This form is used as an application for qualification of indentures pursuant to the Trust Indenture Act of 1939, but only when securities to be issued thereunder are not required to be registered under the Securities Act of 1933.

- **T-4:** This form is used to apply for an exemption from certain provisions of the Trust Indenture Act.

- **T-6:** This form is used by a foreign corporation as an application to act as sole trustee under an indenture qualified under the Trust Indenture Act.

Index

Note: **Boldface** numbers indicate illustrations.

About the Author

J. Dennis Jean-Jacques is a former senior analyst with Mutual Series Funds. His work has been featured in top financial publications including *Barron's*, *Fortune*, and *Business Week*. Prior to joining Mutual Series, Jean-Jacques—who received his MBA from Harvard Business School—was an investment analyst at Fidelity Management & Research Company, adviser to Fidelity mutual funds.